THE FEASIBILITY OF
DEMOCRACY IN AFRICA

ABOUT THE AUTHOR

The death of Claude Ake in a plane crash in November 1996 robbed Africa of one of her most distinguished political scientists, democrats and social commentators. The present volume, in the press at the time of the author's death, probes with passion and insight Ake's lifelong concern with democracy and its future on the continent. It is offered, unrevised, as a tribute to the memory of a great scholar and concerned African.

Claude Ake was born in February 18, 1939, Omoku, Nigeria. He studied and held various teaching positions in Canada, Kenya, Nigeria, Tanzania, and the United States. He was founder and Director of the Centre for Advance Social Sciences, Port Harcourt, Nigeria.

Among his previous publications include *A Theory of Political Integration* (Dorsey Press, 1967); *Revolutionary Pressures in Africa* (London, Zed, 1969); *Social Science as Imperialism: The Theory of Political Economic Development* (Ibadan University Press, 1974); *A Political Economy of Africa* (Longman, 1982); *Political economy of Nigeria*, co-author (Longman, 1985); *A New World Order: A view from the South* (Lagos, Malthouse, 1993); *Democratisation of Disempowerment in Africa* (Lagos, Malthouse, 1994); and *Democracy and Development in Africa* (Brookings Institution, 1995).

THE FEASIBILITY OF DEMOCRACY IN AFRICA

Claude Ake

COUNCIL FOR THE DEVELOPMENT OF
SOCIAL SCIENCE RESEARCH IN AFRICA

© Council for the Development of Social Science Research in Africa 2000
Avenue Cheikh Anta Diop Angle Canal IV, BP 3304 Dakar, Senegal

ISBN 2-86978-082-6

Cover design painting by Kalidou Kassé, 'La Causerie' or 'the discussion'

Typesetting by Djibril Fall

Printed in Great Britain by Antony Rowe Ltd., Chippenham, Wiltshire

Reprinted in 2003

Distributed in Africa by CODESRIA

Distributed elsewhere by
African Books Collective, 27 Park End Street, Oxford, OX1, 1HU UK
    Fax: 44-01865-793298   Email: abc@dial.pipex.com
    web site: www.africanbookscollective.com

CODESRIA would like to express its gratitude to the Swedish International
Development Cooperation Agency (SIDA/SAREC), the International
Development Research Centre (IDRC), the Ford Foundation, the MacArthur
Foundation, Carnegie Corporation, the Norwegian Ministry of Foreign
Affairs, the Danish Agency for International Development (DANIDA), the
French Ministry of Cooperation, the United Nations Development
Programme, the Netherlands Ministry of Foreign Affairs, the Rockefeller
Foundation, the Prince Claus Fund, and the Government of Senegal for
their support of its research, training and publications programmes.

Contents

Chapter 1

The Travails of Democracy

Liberal Democracy 9

Theoretical Foundations of Liberal Democracy 12

The Development of Liberal Democracy 17

Democracy and the Market 21

The New Threat to Democracy 26

Conclusion 28

Chapter 2

The Dynamics of Democratization in Africa

Part I: The Context and the Provenance of Democracy 33

The Colonial Legacy 35

Part II: The Rise of the Movement of Democracy 37

Elite Demand for Incorporation 37

The Masses: Demands for Economic Incorporation 45

The Process of Democratization 51

Accommodationist Strategies 53

Preventive Strategies 54

From Democratic Processes to Democratic Outcomes 70

Chapter 3

Democracy and Development

Introduction 75

Part I: Democracy and Economic Development 76

The Case for Authoritarian Regimes 81

Why Democratization of Development Matters 87

Part II: Democratization and Ethnicity 92

    The Concept of Ethnicity 93

    Ethnicity and Conflict 95

    The Case of Nigeria 97

    The Salience of Ethnic Consciousness 109

Part III: Democratization and Political Instability 115

    The State-Building Project 116

Conclusion 125

Chapter 4

The Feasibility of Democracy in Africa

Part I: Introduction 127

    The International Community 128

    The Business Class 130

    Counter-Elites 131

    Activist Elements of Civil Society 139

    The Masses and Peasants 135

    Conclusion 136

Part II: The International Environment 137

    Intervention Through Multilateralism 143

    Political Conditionality and Armament 145

    Positive Incentives 147

    Difficult Assumptions 151

    Conclusion 154

Part III: The Internal Situation 155

Part IV: Necessary Transformations to Feasibility 160

    State Transformation: Towards a Democratic State 160

    State Transformation: Towards a Liberal State 164

    Social Transformation of Society 167

    The Social Transformation of Democracy 174

    Conclusion 184

    Conclusion: The Challenge of Change 189

Bibliography 193

1

The Travails of Democracy

This is an inquiry into the process of democratization and its feasibility in Africa. Africa is by no means the only part of the world where the prospect of democracy is in question. It is in question everywhere for democracy is in crisis all over the world. This chapter examines the crisis of democracy which contextualizes the democratization in Africa.

At the end of the Cold War, democracy appears to be triumphant and unassailable, its universalisation only a matter of time. Democracy has become the unifying discourse which is supposed to tame national and international politics and to foster peaceful coexistence in a world set at odds by the ideological struggles of the Cold War. Unfortunately, the triumph of democracy is more apparent than real. If democracy is being globalized, as appears to be the case, it is mainly because it has been trivialized to the point at which it is no longer threatening to political elites around the world, who may now embrace democracy and enjoy democratic legitimacy without subjecting themselves to the notorious inconveniences of democratic practice.

The trivialization of democracy often occurred under cover of clarifying or operationalizing a supposedly complex and confusing concept. But that was only a blind because there is nothing complex or confusing about the concept of democracy. For a political concept, 'democracy' is uncharacteristically precise. It means popular power, or in a famous American version, government of the people, for the people, by the people. There was agreement on this definition across the considerable ideological divide of classical Athens. The Athenians refined it with obsessive rigour and operationalized it meticulously in practical political arrangements. They left no doubt about who the people are. They let it be known that in the final analysis the people are to be defined in class terms. For instance, Aristotle, no friend to democracy, maintains that 'democracy exists where the sovereign authority is composed of the poorer classes and not of the owners of property' (Aristotle 1981:115).

Ancient Athens was just as precise about what the rule of the people means as it was about who they are. It stuck uncompromisingly to direct rule by the people and shunned notions of consultation, consent and representation. Athenians held that a life deprived of direct involvement in rulership is without merit, for the citizen's involvement in the exercise of sovereignty is the major business of life. Classical Athens did not shy away from the demanding implications of the idea of popular power. For instance, it was understood that it meant strict adherence to the principle of equality as well as the rule of law. The importance of equality was underlined by the tradition of filling offices by lot, the rotation of offices and the adoption of very short tenure to enable as many people as possible to take a turn at holding office.

Finally, the Athenian notion of democracy was not just an ideology. It was actually operationalized and practised at great pains. All citizens formed the sovereign Assembly whose quorum was put at 6,000. Meeting over 40 times a year, it debated and took decisions on all important issues of public policy including war and peace, foreign relations, public order, law making, finance and taxation. The Assembly was regarded as the incarnation of Athenian political identity and collective will. To underline this, it preferred to take decisions by consensus rather than votes. The business of the Assembly was prepared by a council of 500 which had a steering committee of 50 headed by a President who held office for only one day. The executive function of the polis was carried out by magistrates who were invariable a committee of 10 usually elected for a non-renewable term of one year.

Even if there was a chance that anyone had difficulties with the precise Athenian conception of democracy, these political arrangements leave no doubt about what it was as a form of government. We cannot complain of not knowing what the meaning of democracy was to those who invented it and to the only people who have tried to practise it without trivializing it.

Democracy began and reached its peak in ancient Athens. With the decline of Athens, democracy declined too. As Sparta superseded Athens, the ideal of homo politicus which was associated with direct democracy was gradually superseded by the notion of homo militans, its very negation. This ideal prevailed from the ascendance of Sparta to the end of the Roman interregnum.

The Christian Middle Ages did not help the progress of democracy, for the values of respublica Christiana framed a new ideal of being, the homo credens, an inevitable choice in an age of faith, authority and ascriptive hierarchy. While the Athenians tried to realize the good life in the polis, the Middle Ages saw Christians as pilgrims passing through human society. The apoliticism which this bred was a far cry from the overcharged political activism which nourished Athenian democracy.

Even though the Renaissance looked back to the classical age, its classicism was more Roman than Greek, as is clear from the political thought of its leading thinkers such as Niccolo Machiavelli. It is therefore not surprising that the Roman ideal of homo militans resurfaced. The republican bias of the Renaissance did not translate to democratic commitment. The Renaissance was absorbed in the charismatic politics of the Medicis and the Borgias, and in the problem of political instability. Its political morality was framed by the overriding necessity for political order, as is clear from the greatest political theorist of the period, Niccolo Machiavelli.

Europe was confronted with the problem of political order through the interminable gestation of the nation-state which stretched from the Reformation through the age of Absolutism to the French Revolution. The French Revolution was a phenomenal emancipatory struggle which heralded the beginning of the modern polity and the modern world. It changed the world profoundly by introducing remarkable innovations such as universal citizenship and the idea of inalienable rights of humans and citizens.

The French Revolution was a watershed in another sense. It reached back, at any rate, tried to reach back, to the Athenian ideal of popular power. This was aptly expressed in its theory of popular sovereignty and political participation. In this, it created implacable enemies not only against itself but also against democracy. The rising European bourgeoisie which had welcomed the French Revolution because of its hostility to the institutions and values of feudalism was appalled by the implications of popular sovereignty, especially its radical egalitarianism, the emphasis on equality and the prospect of the majority having absolute power over everything including private property. They understood only too well the threat which this posed to their right of property and the privileges which they enjoyed by virtue of their social and economic status. Inevitably, they undertook to wage war against these dreaded prospects.

Liberal Democracy

The European bourgeoisie knew that their interests demanded rejection of the idea of democracy as popular power, and that was precisely what they did. Eventually, they succeeded in replacing democracy with liberal democracy. Liberal democracy is markedly different from democracy even though it has significant affinities to it, for example, in the notion of government by the consent of the governed, formal political equality, inalienable human rights including the right to political participation, accountability of power to the governed and the rule of law. Nonetheless, the differences are highly significant. Instead of the collectivity, liberal democracy focuses on the individual whose claims are ultimately placed above those of the collectivity. It replaces government by the people with government by the consent of the people. Instead of the sovereignty of the people it offers the sovereignty of law.

In the final analysis, liberal democracy repudiates popular power. It is not really a political morality in the sense that classical democracy was to the Athenians but a political convenience, the political correlate of the market, or the political condition for operationalizing the law of value and maximizing its efficiency and sustainability. Also it appealed to the emerging bourgeoisie because it guarantees the rights of the individual, most significantly, the right of property against even the will of the majority.

So much is made of democracy's plurality and confusion of meanings that it is necessary to stress that, in regard to the emergence of liberal democracy, the cause is not the confusion of meanings but a deliberate political choice arising from a careful appraisal of substantive interests. What occurred was the rejection of a political doctrine and a political practice and not the introduction of definitional refinements.

The concept of democracy is bitterly contested to this day. However, by all indications the contestants know what it means. All those who opposed democracy even through the Enlightenment for enthroning the tyranny of numbers, the rule of passion and ignorance, the cult of mediocrity and power without responsibility (actually power without property) knew what they were opposing. They were not in the least confused about the meaning of democracy. They were addressing themselves to the idea of popular power. It was precisely because of this shared understanding of the meaning of democracy that these fears and criticisms arose.

In particular, they were addressing the fear that popular power would pose a grave threat to privilege, especially private property. In the end, the opposition to democracy was so successful that the fear of popular power became well-established. We find it among conservatives and liberals alike and even among the poor. James Mackintosh expressly argued in 1818 that universal suffrage would mean 'permanent animosity between opinion and property'. In 1824, Thomas Macaulay insisted that it would be 'the end of property and thus the end of civilization'. David Ricardo wanted suffrage only for those who did not have any interest in abolishing private property.

Up until the last quarter of the eighteenth century, there was no fundamental disagreement over the meaning of democracy. There was broad consensus among both its supporters and opponents that democracy meant what classical Athens said it was. That was precisely why the fear of democracy was so widespread, especially among the propertied classes, and why democracy was so vehemently denounced and opposed by so many, including some of the founders of the American Republic.

The founders of the American Republic took the momentous historical step of challenging the consensus on the meaning of democracy. Instead of merely denouncing democracy as others had done, they began the process of redefining it specifically as representative democracy. What looked on the surface like an innocuous distinction between direct and representative democracy was actually a radical departure which rejected the accepted meaning of democracy and substituted something different. For according to the accepted meaning of democracy, representative democracy was a contradiction in terms. Citizens had to participate directly in the exercise of sovereignty or there is no democracy at all. The idea of representative democracy repudiated the very core of the traditional meaning of democracy, popular power. However, representation was not invented by the Americans. It goes as far back as the Middle Ages and arguably beyond. But the Americans were the first to connect representation specifically to democracy and to advance the constitutional idea of representative democracy.

To understand the nature and significance of this change, it is important to remember that the founding fathers of the United States were not just making a concession to expediency. They were not trying to come to terms with the obvious difficulties of having direct democracy in a large, complex society. They were offering a new meaning on principle. Far from taking the view that complexity had compelled a necessary compromise in democratic arrangements, they welcomed complexity as a condition which made representation as inevitable as it was desirable:

> It is worth remembering that the Federalist argument—at a time when other options were still in contention—was not that 'representative democracy' was expedient in the conditions of a large republic, but on the contrary, that a large republic was desirable because it necessitated representation. The virtues of the Federalist solution, as against the existing Confederation or any other system which preserved an excessive degree of local autonomy and manageable units of self-goverment, was precisely that it precluded democracy in the traditional sense. Indeed, argued Madison, the larger the republic the better, since the ratio of representatives to represented will be reduced (Wood 1988:5).

When the European bourgeoisie finally succeeded in replacing democracy, what they replaced it with was not so much representative democracy as liberal democracy. It is indicative of the success of the opposition to democracy that we tendentially conflate democracy with liberal democracy and regard anyone who tries to say that liberal democracy is less than democracy as ahistorical. Perhaps, because it makes it easier for us to conflate liberal democracy with democracy, we seem very reluctant to study liberal democracy to be clear about its form and content. Even in the countries which are considered advanced democracies, there is very little knowledge of what democracy is and a great deal of confusion.

The practice of democracy, now largely reduced to multi-party electoral competition, tells rather little about democracy. Democratic practices such as elections, which mean very little in the context of oligopolistic parties and the inordinate influence of wealthy oligarchs, are mixed with fictional notions of 'the noble ideal of democracy'. There is very little interest in the doctrines and theories which are regarded as the classics of liberal democratic theory. Democracy has in some degree been reduced to an ideological representation which is well internalized; facts or realities which challenge this representation do not receive serious consideration.

For the purposes of this study, it is necessary to revisit liberal democracy briefly, especially its classic theoretical foundations. This is perhaps the most effective way of shedding light not only on liberal democracy but also on the confusions of our democratic discourse and democratic practice, confusions which are an important part of the problems of democratization in Africa.

Theoretical Foundations of Liberal Democracy

The classical theory of liberal democracy was developed by the social contract theorists, especially Thomas Hobbes and John Locke. Like Machiavelli, Hobbes was preoccupied with political order. In his time Britain was plagued by civil strife and political instability and threatened by ambitious rivals and neighbours, especially Spain. Hobbes repeatedly acknowledged his obsessive fear of anarchy and timorous nature, and used to joke that his mother gave birth to twins, fear and himself, referring to his rather premature birth in the panic caused by the arrival of the Spanish Armada. Not surprisingly, his political theory was a dedicated search for the most solid foundation for political order. He was convinced that society, every society, has an overriding interest in order and that any order is better than disorder.

For Hobbes, human nature demands political order, for humans are irresistibly egotistical. Their existence is a continuous striving for the satisfaction of an endless stream of desires, a striving that ends only in death. Human nature being what it is, a pre-political state of nature where the dedicated egotists seek gratification and self-aggrandizement, and where everyone is a law unto himself, would be a state of war of all against all. In this condition, there would be no leisure, no peace or culture, only constant fear of violent death. This is the unacceptable alternative to political order which renders the social contract for the formation of political society necessary. In the face of this reality, Hobbes argues that everyone's interest demands the cessation of hostilities, and the establishment of political order, whatever the terms.

How do the combatants in the state of nature get out of it? By contracting among themselves to surrender their right of nature to a neutral person or a group of persons, the Leviathan, who is effectively the sovereign. The sovereign does not ask them to surrender their natural rights and does not enter into any contractual obligation with them. It is merely a beneficiary of an undertaking which they make voluntarily among themselves. The implication of this is important. The sovereign incurs no obligation whatsoever to those who have surrendered their right of nature. The other side of this is that there can be no limit to the obligation of the subject to the sovereign except the overriding rationale of the contractual undertaking, namely self-preservation. When self-preservation is threatened, which for Hobbes means a return to the state of nature, then the question of obligation no longer arises.

This looks more like a theory of political order than a theory of democracy. And yet Hobbes, even more than Locke, is regarded as the father of liberal democratic theory. What is the affinity of this theory to democracy, liberal or otherwise? First, in the fact that what Hobbes offers is a theory of consent of the governed albeit a highly problematic one. It is only the fictional consent of what Hobbes and the other social contract theorists call a thought experiment. The consent is given under difficult conditions of anarchy and pervasive fear of violent death, and what is consented to is political absolutism. In so far as the alternative to the consent of the governed is near certainty of violent death, consent fades into compulsion; it is dissociated from choice. In the end Hobbes nullifies the notion of consent by rendering it irresistible.

Hobbes's liberal credentials do not lie in his theory of consent after all. What makes Hobbes's theory so important for liberal democracy is its peculiar character as a theory of limited government. Paradoxical as it may be for a theory that seemed so supportive of political absolutism this was what appealed to those people who feared democracy and the political radicalism of the French Revolution. Hobbes's political theory reproduces the laissez-faire of competitive capitalism in the political sphere.

For Hobbes, human beings suffer from unbridled egotism, and they are in inescapable bondage to an insatiable appetite. Different people desire different things, and no one always desires the same thing. Appetites shift constantly from one object of desire to another. Hobbes concludes from this that there is no *summum bonum* for the individual, let alone the collectivity. In reaching this conclusion he set aside a concept which had dominated political theory for centuries. The closest thing to a common good in

Hobbes is the maintenance of political order which enables people to go about their selfish pursuits without destroying one another.

It is just this need to avoid mutual annihilation which renders government necessary. According to Hobbes, government exists merely to maintain order for the physical security of its subjects. The government could not do more than that even if it wanted to because it is impossible to conceptualise a common good that makes any sense apart from self-preservation. Hobbes's is the quintessential minimalist government theorized with unprecedented rigour. It is even more minimalist than that of Adam Smith's *The Wealth of Nations*. That is why Hobbes is regarded as the father of liberal democracy. Among other things, what Hobbes's exalted place in the liberal tradition tells us is that the salient doctrine of liberal democracy is that the government which governs least, governs best.

Interestingly, the classic of liberal democracy has very little to do with democracy. While the Athenians were concerned with people governing themselves for themselves, Hobbes's only concern is how people might be protected from themselves and from others. In its classic sense, democracy is the realization of human potentialities through active participation in rulership, but in liberal democracy, it offers only protection. In the one case, freedom is positive and activist, in the other, it is a passive acceptance of immunity. The one enables and empowers, the other prevents and protects. So much for Hobbes.

The political theory of John Locke makes markedly different assumptions from those of Thomas Hobbes. His point of departure is, like that of Hobbes, a pre-political state of nature, which, though not so fearsome and violent as Hobbes's, was unacceptably 'inconvenient'. Because of its inconveniences, its denizens contract out of it into political society. However, for Locke, the state of nature is a state of peace rather than war. It is not without governance. God rules it through the law of nature which humans understand through reason. The law of nature allows humankind rights, especially the right to self-preservation. It also enjoins obligations, especially the obligation to enforce the law of nature. Whether in or out of political society, human beings have rights and these rights are inalienable. In or out of the state of nature, human beings are governed by laws and they must fulfil the obligations arising from these laws. The state of nature is lawful and reasonably peaceful.

However, useful and necessary as it is, the enforcement of the law of nature poses problems because everyone is an enforcer of this law. This often leads to a situation of being judge in one's own case with the result that objectivity is invariably compromised, injustices are perpetrated and conflicts ensue. It is to remedy these inconveniences that people contract to come out of the state of nature.

In Locke's case, the contract is made in two stages. The people in the state of nature first contract among themselves to form political society. Having done so, they then contract to set up a government by surrendering their right to enforce the law of nature, a function now performed solely by the government. Unlike the case of Hobbes, where the executive is only the beneficiary of an undertaking which other people have made among themselves, the executive in Locke is a party to the contract to set up government and is obligated by the terms of the contract, especially to enforce the law of nature and the right of nature judiciously.

At first sight, it is easier here than in Hobbes to see the democratic prospects of this theory. It is emphatic on government by consent and on the obligations of rulers to the ruled. Also it posits human rights, particularly the right of self-preservation and the right of property, which are inalienable. But what is the actual democratic content of these elements?

On closer examination Locke's theory of consent has serious problems, especially regarding the critical question about how consent is given or withheld in actual historical societies. Confronted with this question, Locke replaces the concept of consent with implicit consent and rationalises just about any link with government as implicit consent. Thus when we use the highways, we have consented to the government of the territory. Since it is difficult not to be associated in some way with some government facility or its jurisdiction, it is difficult to imagine a situation of non consent. It turns out that the only circumstances in which we can signify non consent is when we are in active revolt. But if we can only signify non consent in such an extreme and dangerous way, the right to give or withhold consent effectively ceases, for a right does not really exist if it cannot be enjoyed in relative ease and freedom from danger.

The theory of consent also reveals that Locke does not have a democratic commitment to human rights. Locke is totally focused on the right to self-preservation and the right to property. However, it turns out that the right to self-preservation is only an aspect of the one right that matters to Locke, which is property right. It matters so much to Locke that he upholds it even when it entails someone else's death by deprivation. In the *Second Treatise*, Locke accepts that God has given the earth and, everything in nature to humankind but he says that by mixing the common property with our labour we legitimately create private property. He then raises the question of appropriating so much from the common stock that others are deprived of the benefits of our common heritage and possibly of self-preservation as well. But instead of limiting private appropriation so that all can partake and survive—the position most consistent with Locke's privileging of self-preservation—he argues that as long as we are able to prevent what we appropriate from going to waste, our right of private property cannot be limited.

Locke proceeds to prioritize the right of private property more still by reducing the right to self-preservation to the right to private property. He does this by defining property to include ourselves. Property for Locke means 'lives, liberties and estates', our persons are our primary property and the right to self-preservation is the protection of our property in ourselves.

Not surprisingly, Locke's defence of rights and liberties becomes an obsessive defence of the right of property. We soon learn that the 'inconveniences' which motivated the transition from the state of nature to political society are essentially about threats to property defined to include physical being. But if political society and the state are instituted primarily to protect property, then those who have no property have no interest in political society and no claim to political participation. In line with this logic, Locke the advocate of inalienable human rights, supported a property qualification for the franchise.

The strength and the appeal which made the Second Treatise a classic of liberalism is not its advocacy of human rights or government by consent, let alone popular participation in government. What made it a liberal classic is its unabashed privileging of property as the one right that counts, the right which called government into being in the first place.

Locke and Hobbes seem quite different in their concerns and the methods of their theory, and yet they are regarded as the fathers of liberal democracy. What is it that is common to them in articulating the kernel of liberal democracy? It is something whose link to democracy is quite tenuous: minimal government. In Hobbes, the minimization of government is inevitable because there is no common good except self-preservation, and there is only one thing the government can do that will be in the interest of everyone, which is to keep order. For Locke, the need for minimal government arises partly from the fact that government is barely necessary to begin with. Reaching back to the original Stoic idea that humankind is one country, God is its ruler and reason its constitution, Locke barely recognizes the need for government. The need arises, only because of the need to remedy some inconveniences. Government exists just to prevent disorder which may be caused by everyone enforcing the law. It prevents harm but it does not seek to do good. Indeed, it cannot be activist, however well-intentioned, without doing harm by encroaching on the right of property.

We may conclude that the classical theory of liberal democracy is less an expression of democracy than its restriction. It does away entirely with the idea of popular power and it replaces the idea of self-government with that of the consent of the governed. Even so the consent of the governed is largely an abstraction which is not operationalized, especially by universal suffrage. It does not set much value on the idea of political participation or the active development of human settles for a negative conception of freedom as the absence of constraint by the state. It is not about involvement in government but about minimizing government and its nuisance value.

The Development of Liberal Democracy

Liberal democracy has not stood still. It has been evolving continuously, and nothing useful can be said about the status of democracy in the contemporary world without taking account of its development. Those who have contributed to its development include Weber, Schumpeter, Michels, Pareto, Durkheim, Truman, Lipset, Dahl, Almond, Verba, Green, Hart and Berlin. Space does not permit a comprehensive treatment of the evolution of liberal democracy. A few examples will be given here just to illustrate the main thrust of this development, which is towards the trivialization of democracy.

Weber's work was particularly useful in placing democracy in the context of industrial capitalism, which he portrayed (in *The Protestant Ethic and the Spirit of Capitalism*) as uniquely different from other civilisations. It is particularly so in its rational calculating attitude, a tendency epitomized by the scientific method. Weber insists that this calculating attitude goes beyond the realm of science into production, culture and institutions. For instance, it underlies capitalist production, which is driven by technical improvement, information, knowledge and unrelenting pursuit of efficiency and profit. This calculating attitude, which is a break from the metaphysical consciousness of the past, has weakened the grand moralities and ideologies of the past and thrown people back on themselves and their value-maximizing strategies.

Weber argues that these changes also undermine some of the presuppositions of liberal democracy, especially the idea of an accepted political morality and metaphysical notions such as natural rights. He holds that the consummatory orientation of the liberal project has to change to a procedural one. In other words, it has to be conceived more modestly as just a political arrangement which accommodates competing values and interests and allows them to make their own choices according to their values and to fend for themselves.

The rationalistic orientation militates against liberal democracy in another sense. A particularly significant sedimentation of the calculative culture is bureaucratic organisation and its spread as the means of administration. As a social structure, bureaucratic organisation is hierarchic, functionally specialized and rule-bound, features which render it conducive to accountability and predictability. All of which is good for capitalist production but bad for democracy. Even those organisations such as political parties and interest groups which are vehicles of democratic expression cannot avoid being bureaucratized and de-democratized, and yet the tide of bureaucratization in modern society cannot be stemmed.

While Weber is content to show how the social context of modern industrial society must limit democratic participation, Schumpeter launches a direct attack on participatory democracy. Schumpeter can only think of democracy as representative democracy. He defines it as the political arrangement by which those who make public policy do so by virtue of winning a mandate. Its essence is not the opportunity to rule or to participate in rulership but the opportunity to replace unwanted rulers:

> Democracy does not mean and cannot mean that the people actually rule in any obvious sense of the terms', people' and 'rule'. Democracy means only that the people have the opportunity of accepting or refusing the men who are to rule them (Schumpeter 1978:284-5).

In saying this, Schumpeter does not pretend to be merely recording how things are or suggesting how democracy is obliged to bend to expediency. He is prescribing how things should be. He had a very low opinion of ordinary people whom he regarded as generally apathetic, lazy, fickle, ignorant, prejudiced and of unsound judgment (Schumpeter 1978:256-64). It cannot be in their interest or that of the state for them to rule. To underline this, he made a distinction between the sovereignty of the state, which he considers entirely appropriate, and the sovereignty of the people, which is dangerous. The people have to be led; it is enough if they are consulted about who should lead them and if these prospective leaders compete for the popular mandate in what is now called 'competitive elitism'. But for the people to actually rule is anathema.

Contemporary social science has played a highly significant role in the trivialization of democracy through successive waves of theorists who theorized democracy ostensibly to make its meaning clearer and more relevant to the actual world of politics. It is not clear how far these revisions were motivated by science or interest. But the outcomes of these waves of revision reflect a clear class bias and they have contributed to the trivialization of democracy.

One of the most important of these waves was the pluralist wave. This school of thought rose partly from the inspiration of Schumpeter and partly as a response to the limitations of his theory. Following Schumpeter, the pluralists dismissed the feasibility and even the desirability of classical democracy as well as the nineteenth century theorists of representative democracy including John Stuart Mill. They held that ordinary people never really exercise influence in politics, being ignorant, apathetic and lacking power resources, nor do the representatives of the people really ever represent them. More often than not, they lead, manipulate or dominate them. Like Schumpeter, the pluralists accepted that the essence of democracy is not participation in rule but the choice of those to rule. These affinities reflect the fact that the pluralist school largely shared Schumpeter's prejudices regarding the moral, psychological and intellectual limitations of the masses.

Having concluded that classical democracy as well as representative democracy are not feasible, the pluralists proceed to show how democratic politics actually works without bothering to explain how they came to characterize as democratic the politics they describe. In effect they discard the meaning of democracy and arbitrarily select another one. But this need not detain us here.

The pluralist model of politics treats 'political man' as homo economicus, the calculating utility-maximizing egotist on the prowl. Political society is treated like the market where people individually or collectively seek to maximize utilities and where political interests are negotiated and promoted just like economic interests amid intense competition. This, the pluralists say, is not the ideal world of Athenian or Rousseauan democracy but the real world.

What is interesting is that the pluralists do not see their project as the underwriting of the defeat of democracy. On the contrary, they see it as the prevailing reality which they describe as being positively associated with democracy. Essentially, they see a world of interest groups which are not so unequal and which remain reasonably competitive. An interest group may have a competitive advantage in some respect, and others in other respects. The disadvantages and advantages cancel out on balance. Thus interest groups allow individuals to be more effective politically by forming a critical mass, aggregating and articulating their interests in ways that are more likely to achieve results. In being all this they are an asset to political participation. And because of the general balance of power, they prevent the stratification of the polity and thus serve the cause of democracy. By facilitating the competitive distribution of political power in society, interest groups encourage bargaining, consensus-building and inclusiveness. According to pluralists such as Dahl and Truman, what determines public policy is actually the net effect of the pressures of interest groups which are usually so many and balanced that no single one wields excessive power. Democratic decision-making is secured by polyarchy.

The problems of pluralist theory are easy enough to see. In the name of realism, pluralist theory adopts the prevailing political practice in the West and arbitrarily redefines democracy in terms of this practice. It represents issues of interest group competition as the salient issue of democracy and frames a discourse which is not really about democracy.

It does not deal with the issue of consent or the problem of political allegiance generally. Nor does it deal with the accountability of power or even the rights of individuals. It evades completely the issue of self-government and even representation. Democracy is no longer about government by the people or even government by representatives of the people or about participation in any meaningful sense; it is merely a matter of joining groups which strive to influence policy or to realize interests. Democracy comes very close here to being reduced to the pursuit of group interests.

Even the prospects of realizing interests or influencing policy through pressures are not problematized. The assumption that groups are generally competitive in the sense of being more or less equal in their power resources, at any rate, equal enough for a general balance of power, is patently false. Interest groups in industrialized societies are, to use John Porter's famous phrase, a vertical mosaic. The vast majority of them which are at the bottom of this mosaic have no significant power while a few are enormously powerful, powerful enough to have their way quite often. The best argument for this has been made by a pluralist who began to question the empirical validity of pluralist assumptions. In *Politics and Markets*, Charles Lindblom shows that the power which big business could exercise in politics and society generally was far above the power that any other interest group could muster (Lindblom 1977). More often than not, the power of these interest groups is informal and dissociated from responsibility and accountability.

Another notable theoretical wave which contributed to the devaluing of democracy is the protectionist theory of democracy. According to this theory, the democratic polity is one in which the citizen is protected against the state. It is invariable a polity which has a vibrant civil society that is able to check state power, particularly its propensity to be oppressive. This theory has accentuated the contrast between the state and civil society and helped to transform it into a dichotomy, the state being the sphere of necessity while civil society is the realm of freedom.

The protectionist theory of democracy goes back to the antipathies against state and government which constituted the phenomenon of minimal government. The theory gives the misleading impression that the state is simply a threat and not also a fundamental condition of freedom, that civil society is never oppressive. In the protectionist theory of democracy, the idea of sovereignty disappears as does the idea of positive freedom, leaving us to the idea of negative freedom. Democracy is no longer about active self-determination or involvement in the collective enterprise of democratic citizenship but about securing immunities against threat.

Some recent theoretical waves in the extension of democratic theory stand out for making virtues of the failures of existing democratic practices. For instance, in *The Civic Culture*, Almond and Verba (1963) suggest that political apathy is good for democratic stability. In similar vein, Nelson Polsby argued in another notable book, *Community Power and Political theory*, that political apathy is a sign of satisfaction with the performance of the government in power and that most people, in any case, prefer to go about their business than to take interest in politics (Polsby 1963).

Finally, in *An Economic Theory of Democracy*, Anthony Downs agrees with Schumpeter that the main event is the struggle for power, wealth and office, and that any social outcome in politics is incidental, in the same sense as production is incidental to profit-making in economics. Downs insists that the reality is that the rational men in democratic politics are interested in their own 'utility outcomes' rather than public policy as such, and that interest groups and political parties are not interested in realizing an ideal, democratic or otherwise, or in making a better society, only in office and its rewards (Downs 1957:96).

Democracy and the Market

Downs and Schumpeter raise the issue of the relation between democracy and industrial capitalism which bears importantly on the demise of democracy. Liberal democracy developed alongside the development of industrial capitalism, and was largely driven by industrial capitalism. In effect, liberal democracy reproduced in the political sphere the core values of the market, with the result that it appears to be the political correlate of the market. This has become a source of considerable contestation and confusion. When we declare our commitment to these core values, are we committed to the market or to democracy? Which of these two elements has priority?

Before going into these questions, it is necessary to take cognizance of the homology of liberal democracy and industrial capitalism. All the classical sociologists and political economists, for example, Spencer, Toennies, Durkheim, Marx, Maine, Conte, Schumpeter, Adam Smith and Weber, agree that capitalism created an entirely new society, the market society. Market society is based on a principle of solidarity which is radically different from the primordial ties and the traditional authority of feudal society. Its basis of integration is the nexus of exchange relations. Because everyone is self-seeking and regards others as a means to its ends, all become interdependent, for without using others as means, none can attain the selfish goals which they seek. Hegel, who theorized this phenomenon exhaustively, puts it this way:

> When men are thus... reciprocally related to one another in the work and the satisfaction of their needs, subjective self-seeking turns into a contribution to the satisfaction of the needs of everyone else. That is to say by a dialectical advance, subjective self-seeking turns into the mediation of the particular through the universal, with the result that each man in earning, producing and enjoying on his own account is *eo ipso* producing and earning for the enjoyment of everyone else (Hegel 1942).

Adam Smith makes the same point in his discussion of bourgeois society in *The Wealth of Nations*. He argues that bourgeois society epitomizes the development of the unique qualities of human beings, namely, egotistical entrepreneurship and dependence. The paradox of egotism and dependence is resolved in the necessities of commodity production and exchange by which the self-seeking of each binds him to all:

> It is not from the benevolence of the butcher, the brewer, or the broker that we expect our dinner, but from their regard to their own interest. We address ourselves, not to their humanity but to self-love, and never talk to them of our own necessities but of their own advantages (Smith 1937).

Market society has its own logic which determines its own form of government and administration and its political ideology. This is reflected in the fit of the capitalist economy and liberal government in Adam Smith. Smith posits that the social order created by the interdependence of commodity production and exchange is the frame of government. The state is formally engendered as support for the liberties whose dialectics constitute this social order. For Smith, the basic operational principle of the state is that 'every man as long as he does not violate the laws of justice, is left perfectly free to pursue his own way and to bring both his industry and capital into competition with those of any other man, or other men'.

The affinity between the core values of the market and liberal democracy can be clearly seen by reflecting on the presuppositions of commodity production and exchange. First, the commodity bearers in exchange act self-interestedly. Each is concerned with maximizing utilities, and regards all others only as means to that end. To be sure, everyone is locked into commodity relations which require that they produce for others. However, people become the means of others only because they posit themselves as ends, that is to say, they become the means only to underscore and serve their selfishness.

Second, the exchange relation is a relation of property owners. If one does not have a commodity which has some use value for some other person, one does not participate in exchange, one offers no value and gets none. Third, the commodity bearers are free. They posit themselves as ends and out of their own free will dispose of their commodities through contractual agreements to which they freely enter. Indeed, if exchange was not free, resources would not be allocated efficiently, and the law of value would not be operationalized. Fourth, the commodity bearers are equal. All qualitative distinctions are masked behind the formal sameness of buyers and sellers. With qualitative distinctions masked, everyone sees everyone else in the uniformizing role of exchanger. As they exchange equivalents, each person sees the other as equally worthy. In sum the values of the market are essentially the same as the core values of liberal democracy: egotism, property, formal freedom and equality.

The relation between industrial capitalism and market society on the one hand and liberal democracy on the other can be seen in clearer relief by reflecting on the nature of the law in market society. As is well known, law occupies a pivotal role in liberal democracy; the repudiation of popular power in liberal democracy is expressed in the replacement of the sovereignty of the people with the sovereignty of the law. The form and content of law in liberal democracy and market society expresses the fundamental attributes of market society.

To begin with this law reflects the revolutionary changes inherent in the shift from feudalism to industrial capitalism. Emile Durkheim's typology of law in *The Division of Labour in Society* is instructive here.

He distinguishes between penal law and restitutive law. Penal law, which is characteristic of pre-capitalist societies ordered around shared beliefs and sentiments and a strong orientation to collective identity rather than individualism, is punitive, reflecting the perception of offence as crime. Restitutive law, which prevails under a market society and presupposes that interests are individual and potentially in conflict, is concerned with reestablishing damaged relations. It tends to be highly codified and to require a specialized enforcement machinery because, being a mediator between conflicting private interests, its application needs to be objectified.

Another aspect of the homology of law in liberal democracy and market society is that it rests on the values of commodity production and exchange. That is why this law is abstract, universalistic and highly focused on private property. In the relation of commodity bearers individuality is extinguished. Everyone is collapsed into the homogeneous category of buyer/seller, exchanger; each one exists for the other only as the owner of a commodity or the producer of exchange values; and the commodities themselves become homogenized as exchange values.

The use of money as the medium of exchange underscores this homogenization, for in circulation values are moving constantly from commodity form and money form, reducing all differences to quantitative differences. Following this tendency towards homogenization, the law which arises among people in exchange relations must have a universalistic thrust, for laws applying to categories which do not permit differentiation cannot be particularistic. Also laws made by subjects which are equal (as commodity bearers) for themselves as equals apply equally, universally.

The homogenization is also a process of abstraction. In the market the existence of the producer as a human being is masked. In place of the natural person, there is only an abstract being, the buyer, the seller, the exchanger, the commodity mask. It is only in the emergence of this abstract and disembodied person that rights, including the all-important right of property, fully develop. For it is the fixity of the bearer of rights achieved in the abstraction of the commodity bearer into a generic person, so to speak, which gives property rights stability and definition. We no longer think of the conjunction of particular properties and particular persons, a conjunction that is ephemeral, for it is only a matter of history that particular persons and particular properties exist and are linked in a relation of ownership. In the emergence of the legal subject, subject and object, property owner and property are linked inseparably. It is rather like moving from the realm of contingence to one of necessity.

Apart from being abstract and universalistic, the law of market society is formalistic. This is associated with the distinction between the universal categories such as property owner and actual persons. Of course what appears in court as an abstraction, the defendant, is also a person and his or her physical presence cannot be entirely denied. But in keeping with the universalism of the law, he or she has to be dealt with very formally or the law will be particularized. Thus in its procedures, the law relies heavily on rational proof and, as much as possible, avoids expedential considerations. In the same vein, it appears to be more interested in logic than in truth and in formal justice than in substantial justice.

Finally, one aspect of law under liberal democracy which underlines its historical specificity to capitalist economy is that this law is mainly about property. The exchange relation is a contractual relation between free persons who mutually recognize each other's rights. In the act of exchange, the exchangers constitute a contractual relation and posit the recognition of their rights of private property and its free disposal. As Ferdinand Toennies has argued, 'as a product of the rational will, the law centers around the elementary phenomenon of property transfers or the exchange of goods' (Toennies 1963). This characteristic of the law so obvious in substantive law is also evident in the nature of legal proceedings:

> Civil procedure takes the basic form of private claims by an individual (or aggregation of individuals) which is basically a claim for damages quantified in money. This means

that as procedural requirement, any interest to be thought of in legal terms must be expressed as a commodity. Legally protected interests boil down to the individual's person or property. But even rights in respect of the person are reified: the physical person is considered as an income-producing asset (so it is cheaper to injure a poor person than a rich one); the only non-physical personal interest recognized in English law is 'reputation'. Hence all kinds of needs or demands are forced into the commodity form when put forward as legal rights—for example, proposals to control the extent of corporate and state surveillance tend to be discussed in terms of the right of the individual to 'privacy' (Holloway and Picciotto 1979:172).

Let us return to the question whether our commitment to democratic values is a commitment to democracy or to the market and whether the market or democracy, economy or polity, has priority. The theory of liberal democracy clearly answers this question in favour of the market. It is not the economy that gets politicized, it is the polity that gets economicized. As the quote from Adam Smith indicates, the overriding principle of the polity is to facilitate laissez-faire. For Hobbes, the state is just a facilitator which provides the necessary order to ensure that the dedicated egotists can get on with their self-seeking without killing themselves. For Locke, government arises from the need to preserve the right of property. For all of them the less the government tries to do beyond maintaining order, the better. Indeed, government cannot be activist without doing more harm than good. Liberal democracy allows the subordination of politics to economics and the state to the market by offering a concept of politics which is a radical departure from previous concepts of politics and which nullifies the very raison d'être of politics.

In previous political theory, politics was always the moment of universality, the acting out of collective identity, the occasion for marrying the individual to the collectivity, setting collective goals and realizing them. It has always been the defining moment of our sociability. Liberal democracy changes this completely. In liberal democratic theory, polity and politics become the moment of particularity, completely divorced from those considerations which led humankind to refer to the state as 'res publica' or even 'the commonwealth', the instance of sociability and solidarity. Liberal democracy economicizes politics so that it is all about egotism, interests in conflict and no common interest. This is the antithesis of politics.

Given the fact that liberal democracy and the market have the same core values and the primacy accorded to the market over the state and economics over politics in the liberal tradition, it is difficult to take for granted the declared commitment of the market economies to democracy. And it may be reasonably assumed that when commitment to democracy is declared, it may be derived from a primary commitment to the market. This assumption may be borne out by the fact that the industrialized countries and the international development agencies which are currently insisting on structural adjustment and democratization in the developing countries are often inclined to give priority to structural adjustment over democratization.

The development of capitalism has been reflected in the development of liberal democracy. The classical contractarian liberalism which emerged from the state of nature corresponds to the ideal conception of the market with perfect competition. As capitalism took hold, developed into monopoly capitalism and went into what following Foucault may be called a panoptic mode, liberal democracy in turn abandoned political participation in any meaningful sense, embraced competitive elitism and finally, degenerated into apoliticism. Now democracy tends to refer to multi-party elections.

The New Threat to Democracy

In the contemporary world, democracy faces a new and deadly threat from the process of globalization, which we may define rather simplistically as the stretch of processes, practices and structures across space, especially the national space to globality or the transnationalization of things. In the wake of globalization the traditional assumption to the effect that the nation-state is the inevitable basic political organisation of humankind has become highly problematic because globalization is undermining the nation-state and its relevance, leaving its future in doubt.

As the relevance of the nation-state diminishes, so does that of democracy, especially liberal democracy. For democracy is ideally articulated in the context of the national organisation of political power. The nation-state, the traditional repository of sovereignty, has the consummate power which no sub-state or super-state political formation can legitimately claim or exercise. This consummate power, including the power of life and death within the national territory of the nation-state, is the other side of democratic freedom and self-realization. For it is what gives concreteness to them since there is no freedom in powerlessness and no point in democratic arrangements when power resources are minimal or nonexistent. When we apply the concept of democracy to any social or political formation apart from the nation-state, its use is largely metaphorical. We can and do apply the concept of democracy to the government of the family but that is clearly not a strict usage of the term. The democratic intensity of the family is low because a natural sense of minimal obligation makes democratic arrangements less compelling, as does the family's lack of anything remotely close to consummate power. Similarly, political formations such as the European Union and the United Nations are democratic in a largely analogical sense; they too have low democratic intensity lacking consummate power.

One way in which global processes have been significant for democracy is how they have been whittling away the power of the nation-state. With the transnationalization of more and more activities, decisions which affect people's lives and shape public policies are made in distant places, often anonymously by agents and forces we can hardly understand, much less control. Therefore, it is not always clear what people are choosing or controlling at national elections. The dilemma is that the political entity which ideally materializes popular sovereignty has less and less power while the amorphous space of transnational phenomena which is not amenable to democratic control has more power. A polarisation appears to be occurring: on the one side, democracy without empowerment, and on the other, power inaccessible to democratization.

Global processes are affecting the prospects of democracy more radically still by threatening the annulment of the social. This is connected to the constitution of capitalist hegemony at the end of the Cold War. Already liberal theory privileged the market over the state, studiedly prohibiting the state from being an entrepreneur to avoid giving it any financial independence and positing that the less state, the better. Now the status of the market is higher still. The market looms so large it effectively subsumes society as well. Market society is no longer simply a metaphor or an analytic concept. It is a living reality.

As the market subsumes society and consumer identity becomes the overriding identity, democratic politics, any politics for that matter, becomes very difficult. This is so because the market is about self-seeking and private concerns; it is the moment of particularity. Democratic politics, on the other hand, is the moment of universality. It is about collective enterprise, about how common concerns are to be addressed. Indeed, without the presupposition of common cause, and relative homogeneity of the population which makes common cause possible in the first place, the basis for democratic participation disappears for we cannot expect to participate where we have no interest in what is strictly other people's business.

One aspect of the desocialization of life in market society deserves special mention because of its special significance for politics. Advances in communications technology driven by global marketing and the information revolution which it has spawned are reconstituting consciousness as information, information delivered in ever-increasing profusion and speed. Since this information is only a record encrusted in technology and carries no social meaning, it does not integrate socially. Rather it isolates, partly because of the structure in which it is delivered and consumed. The technology connects us as discrete units in an electronic coherency while isolating us socially, for, among other things, it is delivered through the privacy, of modems, storage devices and computer screens.

In this context, there can only be a politics of disempowerment, for here is a context in which the critical role of political mobilisation is abstracted and concentrated in the mass media. The mass media constitutes and instrumentalizes contemporary politics but in a manner that amounts to self-constitution. It promises politics and participation only to deny them by crystallizing itself as a formidable power and a formidable obstacle to politics. It denies them by creating a realm of necessity which demands submission rather than one of freedom which facilitates and enjoins creativity.

Global processes have framed a syndrome of isolation and desocialization at the confluence of the singularities of the new communications technology, information and the public sphere. For a start, the technology delivers the information to us in relative isolation devoid of social experience. Then the information itself is isolating. And both technology and information define a new public sphere which is mediated in complex ways that desocialize it. This is not the bourgeois public sphere of Habermas so conducive to democratic politics (Habermas 1976) for it is decidedly nondialogical.

Our visibility to each other in this new public space is abstract as is the space itself. It has hardly any boundaries, it is too fluid, too amorphous to elicit a sense of sharing in a social entity or to nurture political projects and democratic activism. How can people organize against oppressive power which is impersonal, invisible and fluid, power which is always flowing into spaces beyond our grasp and immune to the institutional constraints in our locality? It is not just power that is fluid. We too are fluid. We too are fluid and despatialized. Unfortunately, the expansion and porosity of our space gives us only a disorienting sense of spacelessness and very little room for political action.

Conclusion

These reflections show that the triumph of democracy may be more apparent than real. Democracy has had an embattled history struggling to survive in an environment in which support for it was rarely ever more than lukewarm and invariably ambivalent, confused or opportunistic, and opposition to it powerful, resourceful and unrelenting. By all indications it would be more appropriate to be lamenting the demise of democracy rather than celebrating its universal triumph.

Democracy was displaced by liberal democracy which has itself atrophied in a long process of devaluation during which it lost much of its redeeming democratic elements. Under pressure from political reaction, liberal values have lost ground. In most of the 'established democracies', in the contemporary world, liberal is now a term of abuse, a label to be avoided by anyone who wants public office.

As for democracy, it has been defined and redefined in an endless process of appropriating democratic legitimacy for political values, interests and practices that are in no way democratic. At the same time, the process has yielded an anarchy of meanings of democracy and spread confusion, to the detriment of democracy, which now means too much and too little.

And now with globalization, democracy faces yet another problem which is uniquely different and extremely threatening. It is not a problem for democracy in the sense of redefining it in theory and practice or bending it to the service of specific interests. It is not a problem of appropriating democratic legitimacy for something else, or trivializing it or even rejecting it. What globalization is doing is rendering democracy irrelevant, and in this it poses the most serious threat yet in the history of democracy.

This is the context in which Africa is democratizing. What are the implications of this context for the democratization in the developing regions of the world, especially Africa? To begin with it is now necessary to reexamine the assumption that there is a 'real' world of democracy out there, a world of established and flourishing democracies which Africa can and should join, a word which is anxious and able to play midwife to the birth of democracy in Africa. By all indications, the 'established democracies' are not able to offer the developing countries clear and meaningful standards of democratization to relate to. This is because they themselves have no clear and meaningful standard of democracy, a condition arising from the growing alienation of the practice of democracy from the Western ideology of democracy and the concerted effort by powerful interests to deradicalize democracy by offering a profusion of definitions which trivialize it.

In the midst of the contrived confusion over the meaning of democracy, all kinds of ideological representations, most of them inconsistent or incoherent, are put out in response to changing political and economic conditions of democracy and internalized. In these circumstances, some people in the West are unable to be critical about their own democratic practice, and they tend to relapse into regarding democracy as 'the way we are' and what we do. This renders them ineffective as promoters of democracy, making some developing countries suspicious that democracy is another ruse to conceal westernization.

The confusion over what democracy is has translated into confusion over what to do to support democracy. Democracy is being supported variously by economic liberalization, Structural Adjustment Programmes, political conditionality, the cutting-off of aid to dictators as a sanction, the continuation of aid to dictators to avoid causing economic conditions which encourage extremism, the weakening of the state and the strengthening of the state. Equally, democracy is being supported by urging the need for consensus-building for policy as well as urging political will (a euphemism for authoritarianism) for implementing adjustment programmes, by advocacy of the democratization of development so that the people possess development, and also by top-down approaches, to overcome the resistance of vested interests.

The trivialization of democracy has in turn trivialized notions of what democratization entails and what it takes for others to support democracy; it has led to the confusion of democratic processes with democratic outcomes. Thus external support for democracy has tended to be focused on multi-party elections, easy tolerance of noncompetitive electoral contests and the presumption that voting amounts to choosing.

Africa is democratizing in an international context in which there is apparently no allowance made for the fact that liberal democracy is a historical product. Similarly, little or no attempt is made to separate the values and principles of democracy or liberal democracy from the particular historical practices which operationalize these values and principles in specific historical settings. Since this issue is not usually raised, the question of finding solutions to it does not generally arise. And, if the question had been raised, it would have been quite difficult given the rich harvest of meanings of democracy which have come from decades of trying to mystify it and to appropriate it for political practices that are far from democratic. One serious danger, which looms large for democratizing Africa, is the daunting task of operationalizing the principles and values of democracy in historical conditions that are markedly different from those of the established liberal democracies.

As we have seen, liberal democracy is a child of industrial capitalism, a product of a socially atomized society where production and exchange are highly commodified and thus of a society which is essentially a market. It is the product of a society in which interests are so particularized that the very notion of common interest becomes problematic, hence the imperative of democratic participation.

Contemporary Africa remains a far cry from this. It is still predominantly pre-capitalist and pre-industrial. Primordial loyalties and pre-capitalist social structures remain strong. Apart from the urban enclaves, most African rural societies are still constituted as what Durkheim calls mechanical solidarity; they are still communal, and it is communalism which defines the people's perception of self-interest, their freedom and their location in the social whole. Liberal democracy presupposes individualism but there is little individualism in the communal societies of rural Africa; it assumes the abstract universalism of legal subjects, but that applies mainly in the urban enclaves. The political party system of liberal societies make little sense in societies where the development of associational life is rudimentary and interess groups remain essentially primary groups. In the light of such differences, it will be very misleading to think of democratization in Africa as multi-party electoral competition.

In Africa's search for democracy, there is very little in the experience of the established democracies to guide it and a great deal to mislead it. That makes the task of democratization in Africa all the more difficult and the outcome all the more uncertain. But the democratization of Africa is an event of enormous historical significance—not only for Africa, but for democracy and the possibility of civilisation.

While the relevance of democracy is diminishing and its potential for development appears to be dissipated in the North, it is gathering tremendous impetus in Africa and looks set to make a decisive impact not only on the history of that part of the world but also to use its resurgence in Africa as its defining moment.

To begin with, all the major players in Africa agree on the overriding importance of democratization. Of particular significance in this regard is the desire of the ordinary people of Africa for democracy in the name of a 'second independence' from their own leaders as opposed to the first independence from the colonizing powers. The language of this demand suggests that it is a matter of survival; the demand arises from a shared feeling that the economic mismanagement and the brutal repression of the indigenous leadership in most of post-colonial Africa has become life-threatening for ordinary people. They see their political empowerment through democratization as an essential part of the process of getting the economic agenda right at last, as well as managing the development project better, so as to address the intensifying poverty and the prospect of physical extinction. The debates in the National Conferences shed light on these motivations.

The United Nations development agencies have also come to the conclusion that democracy is essential for improved development performance, as is evident in official policy documents such the United Nations Program of Action for African Economic Recovery and Development (UNPAAERD) of 1986-1990. The Bretton Woods Institutions, in a significant break from their traditional apoliticism, have come to much the same conclusion. So has the Organization of African Unity, although it is unclear if this is a grudging concession to the spirit of the times. The rich donor countries have also reached the same conclusion, hence the currency of political conditionality.

The importance of democracy in Africa goes beyond this. Increasingly democracy looks like the necessary condition for dealing with the political question which underlies the deepening crisis of underdevelopment. The state-building project, always violent, has been particularly so in Africa, where it is has been stoutly resisted by African culture and retarded by the failure of capitalist development. Instead of breaking down competing power centres to the state and abolishing other foci of loyalty, it has tended to consolidate them as people fall back on traditional solidarity groups embracing national, ethnic and communal identities. The clash of these solidarity groups with the uniformizing state project has been all the more violent because such groups with cultural holistic identities are taken by their members to incarnate their very being and so worthy of being defended at all costs. By giving the state the image of a hostile and threatening force and causing people to embrace traditional solidarity groups, the state-building project is effectively dissolving the state in Africa; often there is neither the political coherence nor the political order for it to be anything like a going concern.

Clearly, the state project is not winning yet in Africa. Somehow, this condition does not appear to be passing away. If anything, as the examples of Sudan, Djibouti, Nigeria, Cameroon, Zaire, Somalia, Sierra Leone, the Central African Republic, Liberia, Rwanda and Burundi show, the disorganization and violence appear to be escalating, and some discern encircling chaos. It is becoming increasingly difficult to escape the conclusion that the only response to this situation and the one way to reduce the hostilities and begin to achieve incremental political coherence is to embrace democracy in the sense of participative negotiated consensus.

If these expectations are correct, then democracy has a role of unprecedented importance to play in Africa. But it cannot play this important role by following the line of least resistance or by mimicking the liberal democracy of the West. It has to be articulated in an extraordinarily creative way. To the extent that this happens, it may open new possibilities of political civilisation. Paradoxically, it may well be that it is in the late-start regions, especially Africa, that democracy will finally fulfil its historical mission or betray it.

2

The Dynamics of Democratization in
Africa

Part One

The Context and the Provenance of Democracy

The history of Africa has been one long emancipatory struggle against all manner of oppression—by Portuguese and Arab slave traders; overzealous missionaries; French ideologues and British colonizers; homegrown dictators and foreign imperialists; intensifying underdevelopment and development bureaucracies. Through it all, it was generally agreed that democracy is not relevant to Africa. These struggles were hardly treated seriously by the outside world, especially the developed market economies which had appropriated democratic legitimacy for their political practice as the emancipatory projects which they were. Nor were they accorded the status of democratic struggles. To the extent that democracy was talked about at all in the African context, it was only to problematize its relevance and to dismiss its possibility.

Powerful factors conspired against democracy in Africa and even the admission of its possibility. The colonial powers could only justify colonialism with the fiction that Africans were less than human and could not be entitled to the amenities of civilisation, especially democracy. In the colonial era, political discourse excluded not only democracy but even the idea of good government. Colonial politics was, in the final analysis, the clash of two exclusive claims to rulership.

After political independence, the African nationalist leaders continued this legacy by turning against democracy. Having decided to inherit the colonial system, instead of transforming it in accordance with popular nationalist aspirations, most African leaders found themselves on a collision course with their people. Faced with pressures for the expected structural transformation of the colonial system, they insisted that it was necessary to pursue development first and that this was better done by giving unquestioning support to the leadership. When voluntary conformity did not come they resorted to repression and criminalized political opposition.

The rest of the world encouraged these political tendencies. Africa's former colonial masters, anxious for leverage with the new holders of power, gave indulgent support. Bowing to the necessities of the Cold War, the great powers ignored human rights violations and sought allies wherever they could. All these factors helped to crystallize a climate of opinion in the West hostile to democracy in Africa. From time to time (for instance, during the Carter Administration in the United States), human rights abuses in Africa became an issue but never democracy. This implicit indifference to democracy was true even for human rights organizations which had made strenuous efforts to check human rights abuses in Africa. Inexplicably, they too appeared not to connect human rights concerns with democratization.

But this has changed. Issues of democratization and human rights now dominate the world's interest in Africa, overcoming this legacy of indifference. Indeed, interest in the democratization of Africa, which external donors now link to political conditionality, is so strong that some are beginning to fear a new imbalance. Why is there so much interest now in the democratization of Africa?

The 'revolution' in Eastern Europe has certainly contributed to this change of heart by providing the West with a dramatic vindication of its own values and a sense of the inevitability of the triumph of democracy. The aggressive vacuity of the Cold War has been replaced with the mission of democratization, a mission which, it is widely believed, will firmly consolidate the hegemony of Western values throughout the world. Thus the West has come to regard democracy as an important item on the African agenda. This change in attitude also reflects the fact that the long struggle for democracy in Africa is beginning to show results too impressive and too widespread to be ignored. These include the popular opposition to military rule in Nigeria, the demise of apartheid in South Africa, of Samuel Doe in Liberia, Kérékou in Bénin Republic, Siad Barré in Somalia and Moussa Traoré in Mali; other noteworthy results include the modest gains for pluralism and multipartism in Niger, Togo, Madagascar, Gabon, Ivory Coast, Guinea, Mozambique, Angola, Sao Tomé and Principe, and the Congo; the deepening crisis of democratization in Kenya, Somalia, Sudan, Cameroon, Ghana, Sierra Leone, Ethiopia and Zimbabwe.

The West's changing attitude towards democracy in Africa has also drawn additional impetus from Africa's economic and strategic marginalization. As is well known, the world economy has been shifting from the production of goods to services and from material-intensive to knowledge-intensive industries, a trend which is reducing the economic importance of primary producers. At the same time, advances in science and technology have yielded an increasing number of synthetic products which are more flexible and more versatile than those which Africa traditionally exported. These changes have made Africa's primary economies far less relevant to the current economic needs of the industrialized countries. Now with the winding down of the Cold War, Africa's strategic significance to them has also declined considerably. As Europe draws closer to unification, even the former colonial powers—notably France—are finding it necessary to downgrade their special relationship with their former colonies, relations which seem far less useful now than previously.

The economic and strategic marginalization of Africa has given the West much more latitude to conduct its relations with Africa in a more principled way. As we have seen, in the past, the West adopted a posture of calculated indifference to issues of human rights and democracy in Africa in order to avoid jeopardizing its economic and strategic interests and to facilitate its quest for allies against communism. As soon as the significance of these concerns diminished, the West became more inclined to bring its African policies closer to its democratic and human rights commitments.

While some of the impetus to democratization may have come from these developments in the external environment, the drive for democratization in Africa is predominantly internally generated. To all appearances the movement for democratization is being driven by the dialectics of underdevelopment in Africa. It arises from the contradictions of the very conditions which constituted political authoritarianism in Africa.

The Colonial Legacy

The conditions in question go back to the colonial legacy. The colonial state in Africa was all-powerful and arbitrary. It had to be because it was an occupying force. It gave itself rights over everything in the territory and the privilege of doing whatever it could to advance its purposes. For instance, it imposed taxes, redistributed land, instituted forced labour, decided where everyone could live, who should produce what and how. As if to underscore the absolutism and arbitrariness of the power of the colonial state, its officials showed little interest in transforming domination into hegemony beyond the notion that their domination was also a civilizing mission. There may have been circumstances in which the use of state power was not arbitrary in practice, but it was always arbitrary in principle.

Since the colonial state was, for its subjects at any rate, an arbitrary power, it could not engender legitimacy even though it made rules and laws profusely and propagated values assiduously. Accordingly, in struggling to advance their interests, the colonial subjects were not particular about conforming to legality or legitimacy norms. As rulers and subjects alike extended their rights to their powers, the idea of lawful political competition became impossible; politics turned into the forceful determination of two exclusive claims to rulership.

The coming of political independence did not change this. Independence changed the composition of the managers of the state but not the character of the state, which remained much as it was in the colonial era. Its scope continued to be totalistic and its economic orientation highly statist. It presented itself often as an apparatus of violence, its base in social forces remained extremely narrow and it relied for compliance unduly on coercion rather than authority. With few exceptions, the elite who came to power decided to inherit and exploit the colonial system to their own benefit rather than transforming it democratically as had been expected. This alienated them from the masses whom they now had to contain with force.

The use of force only increased the mutual alienation of the elite and the masses, which in turn increased the reliance of the rulers on coercion. A great deal of coercion was required not only to constrain the political expression of mass discontent but also to impose 'political unity' in the midst of considerable social pluralism, which was now all the more divisive for being exploited by leaders desperate to paper over a growing class divide. This is the background to Africa's single-party systems and military rule which continued to fan discontent while attempting to suppress its political expression.

Most of the leaders of the early post-colonial period in Africa were operating in a state of siege. Besieged by the multitude of hostile forces which their betrayal of popular aspirations, exploitative practices and political repression had bred, they became completely absorbed in the very difficult task of surviving in a hostile political environment. All aspects of social life were suffused with politics and the premium on power grew exceedingly high. Everything else including development was marginalized. It is not surprising that for most of the post-colonial period, the only thing which has been developing is underdevelopment.

We usually think of the crisis of underdevelopment in Africa as an economic crisis. But it is in fact primarily a political crisis. To be sure, it has an economic side which is serious, but this could be incidental. It would appear that the problem is not so much that the development project has failed as that it never started in the first place. It never started because the political environment has been inclement.

To appreciate this, it is necessary to remember that development strategies and policies do not simply emerge and get implemented, their feasibility and success being determined by their formal character. Strategies and policies are made and managed by a government in office and a political elite in power in a determinate historical state, and a particular configuration of social forces. In post-colonial Africa most countries did not really have a development project because the character of the state and the political class were not conducive to that enterprise. Instead of being a public force, the state in post-colonial Africa tends to be privatized by the ruling elite. The nature of the state and the political context of development in most of Africa is such that, with minor exceptions, the commitment of most African leaders to development is at best ambiguous and, at worst, nonexistent. When they pursue development, they invariably do so in a manner that is perfunctory, contradictory and ineffective. The tragic consequences of this are all too clear in the intensifying poverty and the diminishing viability of African economies and polities.

Part Two

The Rise of the Movement of Democracy

It was this condition of political monolithism, repression and persistent underdevelopment which engendered the democracy movement. The movement arose initially as a demand by marginalized elements for incorporation. This demand occurred on two levels, on the level of elites as a demand for political incorporation and on the level of the masses as a demand for economic incorporation.

Elite Demand for Incorporation

What is the elite demand for incorporation and how did it arise? As we have seen, in post-colonial Africa the state was everything. It controlled the economy, polity and society, its presence was ubiquitous and its power enormous, unchecked by constitutional constraints, a mature political culture or a vibrant civil society. Those who did not have access to state power were at the mercy of those who did. In most of post-colonial Africa the only way for elites to secure life and property and some freedom was to be in control, at any rate, to share in the control of state power. As Kwame

Nkrumah, the first President of Ghana, put it, one had to 'seek the political kingdom first'. That was part of the reason why state power was sought with such desperation that political competition tended to degenerate into warfare. Those who prevail in this struggle privatize the state and take what they can, and those who lose effectively lose all claim to the resources of the state, including protection by the law, and suffer what they must. In these circumstances, everyone desperately wants to be incorporated in the sharing of state power.

Incorporation should not normally be a problem even in authoritarian one-party states or military regimes. Within such political monolithism, it could be operationalized in a consensual arrangement. Indeed, these authoritarian political structures were justified on grounds of avoiding exclusion, opposition and unnecessary conflict, and facilitating inclusivity and solidarity. The ideologues of the single-party system such as Sékou Touré, Julius Nyerere and Jomo Kenyatta defended it on the basis that it was more akin to the African tradition of consensus-building in which people talk about community affairs at great length until they agree and then they insist on broad conformity to the agreement. Indeed, the pursuit of development was put in much the same perspective, namely, that the need for development is so obvious and its problems so demanding that it is better to proceed in unity. Clearly, the need for inclusion was recognized. And yet there was such a strong tendency to exclusion that the demand for incorporation became a major force in society which fathered the process of democratization. How did this happen?

To begin with, there was an essentially Hobbesian situation where the premium on power was so high that the appetite for power was insatiable. That frames a competition for power in which workable power-sharing arrangements do not hold because power is too important to respect such arrangements when opportunities for more power arise, and because there is nothing to guarantee power-sharing arrangements or anything else except power. On this score, it is significant that it is on the level of elites that the premium on power is at its highest; it is at this level that the struggle for power is most Hobbesian. One implication of this is that the elite in Africa is generally too undisciplined and incoherent to initiate and carry out a development project. That is one of the major differences between them and the elite in the fast-developing Asian economies, notably Hong Kong, South Korea, Singapore, Thailand and Taiwan (The World Bank 1993).

In this situation, where there is pervasive insecurity about power and the appetite for power is insatiable, the social base of power will tend to be very narrow. To be sure, those who have power are obliged to share its exercise; the more power they have, the more they have to share. The dictator cannot also be the field commander of all regiments, the chief justice, the governor of the central bank and the chief of police. But in the face of pervasive insecurity of power, the rational dictator will share with as few people as possible. And these have to be people who are close, loyal, and as much as possible with identical interests. This is an extremely restrictive criterion of sharing, so restrictive that it is more appropriate to call it a criterion of exclusion.

That is the prevailing practice in much of post-colonial Africa. Those in power are inclined to share it only with a very small coterie of collaborators. Often the state is effectively privatized in the control of this small group, whose most powerful members are usually drawn from the leader's community, religious faith, geographical region or ethnic base. This was the case in Liberia under Samuel Doe, Nigeria under General Ibrahim Babangida, Cameroon under Paul Biya, Kenya under Jomo Kenyatta and even more so under Arap Moi, Somalia under Siad Barré, Togo under Eyadéma, Ethiopia under Mengistu, Rwanda under General Habyarimana, Bénin under Kérékou, Mali under Moussa Traoré, Burkina Faso under Compaoré, Uganda under Idi Amin, Sudan under Niemeri, Niger under President Diori and Zaire under Mobutu. The list can be much longer. There are very few countries in Africa, even the more liberal countries, which escape this phenomenon of exclusion and the monopoly of power.

Since exclusion is such a dreaded fate in countries where state power is everything, Africa is in constant turmoil from struggles between people who must secure power by exclusion and those who must access it by incorporation. It is well to note that the struggle of those who want incorporation is not necessarily emancipatory. Some of them, the most privileged of the marginalized who see themselves as alternate dictators, want to appropriate state power and act just like those who oppress them. It is doubtful that the struggles of these kinds of people can be called emancipatory. A good example is Samuel Doe's Krahn kinsmen fighting for power and incorporation after his death. But these people are the minority among the political elite who want incorporation. Most of the people who join such struggles can only hope for incorporation, a right to be involved in common concerns, to share in the rewards and burdens of common citizenship. This is decidedly emancipatory.

More often than not, the elite struggles for exclusion and incorporation spill over and engulf the rest of society. To engage in elite competition effectively, it is necessary to mobilize power resources, especially as a political constituency. Those like Idi Amin, Siad Barré and Arap Moi who monopolise power and privatise the state in Africa, including military regimes such as Mengistu's in Ethiopia, have to do this. Most single-party and military regimes wage their struggle for exclusion and monopoly by cultivating the military as a constituency, playing them against the civilian population and cultivating them with privileges and vast military budgets spent with indulgent disregard of transparency and accountability. The military regime of General Ibrahim Babangida, which ruled Nigeria from 1985 to 1993, was very good at this. So was that of Samuel Doe in Liberia, General Compaoré in Burkina Faso and Idi Amin in Uganda, Eyadéma in Togo and Abacha in Nigeria.

By far the most widely used strategy for developing a political constituency for supporting exclusionist regimes is ethnic appeal. Even military regimes use it as well. Examples which readily come to mind are the military regimes of Idi Amin in Uganda and Eyadéma of Togo. Idi Amin tried to base his support on the army, paying it lavish attention, indulging its excesses and playing it against civilians. But he ensured the concentration of key positions in the hands of people from his own ethnic group. Paul Biya in the Cameroon, Eyadéma in Togo, Milton Margai in Sierra Leone and Samuel Doe in Liberia are notable examples in the use of this tactic. There are several variations on this theme: the appropriation of the state in the name of a racial group such as in Apartheid South Africa, Mauritania, Sudan and Apartheid Namibia. In some cases it is appropriated in the name of religion, as fundamentalists, following the example of Iran, are trying to do in Sudan, Algeria and Egypt.

One of the most blatant instances of this strategy of power is the Arap Moi regime in Kenya which came to power following the death of President Kenyatta in August 1978. In power Moi was very insecure because he lacked the charisma of Kenyatta and did not come from any of the major ethnic groups, Kikuyu, Luo or Kamba; he feared that the Kikuyu, who were dominant in commerce and industry as well as the public service and the military, would oust him.

These fears came to a head during the Air Force mutiny in 1982. Moi then moved to concentrate state power in his own Kalenjin ethnic group and a few trusted friends. He filled the security services with the Kalenjin. He put Hezekiah Oyugi in charge of internal security and provincial administration. Although Oyugi is Luo, he and Moi were very close, especially after Oyugi saved his life during an Air Force mutiny. The security services were flooded with Kalenjins. Joseph Arap Letting, a Kalenjin, became the Cabinet Secretary and head of the Public Service. General Mahmoud Mohammed, an ethnic Somali who posed little danger by virtue of not having a powerful ethnic base was made Chief of General Staff of the Army, and the Army Command was given to Lt General Lengees, a Samburu, who again would not have a significant ethnic base. The deputy head of the Air Force, Brigadier Chelgegat, and the deputy commander of the Army, Major-General Chiruiyot, were both Kalenjins. At the critical operational level, that is the level of commandant or deputy commandant, all major military bases were headed by Kalenjins.

The Director of the Criminal Investigation Department, Noah Arap Too, was Kalenjin. The feared General Service Unit, which deals with riots and attends to real and imagined threats to security with brutality, was under the headship of Koskei, a Kalenjin, as was the Presidential Escort Unit, which is headed by Arap Kiptun. The monopolisation of power extended beyond the machinery of the state to the commercial, industrial and sectors. The highly regarded Finance Minister, Mwai Kibaki, who was also vice-president, was replaced with George Saitoti, a mathematician who has no access to a threatening ethnic base. Control of the Central Bank went from Duncan Ndegwa, a Kikuyu, to Ben Kipkorir, a Kalenjin.

On the political front, Moi frustrated the bid of Oginga Odinga, the veteran radical Luo leader whom Kenyatta had imprisoned, for readmission into the ruling Kenya African National Union (KANU). Attempts of opposition politicians and those ousted from KANU to register a party, for instance, George Anyona's attempt to register the Kenya Socialist Alliance, were frustrated by a hasty constitutional amendment which made Kenya legally a one-party state. Opposition politicians were kept in line by threatening their businesses with denial of import and export licences, closures, harassment with investigations for malpractices such as tax evasion, the confiscation of passports and the denial of international travel.

The Republic of Niger is a better example yet of the strategy of exclusion from power. In this case, as in many others such as Nigeria, it was done with the active support of the colonial power. Niger is ethnically heterogeneous, consisting of Hausa (about 50 per cent of the population), the Zarma/Songhai (about 20 per cent of the population) and several smaller groups, namely, the Kanuri, Toubours, Tuaregs and Fulani. After the referendum of 1958 in which France offered the colonies the option of self-government within the French community or immediate independence, the French decided to back Hamani Diori and his Parti Progressiste Nigérien (PNP), which had been formed in 1948 by an influential faction of the Zarma elite, many of them acquaintances from the Ecole Normale William Ponty. After the referendum the French governor of the colony forced the cabinet of Djibo Bakary to organize an election and by heavy-handedness, including cancelling the election in places such as Tessawa and Zinder where Bakary's party had won, ensured the victory of Diori, who duly became President.

Then the repression began in earnest. The opposition party SWABA was banned and its leadership forced into exile or imprisoned, and mass organisations, especially the labour unions affiliated to it, were similarly attacked. People were persecuted for merely being members or sympathizers of SWABA and even for not belonging to the ruling party; villages in parts of the country known to be sympathetic to SWABA were terrorized by the gendarmerie and 'dissidents' rounded up, tried and executed or imprisoned. Between 1956 and 1974 no non Zarma/Songhai was a member of the all-powerful politburo, and from 1956 to 1990 the two most powerful offices in the state were held by Zarma/Songhai (Adji 1991:234; Ibrahim 1992:56-57). At the same time development projects were concentrated in the western part of the country where the Zarma/Songhai live and where the bulk of the officer corps of the armed forces came from.

On April 14, 1974 the French overthrew their client, Hamani Diori, for wanting to renegotiate the terms on which France took Niger's uranium and installed Lt Col. Seyni Kountché. Fearing a rise of nationalist fervour which might jeopardize French access to vital resources, France gave unflagging support to Kountché to intensify repression and the monopoly of power even more than Hamani Diori. Indeed, Niger graduated from repression to the militarization of society and state terrorism. People suspected of not being conformist enough were often eliminated, including many members of the ruling military council. Hundreds of troops patrolled the streets daily and meted out terrible punishment publicly and at will. The movement of people was controlled. What was left of the opposition was obliterated, except the Tuareg and Toubours nomads and students who paid dearly for continuing to resist. In 1983 President Kountché was obliged to announce a cautious programme of return to civilian rule.

In these modes of exclusion and power monopoly, ethnicity is only an ideological representation, even though it suggests the image of ethnic domination and ethnic conflict. Nonetheless, the phenomenon of ethnic domination and ethnic conflict is derivative, not original. It is interesting to note a strong tradition of academic writings which justify this strategy of power by arguing the necessity and the desirability of the domination of one ethnic group in plural societies. This is seen as the means of maintaining political and social order in such societies. The idea goes back to J. S. Furnivall, who is credited with the concept of the plural society, a society of social and cultural diversity, in which each group holds to its own ways, so that these divergent entities are not integrated. They live side by side rather than together. Furnivall posits that the only way to maintain coherence and order in such societies is to establish a domination over its divergent elements as the colonial governments did in their colonies. Without such domination, he argues, there would be collapse (Furnivall 1949).

This theory quickly became a scholarly tradition. Smith distinguished between institutionally homogeneous societies with institutions which motivate people to conformity to social norms and institutionally 'split' societies which lack such motivation. He argues that 'given the fundamental differences of belief, value, and organisation that connote pluralism, the monopoly of power by one cultural section is the essential condition for the maintenance of the total society in its current form' (Smith 1965). Among others who have argued in this vein is Kuper (n.d; 1982).

This theory assumes too much. Premdas is right in arguing that even if plural societies have displayed a tendency to throw up repressive regimes, we must not confuse description with prescription and conclude that this is the way these societies ought to be governed (Premdas 1993). There are other options for dealing with their social heterogeneity. For example, A Theory of Political Integration (Ake 1967) suggested a paradigm of elite accommodation by which the elites from the different social groups could reach a consensual arrangement and rule as coalition. Under this arrangement, some integration and political stability can be achieved by virtue of the fact that members of the diverse social groups can identify with the ruling elite or part of it and even feel that they have a stake in the government. Later, Lijphart (1977) developed a similar solution in his well-known consocietal arrangement.

Exclusionary tendencies extended the struggles among elites to engulf the rest of society. When this strategy is used, it also elicits by way of response a struggle for incorporation which also reaches beyond the elite to the rest of society. Eventually it leads to a clash of identities, especially ethnic identities. This is because once state power is appropriated in the name of an ethnic or primary group, as was the case in Kenya under Arap Moi or Rwanda under Barianyamaria or Paul Biya's Cameroon or Sudan under Hassan, the organization of the struggle for incorporation along ethnic lines is virtually assured.

The residual category of excluded ethnic or primary groups confronting the exclusionist group is necessarily constituted as a primary group formation. The ensuing conflicts in this kind of struggle are often very highly emotionally charged and very bitterly contested, often with fearsome violence, as in Burundi, Liberia, Rwanda, Sudan and Somalia. This is because primary group identities such as ethnic identity are cultural and holistic, while their claims on those who respond to them are totalistic, which is to say that they regard this identity as the definitive expression of their uniqueness and their entire way of life.

Characteristically, this identity takes itself for granted irrespective of its historicity, asserts its claims categorically, and sees other groups dialectically as the otherness by which it defines itself in oppositionality. When political struggles are constituted around such ideas and social formations, they tend to be very intense and violent because the people involved believe that their entire way of life is at stake. These 'ethnic' conflicts occurring all too often have given Africa the negative image of eternally ethnic people who are forever trapped in violent conflict.

But it is misleading to regard these conflicts as ethnic conflict. They are only superficially so. Appearances notwithstanding, they are usually emancipatory struggles, a striving for access, fairness, equal opportunity, political expression and participation in the collective enterprise of a political community. It is incidental that the interest which appropriates and privatizes state power wears the ethnic mask, which detracts us from seeing that what is being opposed is not ethnicity but something else which is hiding behind ethnicity; that the seeming ethnic opposition is conjunctural and deceptive because it is constituted, not by ethnics wanting to oppose holders of state power, but by holders of state power trying to conceal injustices and undemocratic tendencies behind an ideological mask.

The insertion of these emancipatory struggles in an ethnic universe is highly significant. It devalues them, gives them a negative even primitive face and undermines them, although it does not eradicate their democratic significance. These struggles have resulted in some important gains for democracy. For instance, in the very early 1960s, just when most of the nationalist movements were on the verge of gaining power, a power struggle developed within the leadership as individuals and factions began to manoeuvre to be in positions of power in the incoming national government.

In the course of these manoeuvres, alienation within the nationalist movement, which was usually a marriage of convenience held together by shared grievances rather than mutual undertakings, led to exclusionary strategies of power being used and struggles of incorporation or more accurately struggles to avoid exclusion being launched. In Nigeria, for instance, the nationalist movement was so embroiled in such struggles in the late 1950s that it almost broke down. There was a massive movement of minority groups such as the Tiv, the Edo, the Izon, Efiks, Urhobo and Ishekiri which tried to prevent the leaders of the major ethnic groups, Ibo, Yoruba and Hausa-Fulani, from conniving to control the new government in their own interest and exclude everyone else.

For all its problems, this movement was an asset of considerable value to democratization because it advanced political mobilisation among ordinary people almost as much as the nationalist movement itself. It relocated the democratic discourse of the nationalist movement from its orientation to the coloniser, an easy target of resentment, to the internal political relations of Africans themselves. Most importantly, it put on the table for the very first time and in a serious and concrete manner the difficult problems of democratic governance: the guarantee of fundamental human rights, the rights of minorities and the weak, the balance of power, the rule of law, the distribution of burdens and rewards, the right of every group to cultural expression and access to power, the tyranny of the majority and so on. This made a major contribution to the development of democracy by bringing home to the African elite some of the demanding obligations of democratic practice, obligations which could clash with their self-interest.

The movement not only raised these issues, but it also led to political arrangements to improve the prospects of democracy. To return again to the Nigerian example, the Minorities movement forced the colonial government to set up a Minorities Commission to look into the fears and demands of the minorities and to suggest what might be done about them. While rejecting options such as the right to secession and confederation, the commission recommended political and constitutional arrangements that would ensure local autonomy in a truly federal structure, the rule of law, protection of rights including the political and cultural rights of ethnic groups and subnationalities, fair sharing of national amenities and also electoral arrangements to ensure that the votes of the minorities were not irrelevant to electoral outcome. By reflecting these concerns, the independence constitution of Nigeria was more democratic than Nigeria's subsequent constitutions. The subsequent deviations from this constitution, especially the move from federalism to de facto unitarism under military rule, was a major cause of Nigeria's recurrent political crisis.

The struggle for exclusion and incorporation intensified after independence in response to the poor governance and human rights record of most African governments and the failures of the development project. Political and personal insecurity, the fiscal crisis of the state and a diminishing surplus made the hegemonic factions of the elite more prone to exclusionary regimes and intensified the struggle for incorporation. By the 1980s these struggles were increasingly expressed in the rise of NGOs as a form of exit option, civil rights movements, demands for local autonomy, more progressive distribution, economic liberalization and general de-statization. These developments are already the makings of an incipient democracy movement.

The Masses: Demands for Economic Incorporation

The other source of the democracy movement in Africa is the demand of the masses for economic incorporation. This demand goes back to the nationalist movement, which was itself a democracy movement. The language of the nationalist movement was the language of democracy, as is clear from: *I Speak of Freedom* (Nkrumah), *Without Bitterness* (Orizu), *Facing Mount Kenya* (Kenyatta), *Not Yet Uhuru* (Odinga), *Freedom and Development* (Nyerere), *African Socialism* (Senghor), and *The Wretched of The Earth* (Fanon). It denounced the violation of the dignity of the colonized, the denial of basic rights, the political disenfranchisement of the colonized, racial discrimination, lack of equal opportunity and equal access, and economic exploitation of the colonized.

The people were mobilized according to these grievances and expectations of a more democratic dispensation.

However, these expectations largely failed to materialize, as the new rulers tended to settle for exploiting the colonial system to their benefit rather than transforming it according to the democratic expectations of the nationalist movement. Because of their subsequent alienation, and repression, and the political dynamics engendered by these factors, the development project stalled. In retrospect, Africa is generally taken to have done reasonably well economically in the first decade of independence. But the performance was bad enough:

> ... after a decade of independence, 34 countries of Developing Africa, accounting for about 94% of total population in the area, still record incomes per head of less than $200 per annum. This pitifully low lever of economic performance is brought out even more dramatically when comparisons are made with other countries. The total GNP for forty-four developing countries of Africa is less than that for the Benelux countries, while that of fourteen countries of the West African sub-region is less than the GNP of Turkey. The total GNP of the eight countries of Central Africa is less than that of Peru, while that of the sixteen countries in East Africa is less than that of Finland and only just equal to Norway. More startling results are revealed when comparison is made in the different economic sectors. For example the total imports of West Africa (fourteen countries) are less than those of Mexico, while imports into the sixteen countries of East Africa are at about the same level (Onitiri 1973).

Things did not get better. They got a lot worse in the next two decades. The average annual growth rate of per capita income for Sub-Saharan Africa between 1973 and 1980 was a mere 0.1 per cent; between 1980 and 1989 it was -2.2 per cent. On some social indicators Africans are worse off at the end of the 1980s than they were in the 1960s. Negative growth rates over a long period translated to collapsing infrastructures, rising debt burdens, rising social tensions, intensifying poverty, chronic malnutrition for many and premature death. The failure of the leadership in most parts of Africa had become life-threatening to ordinary people.

With their physical survival under threat, ordinary people were obliged to bestir themselves to meet this tragic crisis. Given the aptly demonstrated failure of the leadership to deliver, the loss of legitimacy by the state and its managers as well as its fiscal crisis which had rendered it incapable of delivering services or even of stemming the threat of lawlessness from unpaid soldiers, policeofficers and workers, the people had no option but to seek what they call in Francophone Africa a 'second independence' and to try to possess their own development, that is to say, to insist on incorporation.

This consciousness has been expressed in a variety of ways. At first it took the form of a retreat from the state to the community or primary group. While the state remained fearsome and violent, it lost its relevance except as a nuisance as people resorted to community self-help schemes to stem the decay of infrastructures, to pool resources for economic ventures and to provide some necessary services for the community.

In the last decade, there has been an explosion of associational life in rural Africa. By all indications, this is a by-product of a general acceptance of the necessity of self-reliance, yielding a proliferation of institutions such as craft centres, rural credit unions, farmers' associations, community-run skill development centres, community banks, cooperatives, community-financed schools and hospitals and civic centres, local credit unions, even community vigilante groups for security.

Some have welcomed this development as a sign of a vibrant civil society in Africa. It may well be that. However, before we begin to idealize this phenomenon, it is well to remind ourselves that whatever else it is, it is first and foremost a child of necessity, of desperation even. Also it is important to remember that the traditional relation between the state and civil society is a relation of unity and difference. Ideally the members of civil society accept the basic legitimacy of the state and identify with it. The state is not just force, it is authority. The particularity of civil society is precisely the orchestration of the fullness of the state as the moment of universality, the expression of corporate political identity at the most ecumenical level. But in Africa, associational life is booming from the vanishing legitimacy of the state and the withdrawal of identity and loyalty, fear and suspicion and even hostility. The development is not framing a dialectical unity; it amounts to an exit option, namely, the dissolution of the state.

To return to the demand for incorporation, the people cannot be truly incorporated, neither can they possess their own development by remaining apolitical or submissive. They have to assert their right to participation and to remove, at any rate minimize the authoritarian constraints of the past. Hence the call for a second independence, not from the colonial masters but from the indigenous elite, which presupposes that as in the first independence, it has to be taken, not given, most probably with some force.

From this perspective, the demand for economic incorporation now takes the form of a popular political struggle against the elite in power and relates to the elite demand for political incorporation. But the economic underpinnings of the popular demand remain even then, and it can be discerned from the fact that the hostility of the masses to the ruling elite and their agitation for democratic participation rises with the deepening of the economic crisis. Economic crisis is indeed the instance of the convergence of the masses' demand for economic incorporation and the elite's demand for political incorporation. At such times when the economic surplus is shrinking and the struggle for it is intensifying, the hegemonic elite faction is more exclusionary, that is more inclined to limit the access of others to power.

Extrapolating from this, we may say that the depth, persistence and intractability of Africa's economic crisis has been an asset to democratization. So has the conventional response to the crisis, namely, structural adjustment programmes, because the African varieties of SAP are so draconian that they tend to intensify poverty in the short-run and to exacerbate social and political tensions. The covariance of economic crisis and the agitation for democratization has held for practically every country in Africa, including Ghana, Ivory Coast, Sierra Leone, Mali, Senegal, Niger, Nigeria, Cameroon, Bénin, Togo, Central African Republic, Zaire, Zimbabwe, Burundi, Rwanda, Kenya, Zambia, Guinea, Gabon, Congo, Sudan, Somalia, Lesotho, Mozambique, Tanzania, Uganda, Chad and others.

The 1980s, a particularly low point in the economic crisis for most countries, produced a powerful surge of demands for political and economic incorporation which was a watershed in Africa's quest for democratization. In Bénin Republic the economy had ground to a halt at this time and the fiscal crisis of the state was so deep that the government could no longer pay the wages of civil servants. In Cameroon, a period of unusually deep economic downturn was compounded by a political crisis which was remarkable for the unprecedented intensity of the demand for incorporation that came to a head in the first quarter of 1990; Paul Biya, the President of Cameroon, typically resorted to a crackdown and the situation deteriorated. Yondo Black, former president of the Cameroon Bar Association, was arrested on February 19 and Albert Mukong, a prominent writer, was arrested on February 26. Government started a wave of arrests of pro-democracy leaders, especially those involved in the formation of a political party which emerged eventually as the Social Democratic Front (SDF) led by John Fru Ndi. On March 13, 1990 the government issued a statement to the effect that the detainees were not arrested for forming a political party but rather for clandestine meetings and for hostile acts against the government and for inciting revolt.

The arrest of Yondo Black mobilized the Cameroon Bar Association into the struggle. Over 200 turned up in court to support the defence and the Bar Association decided to boycott all other trials until the determmination of Black's case. On April 4, one of the defence lawyers, Pierre Mbobda, was killed by the police at a road block. In the meantime, the Social Democratic Front's application for registration as a political party filed on March 16 had elicited no response. On March 26, at least seven people were killed in a demonstration called to support the SDF.

The agitation continued and the government was obliged to bow to a multi-party system and to schedule elections. The consensus of the many international monitoring teams at the election was that the incumbent President Paul Biya lost the election to John Fru Ndi despite his misuse of the resources of the government. However, Paul Biya had himself declared winner and stayed in office. And he was able to do this by a massive crackdown, in the course of which over 200 people were killed and thousands detained, including Fru Ndi. While it allowed Paul Biya to stay in power, the new crackdown again raised the level of conflict and worsened the economic crisis. The demand for incorporation among the Anglophone elite has turned into a demand for secession, putting the viability of Cameroon in doubt.

Ivory Coast had been one of the best economic performers in Africa, with growth rates averaging an impressive 11.7 per cent per annum between 1973 and 1980. But by 1980 the tide had turned and Ivory Coast had become another stagnating African economy. Between 1980 and 1987 the country recorded an average negative growth rate of 2.4 per cent per annum. From 1986, Ivory Coast suffered from a steep decline in world prices of its principal exports, cocoa and coffee, a decline that continued into 1989. The extent of this external shock can be gauged from the fact that by 1988 export earnings from cocoa had fallen by 60 per cent.

The crisis was compounded by the dilemma of a government which had encouraged farmers to produce for export with assurance of stable export prices and whose popularity depended on rural support, especially among farmers. Between 1986 and 1989, it was costing the Ivory Coast on average approximately CFA 700 to put a kilo in the international market while the receipts got less and less—from CFA 727 in 1986 to CFA 370 in 1989. Determined to keep faith with producers, the government decided to maintain its old producer price of CFA 400 a kilo, thereby worsening its fiscal crisis. By the middle of 1989, the IMF and the World Bank stepped in with a recovery programme. Under this programme, beginning from the crop marketing year 1989-90, the producer price for cocoa was cut from CFA 400 per kilo to CFA 200 per kilo, and that of coffee from CFA 150 to CFA 100. The programme also included the raising of taxes on salaries. As was to be expected, the programme led to widespread unrest, strikes and demonstrations by a wide variety of groups including students, taxi drivers, port workers and even the police and the army. There was so much tension that the programme was quickly suspended, but the crisis had already set the country on a course of political change.

Pro-democracy groups and other groups, including farmers, wanting political and economic incorporation capitalized on this situation and became very active politically and much bolder in challenging the regime of the aging President Houphouët-Boigny. Openly defying the law, some proceeded to form political parties. Political movements and parties which were already in existence but operating underground surfaced, notable among them history professor Laurent Gbagbo's Popular Ivorian Front which was secretly formed in 1988. The move to a multi-party system began to look inevitable. On April 30, 1990, the government gave in to the demands.

Oil-rich Gabon, no exception to the general tendency towards economic mismanagement, was also badly hit by the economic recession of the late 1980s, with the same effects; more strident demand for better performance backed with political agitation for economic and political incorporation. Under pressure, the Omar Bongo government reluctantly accepted the need for reform. Political talks were held and it was agreed to form a power-sharing, broad-based transitional government of four parties with opposition parties producing six of 28 ministers. The government also promised fair multi-party election in September 1990 by which time a new constitution would have been negotiated and adopted. The new constitution by which Gabon became a multi-party state was adopted on May 22, 1990.

On May 23 another crisis erupted. A leading opposition politician, Joseph Rendjambe, was found dead in the premises of Hotel Dowe in Libreville, which was owned by President Omar Bongo. Rumours spread that Bongo was implicated and popular anger exploded, especially in Libreville and Port Gentil. In Libreville the political character of the riots was emphasized by the fact that the rioters targeted for looting and destruction businesses and premises owned by President Omar Bongo and his close associates and symbolically vandalized the presidential red carpet in Port Gentil Airport.

The rioting was more serious still in Port Gentil, the home of Rendjame. It brought to a halt the operations of Elf-Aquitaine at a loss of about $46 million a day. Shops were looted and damaged, as were several public buildings and the presidential palace. France rushed in troops to protect its economic assets, especially the facilities of Elf-Aquitaine and also to protect the large French community, some of whom (about 2,000) were evacuated amid accusations of collaboration with the corruption and the authoritarianism of the Bongo regime.

In Togo, President Eyadéma might have hoped that Togo would be spared the rash of democratic insurrections and demand for incorporation sweeping through Africa because since 1979 he had renewed his hold on the presidency with periodic elections which were manipulated to ensure his success. But that was not to be. As in most of Africa, the economy of Togo was in deep recession in the 1980s, a decade in which the country experienced a steady decline in incomes. By 1980 the enormous windfall from the quadrupling of the price of phosphates, Togo's main export in the 1970s had been grossly mismanaged and Togo was saddled with a foreign debt of $1.1 billion and 73 inefficient money-guzzling parastatals.

That level of indebtedness was more than 100 per cent of the country's national income. By 1982 debt-servicing obligations was 75 per cent of export earnings. Togo struggled to deal with the crisis with a structural adjustment programme which did not go down well because of massive staff reduction in the public service and budget cuts in the social sector, especially education.

When the agitation started Eyadéma conducted a superficial referendum to demonstrate that the people of Togo did not want a multi-party system and organized demonstrations in favour of one-party rule. But such tactics could not stem the tide of political agitation against his authoritarian rule. Because of his intransigence the agitation escalated, became violent and in the end he conceded to multipartism while plotting to maintain his power in spite of it.

President Kenneth Kaunda, who ruled Zambia from independence in 1964, made the country a one-party state in 1972. Despite the political discontent caused by that, he remained quite popular because of his benign authoritarianism. But economic pressures were soon to change that. Mismanagement, and external shocks, especially the decline in copper prices, Zambia's main export, sent Zambia into a deep economic crisis by the early 1980s. It was in the context of this crisis that opposition to Kaunda's monopoly of power grew first among the political elite, students, organized labour, the church and ethnic groups who felt marginalized. Zambia was obliged to embrace an austerity programme. As usual this increased discontent and intensified the political agitation for incorporation. In December 1986 large demonstrations in the copperbelt frightened Kaunda into abandoning the structural adjustment programme, to the consternation of the international financial institutions. Kaunda survived the riots but the discontent and agitations grew gradually.

In the late 1980s the recession deepened. Kaunda reluctantly turned once more to a structural adjustment programme in the course of which he increased the price of corn meal, the staple food of Zambia, from $2.79 per 55-pound bag to $6.56. Riots erupted and spread for several days. Fortunes in property were lost through looting and arson, at least 24 people were killed and over 150 people injured. This event was a watershed in the political history of Zambia. Badly shaken, Kaunda decided to put the issue of multi-party system to a referendum, which he lost resoundingly.

The Process of Democratization

Such are the ways in which the demand for economic and political incorporation interface and constitute a rudimentary democracy movement. It remains to consider the dialectics of pressures and responses in processes of democratization. However, before going into that, it is useful for expositional convenience to typologize observed strategies of democratization in contemporary Africa. To make this typology applicable to every country in Africa which is a real or potential democratizer (and every country in Africa falls into one of these two categories) the phrase 'strategies of democratization' is being used rather loosely to include instances in which the dictator or political class in power is trying to thwart democratization. Thus when we speak of strategies of democratization, it is really a short hand for strategies of democratization and nondemocratization.

A cursory look at how the rulers of Africa are reacting to pressures for democratization initially suggests two types of strategies. There is the preventive strategy in which the people in power remain steadfast in their opposition to democratization despite pressures. In this case, the pressures only elicit repression or highly contrived devices for frustrating and derailing the democracy movement. The overwhelming majority of African leaders fall into this category. Notable examples are President Eyadéma of Togo, Samuel Doe of Liberia, Ibrahim Babangida of Nigeria, Omar Bongo of Gabon, Paul Biya of Cameroon, Houphouët-Boigny of Ivory Coast, Idi Amin of Uganda, Mobutu of Zaire, Arap Moi of Kenya, Kenneth Kaunda of Zambia, J. S. Momoh of Sierra Leone, Ali Saibou and Kountché of Niger Republic, Blaise Compaoré of Burkina Faso and Jerry Rawlings of Ghana.

The other kind of strategy is accommodationist. In this case, leaders are willing in varying degrees to accommodate democracy. What sets the leaders in this group apart is that for whatever reason, they have come to see some merit in democracy and the need to accommodate it, if possible without losing power. The few instances of this include Cape Verde and Bénin Republic. The willingness of those in power to recognize some merit in democratic arrangements and to try to accommodate them does not guarantee qualitative democratization, if only because even the leaders who recognize the merit of democracy invariably want to maintain their power in the face of democratization.

Similarly, the resistance of leaders in power to democratization does not mean that democracy can never be realized in those instances. Indeed, such resistance could be positive in the sense of leading to a more qualitative development of civil society and democracy, as was the case in South Africa. The typology is not without implications for democratic outcomes but it tells us relatively little about them. Its implications for the politics of democratization, processes of democratization and their contradictions and costs are far more important.

Accommodationist Strategies

President Kérékou's Bénin offers a good example of accommodationist strategies. President Mathieu Kérékou came to power in Dahomey (now, the Republic of Bénin) in 1972 and stayed in power for 17 years notable for

Marxian rhetoric and poor economic management. Like most African countries, the Republic of Bénin was badly hit by the shocks and economic recession of the 1980s. The ensuing fiscal crisis was so devastating that the state could not even pay the salaries of civil servants much less maintain any credible level of social service. It would appear that the crisis led Kérékou to rethink his political and economic policies and to accept the need for political pluralism and a liberal economy.

In this frame of mind he turned to France, the ex-colonial master, which had been an object of public derision for economic assistance and also to the international development agencies. In December 1989 the French ambassador to Bénin communicated the response of the French presidency to Kérékou's principal private secretary. It was to the effect that to get any assistance from France the regime had to accept some power-sharing, especially with the opposition, as well as more transparency.

The surprise was that the French condition for cooperation fell far short of the more radical changes that Kérékou had in mind. Kérékou decided to end the power monopoly of his party and to convene a national conference during which all fundamentals of the political system of the Republic of Bénin would be open for discussion and negotiation. He proceeded to launch this programme even in the face of considerable opposition from members of this party and government who did not want such radical restructuring.

A 'progressive' minister, Robert Dossou was appointed to organize the conference. When it convened in February 1990, the delegates, much against the expectations of President Kérékou, declared the conference sovereign. Supporters of Kérékou including powerful members of the armed forces hatched a plot to rebuff the attack on the powers of the president and possibly put an end to the conference as well. To his credit Kérékou refused to go along with this and instructed his supporters to cooperate with the conference even though it is generally agreed that the plot would have succeeded if he had supported it. The National Conference, now termed the Bénin National Assembly, assumed sovereignty, annulled the old constitution and all national institutions and elected a prime minister, Nicephore Soglo, to head a transitional government and also to be responsible for defence. A high Republican Council was also set up to administer the law until the completion and adoption of a new constitution. After the conference a multi-party election was held. On March 24, 1991, Nicéphore Soglo, the interim prime mnister, defeated Mathieu Kérékou in the presidential election.

An even more impressive example of the accommodationist strategy is that of Cape Verde under President Pereira. This is one of the examples that refute the claim that the process of democratization is driven by political liberalization in Eastern Europe, for the process of democratization of Cape Verde started long before that of Eastern Europe. Much of the credit goes to President Aristides Pereira, who stayed close to the ideals of Amilcar Cabral with whom he had been associated in the struggle for the independence of Cape Verde and Guinea-Bissau since 1950. Because of his commitment to these ideals, his rule in Cape Verde had been exceptional in his respect for human rights, his refusal to privatize the state, or to condone corruption and his prudent economic management which won the respect and support of donors. A series of reforms of the ruling Partido Africano da Independencia de Cabo Verde (PAICV) and the constitution culminated in a constitutional reform of 1990 which stripped the party of supremacy and paved the way for multi-party elections in 1991.

It is all the more significant that President Pereira supported reform in the face of evident risk of being defeated by the opposition Movimento Para a Democracia (MPD) of Carlos Veiga. The MPD was heavily favoured by the business and the international development community because, unlike PAICV, it was not a Marxist party but one which advocated open access to foreign investment, establishing the tourist potential of Cape Verde. More important still, it was clear that the Cape Verde citizens abroad, who are even more numerous than those at home and economically powerful, would support Carlos Veiga and MPD. The most powerful and politically organized émigré community, in the Boston area of the United States, which was led by John Wahnon, entered into a formal alliance with Carlos Veiga. Wahnon also leads a political movement called Uniao Caboverdiana Independente Democratica (UCID). As was expected when the elections were eventually held in 1991, President Aristides Pereira was defeated by Carlos Veiga. Aristides Pereira accepted defeat gracefully and has earned himself great respect in Africa and the world.

Preventive Strategies

In Niger Republic, the process of democratization followed the preventive strategy. Despite the success of his brutal repression in decimating the opposition, Seyni Kountché appeared to have realized that some appearance of concession to democratic pressures was necessary. He accordingly announced on August 3, 1983, a programme of return to civilian rule, which turned out to be protracted and highly controlled. A national charter was commissioned. It was intended to determine the guiding principles of a new constitution and also to determine what the principal agency for democratization would be. Eventually the agency for democratization emerged in the form of the National Council for Development (CND). A draft charter was adopted in May 1987. This charter clearly revealed that Seyni Kountché was more interested in taking the wind out of the movement for democratization than in embracing democracy. The only thing remotely democratic about it was a statement of intention to institute the rule of law (Ibrahim 1993:62; Rayal 1990:397-381). Conspicuously absent in the charter was any plan to hand over power to an elected civilian government.

In November 1987, Kountché died and was replaced as head of state by Ali Saibou, who quickly let it be known that he was committed to the process of democratization. But, soon enough, it was clear that he was no more interested in democratization than his predecessor. He harped on the overriding necessity of order, left no doubt that democratization would not include any prospect of his losing power and rejected the idea of a multi-party system. As it turned out, these were the parameters which defined the 'transition to democracy'. A constitution was made and approved by a referendum by a margin of 99.3 per cent of the vote. This referendum paradoxically underlined the vacuity of the democratic process. Ali Saibou got himself elected President of Niger Republic on December 10, 1989 by 99.6 per cent of the vote.

Shortly after his triumph, Ali Saibou's political strategy fell apart from civil unrest. The unrest began on February 8, when students embarked on a boycott of classes to oppose austerity measures arising from an IMF programme. As part of their protest, the students organized a protest march the next day, February 9, which was forcefully confronted by soldiers. Many students were injured, at least 14 of them fatally. Amid immense public outrage, the trade union movement, the Union des Syndicates des Travailleurs du Niger (USTN) turned against the government to which it had been an important ally and helped to organize, on February 16, a massive demonstration which further deepened the crisis and increased the pressure on the government. Sensing its weakness against the rising tide of public indignation and civil unrest, the government of Ali Saibou sacked the minister for internal affairs and appointed a Hausa prime minister; the Council of Ministers was reconstituted to reduce its Zarma domination and to make concessions to greater participation by other ethnic groups.

Unfortunately for the government, the people were in no mood to settle for minor changes. By all indications, they read the government's concessions as a sign of weakness and pressed on for a national conference to effect a more fundamental political change. Ali Saibou and his ruling party, the National Movement for the Development of Society (MNSD) opposed the idea of a national conference, but they could not prevail in the face of the discontent and civil unrest caused by the massacre of demonstrating students on what came to be popularly called Black Friday. The legitimacy of the government was so eroded and its power was openly challenged by the Tuaregs who seemed strangely emboldened by the brutal assault against them. It was unable to continue holding out against the call for a national conference. The conference ran into many difficulties including lack of money, bad weather, logistic problems, and organizational lapses despite the assistance given by Maitre Dossou, the organiser of the Bénin Republic national conference to its preparatory committee.

In the end the people were so determined to have a national conference that these difficulties were largely overcome, as was the determination of Ali Saibou and his supporters to use the conference to perpetuate their power. For instance, the considerable expense of the national conference, which sat for four months, was raised by the contributions from the people themselves—especially workers, business people and organisations. The conference became a forum for complaints against present and past state functionaries, and testimonies of corruption and abuse of power. Its proceedings were broadcast live on radio, a procedure which immensely promoted popular interest and the spirit of liberty. This contributed in no small measure to making it a defining moment for civil society.

On July 29, 1991, the conference began. Once it finally took off, the Niger Republic National Conference took the pattern of that of Bénin Republic. It immediately claimed sovereignty and insisted that its decisions override all existing institutions and procedures. It deposed the head of the army and rendered President Ali Saibou largely impotent by dissolving his government, putting the ministries under directors-general who were to report directly to the conference. As in the case of Bénin Republic, it elected an interim prime minister, Cheiffou Amadou, who eventually became president after the general elections.

It is tempting to regard Zambia as a case of accommodative strategy. President Kenneth Kaunda's authoritarianism was relatively gentle and the process of democratization was less traumatic than most. However, Zambia remains an instance of preventive strategy. Kaunda's commitment to the single party never changed since the early 1960s. He resisted every attempt to move Zambia to a multi-party system. He might have got away with it if economic austerity had not enlarged and deepened the opposition to his single-party system. From the late 1970s, Zambia was in crisis; got much worse in the early 1980s with external shocks including falling copper prices. President Kaunda was obliged to turn to the IMF and the World Bank, and a reform package, strangely called the Radical Reform Programme (RRP), was launched in October 1985. The austerity of this programme, especially the escalation of the price of the Zambian staple mealie meal from the removal of subsidies, led to civil unrest which forced the government to cancel the programme. The government experimented with a watered-down homegrown programme but it did not take long to realize that this was not viable.

Aware that it had run out of options in the face of deepening economic crisis, the government reluctantly turned to the Bretton Woods institutions again. A new stabilisation programmewas launched in January 1990. By now the legitimacy of the Kaunda government was much eroded, and its confusion and ineffectiveness was much exposed. The Kaunda government and its stabilisation programme elicited determined opposition from students, farmers, workers, human rights activists and supporters of pluralism and democratization. The opposition became more pointedly political than ever. While economic mismanagement and the austerity programme remained a preoccupation, the opposition began to concentrate on ending the single-party system and on democratization. Kaunda was required to put the issue of the continuation of the single-party system to a democratic mandate through a referendum. The government tried to hold out but the pressure was too strong. A decisive factor was the emergence of a formidable opposition political movement, the Movement for Multi-Party Democracy (MMD) which went into alliance with the powerful Zambian Congress of Trade Unions (ZCTU).

In May 1990 Kaunda acceded to the demand for a referendum. But he preferred to look forward to a general election which he still hoped he would win. In the elections, the MMD won 125 out of the 150 parliamentary seats and its leader, Frederick Chiluba, the leader of the ZCTU, soundly defeated Kenneth Kaunda, winning 76 per cent of the votes. Thus failed Kaunda's attempt to co-opt democracy to the service of his political ambitions.

The regime of President Didier Ratsiraka of the Malagasy Republic had tried to give itself democratic legitimacy by holding periodic elections which were managed to favour the incumbent president and his party. The election of March 1989, which Ratsiraka won with 62 per cent of the vote, was his third election. By this time there was considerable disillusion with the Ratsiraka regime, which was popularly perceived as being very corrupt. There was disillusion with the regime's poor management of the economy which had led to a rising tide of poverty and hardship. There was also the frustrating ambiguity of the regime's political character. It had a veneer of liberalism in that Ratsiraka ruled not so much through the single-party system as through a coalition of notables and factions. He was able to maintain power by his control of the institutions of the state such as the civil service by using state power for patronage. But it was by no means democratic because, though seemingly pluralistic, the polity was readily manipulated by the use of state power and corruption to produce political outcomes favourable to President Ratsiraka.

The widespread disillusion and the prevailing democratic struggles in the rest of Africa engendered opposition movements which insisted on political liberalization. In March 1990, the government allowed the formations of parties. Already, numerous opposition and reformist groups had been formed and were operating, some clandestinely. Most of the opposition groups came together in a grand coalition called the Forces Vives (FV). After demanding constitutional reform to no avail, the FV began to insist on a national conference. Following the rejection of its demand for a national conference in May 1991, the movement began to stage protests, demonstrations and strikes. Emboldened by the government's weakness and its growing support, the movement declared the election of 1989 undemocratic and nullified it in July 1991. It then set up its own provisional government with retired General Jean Rakotoharison as president and Albert Zafy, leader of Union National pour le Développement et la Democratie, an affiliate of the FV, as prime minister. Rather surprisingly, government workers and officials including the police cooperated as the provisional government began to take over government institutions such as ministries.

A march on the presidential palace on August 8, 1991 led to about 100 deaths when the soldiers guarding the palace opened fire on the demonstrators. This event only increased the support for FV. Most of the diplomatic community was openly sympathetic. The French asked Ratsiraka to resign. Some Western donors threw their weight on the side of democratization. FV picked up critical support in the powerful Council of Christian Churches (FFKM). The army also began to put pressure on Ratsiraka to negotiate a peaceful settlement with the opposition. Ratsiraka knew that the game was up. On October 31, 1991, a settlement was reached by which a transitional government was to be set up to operate for 18 months while a new constitution was prepared, submitted to a referendum and a national election held. The new constitution was overwhelmingly approved by referendum in August 1993. In the presidential election (run off) on February 10, 1993, Zafy polled 67 per cent of the vote defeating Ratsiraka decisively.

In Mali the democracy movement was up against a military dictator, Moussa Traoré, who had been in power since 1968, having won power by staging a coup against the elected President of Mali, Modibo Keita. Like most other countries in Africa, the pressure for political incorporation and democracy built up significantly in the wake of the economic crisis which began at the end of the 1970s. By 1981 Mali had been driven to the Bretton Woods institutions. And, as in other cases, the cure was a problem all its own, as the austerity programme appeared to add to the political tensions. The Traoré government got nervous about carrying out some of its commitments to the Bretton Woods institutions, as a result of which disbursements were suspended between 1987 and 1988.

But Traoré, desperate to find a solution to the economic crisis, was obliged to return to the Bretton Woods institutions, which insisted on an even more austere programme including revocation of the government's long-standing commitment of guaranteed employment for university graduates. This and other austerity measures led to popular protests in 1991 and more strident demands for political pluralism and democratization, demands which the Traoure government chose to ignore.

. In the meantime the opposition was getting bigger and better organized. Among the growing opposition groups were the Alliance pour la Democratie au Mali (ADEMA), a coalition of several parties formed in 1990, the Comité National d'Initiative Democratique (CNID) and the revival of the ancient party of Modibo Keita, the US-RDA, originally founded in 1946 but now headed by Tieoule Konaté, and the Association des Etudiants et Elèves Malien (AEEM), which was a movement for democratization as well as the defence of the political and economic interests of students.

As the opposition got better organized and more confident, the incidence of public protests increased. The Traoré government, which had imagined that it could ride the tide of protest by benign posturing soon turned to violent repression. From March 22 to 24 there was a rash of student protests in the course of which some government buildings were burnt. The government responded with unprecedented brutality, causing the death of an estimated 100 to 150 students and hundreds more wounded. Amid the inevitable public furore, President Traoré was arrested by Lt Col. Amadou Toumany Touré and the parachutists under his command, the parliament was abolished, as was the constitution, and a Conseil de Reconciliation Nationale (CRN), headed by Lt Col. Touré, later, the Comité de Transition Pour le Salut du Peuple (CTSP) took charge.

Lt Col. Touré announced an accelerated programme of transition to democratic rule. As part of this programme, a national conference was convened for the end of July 1991. It adopted a new constitution which was approved by referendum on January 12, 1992. National elections were scheduled for February 23 and March 8, 1992. 21 parties contested the 129 parliamentary seats, with ADEMA winning a comfortable majority of 76 seats. As expected, the leader of ADEMA, Alpha Oumar Konaré, won the presidential election conducted on April 12 and 26, 1992 and was duly inaugurated president.

In all these cases, the attempt to co-opt democracy by those in power did not succeed, to the benefit of the process of democratization. Predictably, the democratic outcomes in these instances of democratization have been qualitatively low. In Gabon, President Omar

Bongo frustrated the democracy movement by introducing superficial democratic processes and practices and using them quickly to legitimize his rule while the opposition was still off balance. Sensing the mounting pressure for democratization in his country as well as neighbouring countries, Omar Bongo quickly convened a national conference in March 1990.

The opposition, still forming, inexperienced and unprepared, attended the conference in a frame of mind that was more diffident than hopeful, certainly without the feeling of being a major player in the unfolding events. Bongo managed to keep the conference from claiming sovereignty. While the conference took some important and binding decisions, such as the adoption of a multi-party system and a general election, its reforms did not diminish the power of President Omar Bongo. Not surprisingly Bongo's party, the PDG, won the election held at the end of the transition process.

The opposition, now fully awake to the way Bongo had manipulated democratization to maintain power, refused to accept the new government which Bongo formed after the election. The major opposition parties, namely the Parti gabonais du progres (PGP) of Pierre Louis Agondjo-Okawé and the Union socialistes gabonais (USG) of Serge Bekale, protested the handling of the transition to democracy and insisted that the election was not free and fair. Indeed, Antonine Mboumbou Miyakou, the minister for territorial administration, agreed that there were 'disorders, exactions and irregularities' (*West Africa* 1990:2590). The army reportedly intervened in 14 instances in Libreville alone, and voting was cancelled in 32 constituencies which were predominantly opposition strongholds, such as Port Gentil. But their protests got them only agreement on a cabinet of national reconciliation in which some of them could participate.

The Mobutu regime in Zaire has been one of the most determined holdouts against democratization. The demand for incorporation and democratization came somewhat earlier in Zaire because it was also arguably the most corrupt and the most economically mismanaged. Zaire is one of the cases in which economic mismanagement has become life-threatening for ordinary people; real incomes are now only a mere fraction of what they were when Mobutu took power and on many important social indicators, Zaire has been getting steadily worse since then. The fiscal crisis of the state is so severe that infrastructures have collapsed in most urban areas, communications have broken down and parts of the country are beyond administrative control, as are unpaid civil servants, police and soldiers. Unable to deal with the problems of the economy and to arrest the deepening crisis of underdevelopment, Mobutu has nonetheless ensured that the political reforms which would have provided the opening for dealing with the economic and the political problems are bogged down in a stalemate which means that Zaire has virtually no economy and no government.

The demand for a 'second independence in Zaire eventually came to focus on the call for a national conference which Mobutu vehemently opposed, but when he found the pressure irresistible, decided to allow and to subvert. He fought doggedly against sovereignty for the conference and in the end succeeded by exploiting the differences within the opposition as well as by use of patronage. He exploited the social pluralism of Zaire and complexified the arrangements and modalities of the conference to the point of immobilism. He dragged out the preparatory processes for setting up the conference, the basis of representation, the enabling instruments, the agenda, and so on. The accreditation of the unwieldy assembly of 3,000 delegates took an entire month.

Zaire remains bogged down in a stalemate which continues to feed the country's economic and political regression. Despite his eroded political legitimacy and shrinking power base Mobutu still had enough power to obstruct change, although not to govern in any meaningful sense. The opposition, most of which eventually came together under the umbrella of the 'Sacred Union', has not held together partly because of the large number of parties and movements. Even the major ones such as the Union for Democracy and Social Progress (UDPS) of Etienne Tshisekedi, the Democratic and Social Christian Party (PDSC) led by Joseph Ileo and Nguza Karl-I-Bond's Union of Federalists and Independent Republicans (UNFERI) are divided.

Mobutu also draws considerable strength from a core group in the armed forces, mainly from his ethnic base, whom he can count on for protection and for repressing his opponents. The problems of the opposition are compounded because there has been very little new blood in the Zairian leadership, especially the opposition. The prominent leaders of the opposition such as Tshisekedi were either former members of Mobutu's People's Revolutionary Movement (MPR) or former political or business associates who had contributed in no small way to the legacy of Mobutism, many of them too vulnerable to sustain a radical posture. By all indications, many of them see democratization as a convenience facilitating access to power.

Mobutu Sese Seko has succeeded in hanging on to power but not in co-opting democracy to his purposes. Indeed, he is barely in power, governing but not really ruling and what he is supposed to be governing hardly qualifies for the nomenclature of government any more than its territorial base can be called a country without qualification. The democracy movement in Zaire has had some success in undermining Mobutu's authority, reducing his powers and making some democratic reforms through the national conference. But these gains are of no effect in the prevailing political environment of near-anarchy which Mobutu is managing to sustain.

The process of democratization in the Republic of Togo was not unlike that of Zaire. As in Zaire, democratization in Togo faced the formidable opposition of a dictator who had ruled the country for decades and was used to regarding himself as the personification of his country and so entitled to define and actualize its destiny. Known variously as the man of January 13, 'the Helmsman', and 'the Father of Togo', Eyadéma opposed demands for democratization and power-sharing brutally, all the more so because of his paranoia about a vengeful comeback by the family of former President Olympio. He privatized the state, especially the army, which became virtually an ethnic army; the other side was the exclusion of other ethnic groups from positions of power and the free use of the resources of the state to punish and reward.

The economic crisis of the 1980s affected Togo like most countries in Africa, but its impact was cushioned for some time by the flight of capital from Kérékou's Marxist Bénin. But from the mid-1980s a formidable opposition had grown and President Eyadéma was under pressure to end his monopoly of power and to democratize. On September 23, 1986 he survived an attempt to overthrow him in coup. While he blamed this on international subversion, the challenge to him at home got bolder, increasingly taking the forms of demonstrations and civil unrest, sometimes resulting in deaths and injuries. For instance on October 4, 1990 a crowd of about 6,000 demonstrators, protesting the trial of Logo Dossovi and Doglo Agbelenko, activists accused of distributing anti-government material, were set upon by the armed forces and violently forced from the court building into the streets. The youth subsequently went on rampage, and it was not until October 6 that order was restored in Lomé. On October 8, the Bar Association declared a 72-hour strike to protest the government's handling of the demonstrations, which by some estimates cost 17 lives. Many more were injured and 170 people were detained.

As in most Francophone countries, the movement for incorporation and democracy came to focus on the demand for a national conference. President Eyadéma ridiculed and resisted the idea for some time, but found the pressure irresistible. Togo's conference started on July 19, with Monsignor Sanouko Kpodzro, Bishop of Atakpame presiding, amid confusion arising from reports of the arrest of Andoch Bonin, a critic of Eyadéma. Like Mobutu, Eyadéma tried to limit the powers of the national conference and to keep it off balance while projecting power with his ethnic army which he controlled. Eyadéma, who was used to adulation, was shocked by the plain talk and the allegations and criticisms which were aired at the conference. He subsequently suspended the conference by presidential decree on August 26 for a while and sent troops into the streets to assert his power. But the delegates ignored his suspension order, went ahead to prepare a new constitution, set dates for elections and elected a prime minister and a Supreme Republican Council to conduct government business in a transitional period pending municipal, legislative and presidential elections.

When the conference ended on August 28, 1991 Eyadéma excused himself from the closing ceremony claiming a sore throat, but many believed it was to avoid humiliation. What is clear is that despite the conference, Eyadéma remained as unyielding to the pressure for democratization as ever. He rejected the charges of corruption and human rights violations made against him and stoutly defended his stewardship. He was supported by the army to whom he granted high pay increases, which compounded the problems of the economy.

In October 1991, soldiers loyal to Eyadéma took control of the radio station in Lomé demanding that President Eyadéma sack Kokou Koffigoh, prime minister in the transitional government, and dismiss the government. That same evening an emergency meeting of the High Council of the Republic (HCR) demanded that the commander-in-chief of the armed forces General, Bassabi Banfoh, be dismissed. On October 8, soldiers loyal to President Eyadéma forced their way into a hotel where Mr Koffigoh was staying, demanding to see him. When Koffigoh recounted the incident in a broadcast the following day, a substantial crowd converged in his office in a show of solidarity to protect him. The incident led to riots and looting, which were particularly serious in the Northern capital, Adeswi.

This atmosphere of confrontation prevailed throughout the transition period and carried into the election campaign. Not surprisingly, Eyadéma used the coercive resources of the state which he still controlled and his considerable patronage to rig the elections blatantly, to the universal condemnation of international elections observers, some of whom pulled out even before the election, insisting that it was a farce.

The processes of 'democratic transition' in Kenya, Cameroon, Ghana, Burkina Faso and the Ivory Coast were similar to that of Togo in the sense that in each case the person in power contrived a democratic transition programme and used the resources of the state and the privileges of incumbency to 'steal the election' at the end of the process. In this process of appropriating democratic legitimacy some were more crude than others, some more violent, but the principle was the same in all these cases. In Burkina Faso, President Blaise Compaoré firmly and consistently rejected the reforms which the democracy movement and political opponents were pressing for, especially the calling of a national conference. Instead, after violent clashes between pro-democracy groups and government supporters on September 30, 1991, he went on air on October 6, 1991 to announce a referendum on the country's political future as well as the establishment of a tripartite commission which was to include members of the opposition. This announcement, seen by the opposition as part of Compaoré's design to defuse the demand for democratization and perpetuate himself in power, elicited massive demonstrations on October 7, 1991.

Compaoré went ahead with his plans regardless and in the end ran a presidential election in which he was the only candidate, the six opposition candidates having decided to boycott the elections because of Compaoré's high-handedness and his refusal to grant the demand for a national conference. Appeals to put back the election, including that by the highly respected episcopal conference of Burkina Faso, were rejected. Frustration with this process was expressed in civil unrest including demonstrations, looting and the trashing of 42 polling stations, and a voter boycott. But Compaoré went ahead to win his election.

Ghana's transition was similarly manipulated to give the appearance of democratization while ensuring the perpetuation of President Lt Jerry Rawlings in power. In December 1991, Rawlings, who had been a bitter opponent of political pluralism, suddenly announced a time table for return to democratic rule, clearly intending to capitalize on the element of surprise. And his announcement did indeed leave the opposition organized under the rubric of the Movement for Freedom and Justice confused and angry. A committee of experts was to be set up to deliberate on political arrangements and then a constituent assembly was to be convened. Otherwise the programme was vague.

Rawlings and his close associates kept the details of the programme to themselves, put out the occasional detail and used the control of this information to advance their plan while keeping the opposition guessing and off balance. The Provisional National Defence Council (PNDC), especially Lt Rawlings, refused to release its plans regarding the political future. This allowed the PNDC to direct the transition to the advantage of Rawlings prospective presidency. Most important, the PNDC said nothing about the all-important ancillary issues such as government monopoly of the press, human rights issues, amnesty for victims of the regime's repression, and the freedom to form and operate political parties.

This elicited considerable scepticism about the seriousness of Rawlings' transition programme and unfavourable comparison between the Rawlings' transition and Apartheid South Africa. Like Compaoré, Rawlings remained unmoved by criticisms, pressed on with his transition and contrived to have himself elected amid protests, boycotts and demonstrations. But the Rawlings transition appears to have been less violent than that of Cameroon and Togo and was treated with considerable indulgence because Ghana has become the model pupil of the Bretton Woods institutions and the bearer of the image of the success of structural adjustment programmes in Africa.

The political opposition to President Paul Biya and the democracy movement in Cameroon was far better organized and more determined than in Ghana and most other parts of Africa, partly because they were desperate to remove him. The economy, already in crisis when he came to power, had deteriorated during his tenure of office, a condition which the opposition blamed on the corruption of the regime. In the face of escalating economic and political crisis, Biya and his ruling Cameroon Peoples' Democratic Movement (CPDM) seemed strangely inert except in the repression of the opposition. He had privatized the state in a way that his predecessor never did and concentrated a great amount of power in the hands of members of his small Beti ethnic group. This was true especially for the army and the top of the bureaucracy.

The political insensitivity of Biya offended many deeply. He ignored the age-long power-sharing arrangement between the Moslem North and the Christian South. In the 24 years of power, his predecessor always ensured that the two most powerful positions in Cameroon, the President and the Secretary-General of the Presidency never came from one region. But Biya ignored this and appointed secretary-generals who, like him, were also from the Christian South. He enraged Anglophone Cameroon by changing the name of the country from the United Republic of Cameroon to the Republic of Cameroon, dispensing with the view that Cameroon was a negotiated consensus between diverse groups whose diversity had to be recognized and consciously accommodated. Above all, his opposition to democratization was implacable and he was brutally repressive.

All this fed the determination of the opposition and the democracy movement to remove him. As in most of Francophone Africa, the opposition focused on the demand for a national conference, which they camp for with extraordinary courage and ingenuity such as the nonpayment of taxes, YaoundÈ 2, and the 'dead cities' policy. But Biya was equally determined. These were the circumstances which made the pursuit of democratization in Cameroon so costly in terms of social disorganization, economic disruption and the loss of lives and property.

In the end, like Rawlings, Compoaré, and Eyadéma, Biya pressed on with his own tailor-made transition to democracy. By all accounts, including those of the diplomatic community in Yaoundé, Biya lost the presidential election despite his abuse of state power and human rights to get elected. But he remained in power by means of terror and violence amid a monumental legitimacy crisis and popular alienation which has raised doubts about the viability of Cameroon as a country.

Nigeria's case is different still. Like Zaire and Cameroon, the drive for democratization is bogged down in a debilitating stalemate. Here the obstacle to democratization is not a dictator or a single individual, but the military, which has constituted itself as a ruling elite and remains in power with the cooperation of civilian elites who are ostensibly for democracy but for whom democracy is nothing more than a means to power and accumulation which can be set aside as other opportunities and circumstances dictate. In 34 years of independence, Nigeria has been under civilian rule for only two brief interludes, 1960 to 1966 and 1979 to 1983, a total of just nine years. The rest of the time, Nigeria has been under military rule. While in power, the military protests that it is not in the business of ruling and sells itself as the midwife of the transition to a stable democracy, and invariably sets up a transition programme which can be seen from the benefit of hindsight to be designed to be interminable or to fail and bring back the military.

The struggle for democracy in Nigeria is largely a struggle against the military. As in most African countries, the struggle reached a new intensity in the early 1980s with a combination of external shocks and internal mismanagement. Even with external shocks the crisis could have been avoided in Nigeria if the huge fortunes that Nigeria realized from petroleum had been better used. But far from avoiding the crisis, Nigeria experienced a singularly severe version of it. When every attempt to manage the crisis failed, Nigeria turned to the Bretton Woods institutions in 1986; as usual, the solution compounded the problem. By 1986 it was clear that Nigerians were totally disillusioned with military rule and angry that they had to put up with a very harsh adjustment programme which was made necessary by the mismanagement of their rulers. Feelings ran so high that General Babangida, the military ruler of the moment, quickly announced a programme of transition to civilian rule. As it turned out, that programme was meant to reduce popular anger and to buy time, and was not intended to be a transition to anything, much less to a democratic polity.

The programme of transition to civilian rule which the Babangida regime announced was to stretch from 1986 to December 1992. It included the setting up of a Political Bureau to set out the principles, core values and ideology of Nigeria; a Constitutional Assembly to provide a new Constitution; an Electoral Commission to plan elections, educate people on voting behaviour and to hold elections; a Centre for Democratic Studies to teach Nigerians the ways of democracy; a Directorate of Mass Mobilization (MAMSER) to conscientize Nigerians; and a pre-registration programme in which political associations were allowed to canvass and document membership in the hope that they would have a large enough following, spread widely enough in all regions of the country, to be given the privilege of being one of the two political associations to be registered as political parties.

As this long programme unfolded, it became quite clear that instead of being a programme for yielding to civilian successors, it was a programme for ensuring the absence of civilian successors. Periodically, General Babangida issued decrees banning people from participating in politics. By this steady diet of bans, he reduced the civilian leadership and encouraged the emergence of civilian supporters and surrogates rather than successors.

This was achieved by banning the independent-minded and encouraging the subservient and also by making the conditions for political participation so humiliating that people with self-esteem were obliged to withdraw. The regime kept people insecure about participating in politics, subjecting prospective participants to numerous directives and conditions which were changed abruptly and without explanation. When the associations were asked to vie for the privilege of being registered political parties, they were not allowed to use the media to campaign, the politics had to be done in the most demanding manner namely by face-to-face contact. The level of documentation which was required was such that on the day in which the associations submitted their application, the major ones carried six to thirteen lorry loads of documentation. And after all the labour and expense, Babangida decided to set aside the whole process and the mountains of data and form two government-owned parties. To emphasize government ownership of these parties, the government wrote their constitutions and their manifestoes, built and furnished offices for them throughout the country and lavishly financed their operations.

The very idea of a political party was negated. A party is an organisation of people who have evolved some notion of how political society should function and who now strive to elicit a mandate from the society at large to manage the affairs of society in accordance with this notion. In contrast to this, the parties which the government set up, namely, the National Republican Party (NRC) and the Social Democratic Party (SDP), were just assembly points for people with nothing in common except the appetite for power, an appetite strong enough to be undaunted by the humiliations to which political aspirants had to submit.

Not surprisingly, the parties could be nothing other than an anarchy of ambitions, and this meant that the transition did not have much chance of success. Political competition between and within the political parties was indeed anarchic in both a behavioural and a moral sense as legitimacy norms were overridden by efficiency norms in the quest for power. At various points, including the presidential primaries, there was a complete breakdown of the party system and the political process.

Despite all this, General Babangida and the military oligarchy had reason to doubt their control of the transition programme. On the eve of the presidential elections, the last major event of the eight-year programme, the fear had grown to a point in which the government felt desperate about stopping the election. With only two days to go, they contrived a motion for a court order to stop the election. At 9.45 p.m. on June 10, 1993, two days before the election, an Abuja High Court acting on a motion filed by Abimbola Davies on behalf of an organization called Association for a Better Nigeria (ABN) restrained the National Electoral Commission from conducting the presidential election scheduled for June 12.

It was revealed later, and confirmed by its leaders, that ABN was a support group of President Babangida. It is significant for the affiliation of the ABN that the substantive suit asked for the extension of military rule to 1997. Just as significant was the fact that the injunction was granted because, according to Section 19 (l) of the Presidential Election (Basic Constitution and Transitional Provision) Decree 13 of 1933:

> notwithstanding the provision of the constitution of the Federal Republic Nigeria 1979, as amended or any other law, no interim or interlocutory order or ruling, judgment or decision made by any court or tribunal before or after the commencement of this decree, in respect of any intra-party or inter-party dispute or an other matter before it, shall affect the date or time of holding the election or performance by the commission of any of its functions under this decree.

The attempt to stop the election was motivated by the realization that the election would not be deadlocked as the President and his supporters had hoped or won by the candidate more acceptable to the Babangida regime, Bashir Tofa.

The Chairman of the National Electoral Commission (NEC), Humphrey Nwosu, standing on Decree No 13 of 1993, went ahead with the election. By Monday June 14 the National Electoral Commission had started announcing the results, which showed that the candidate of the Social Democratic Party, Chief MKO Abiola, was winning easily. Out of 6.6 million votes counted, the SDP had polled 4.3 million while the NRC had only 2.3 million and taken 11 of the 14 states declared, including Kano, the home state of the NRC candidate. Suddenly, NEC stopped announcing results because the Abuja High Court had on another application by the ABN restrained NEC from announcing more results. Two other court orders enjoining NEC to release the results were of no avail. On June 23, after the meeting of the National Defence and Security Council the Babangida government announced the cancellation of the presidential election and the suspension of the transition programme and its enabling decree as well as NEC.

This caused a great deal of resentment and precipitated an immense political crisis which put into question the viability of Nigeria as a political entity. In the end the popular resentment of the annulment compelled General Babangida to relinquish office on August 27, 1993, but only after installing a surrogate civilian transition government led by businessman Ernest Shonekan. However, this appeased no one. The pressure on the new government made it impossible for it to govern, and the issue of the annulment was so bitterly contested that the country tottered on the edge of a violent disintegration.

On November 18, 1993, General Abacha, who was Chief of Staff under President Babangida, took over from Shonekan in a bloodless coup. He said his tenure would be brief, just long enough to bring Nigeria back from the brink and to arrange an orderly transition. But Nigerians were unimpressed by Abacha's patriotic posture, knowing that he had been Babangida's second in command for eight years and had been responsible for more coups than any one else in the history of Nigeria.

The crisis escalated, especially after June 11, 1994 when Abiola claimed his mandate and proclaimed himself president of Nigeria. The Senate, which was sacked when Babangida, terminated his transition government, had already met secretly to reclaim its mandate on May 30, 1994. So had the House of Representatives on June 3, 1994 when 384 of its members sat secretly. The agitation for upholding the democratic mandate of June 12, 1993 became focused around the National Democratic Coalition (NADECO), The Civil Liberties Organization (CLO), the Campaign for Democracy (CDC) and the Labour Movement, especially PEGASSUS, which called a strike that effectively closed the petroleum industry for several weeks.

General Abacha was just as determined to hang on to power and to pursue his agenda as the democracy lobby was determined to remove him. Chief Abiola was arrested, charged and denied bail, and by all accounts subjected to humiliation and harsh treatment in detention. All the leading newspapers, the *Guardian*, the *Concord* and *Punch*, were closed, virtually all civil liberties were annulled by a rash of decrees, including those that prevented the victims of these decrees from seeking redress in the law courts. The Nigeria Labour Congress was dissolved and a caretaker appointed by the government to manage its affairs. Leaders of NADECO were arrested, as were many supporters of the June 12 election. Demonstrations occurred in various parts of the country, which were firmly put down with considerable loss of life and property. Abacha hung on, his government totally devoid of legitimacy and surviving by sheer force in increasing isolation, too weak to govern but strong enough to resist the opposition.

From Democratic Processes to Democratic Outcomes

What do we make of these glimpses of the processes of democratization in Africa? What do they tell us about democratization in Africa? To avoid misunderstanding, it is necessary to make a point about this typology of processes. The typology only serves expositional convenience. It is not useful to make too much of it as a tool of analysis. This is because, in the final analysis, there is really only one process of democratization, and that is a process of struggle. Democracy is never given, it is always taken. Sometimes with the acquiescence of those in power, but more often than not, it is taken in the face of their determined resistance in a gruelling and costly struggle.

The basic paradox of democratization is that those who have power tendentially have no interest or inclination to democratize, for democratization entails the redistribution of power against those who are in power and those who are privileged. When such people support democracy it is usually for some countervailing compulsion, which may include the force of public opinion or the sanction of popular rejection in the established democracies. So it is entirely natural that, with minor exceptions, those who hold power in Africa are fighting democratization so determinedly.

However, it will be misleading to think of support or opposition to democracy solely in terms of those in power and those who are not in power. To begin with, a distinction should be made between those in office and those in power. Some of those in office, indeed the vast majority of them, usually are not necessarily in power. More often than not, most of those in power are not in office. Among the people who are merely in office but not in power, some will be under the illusion that they are in power and will for all practical purposes act that way. Those who fall into any of these categories tendentially oppose democratization. So do ordinary people who for whatever reason such as primordial loyalties are in solidarity with those in office or in power.

The point here is that democratization always faces a formidable opposition. It is not merely a matter of battling against a dictator. For however much power may be concentrated in the hands of a dictator, one person is never in power. It is always a power elite or a faction of it that is in power. The government in office and its formal powers does not give an accurate notion of the opposition that democratization has to deal with, for it is only a part of the elite in power and sometimes it is not even the most powerful element of this elite. The opposition to democratization is all the more formidable because among the ordinary people there may be a great deal of support for the elite in power. This is especially the case when the ruling elite has transformed its power into authority and domination into hegemony.

But even without that, there may still be considerable support for the ruling elite in its resistance to democratization arising from fear of change, the alienation of ordinary people which sometimes works in favour of those in power by inculcating the attitude that it is futile for ordinary people to engage in the struggle for power, because their plight will never change even if power changes hands. In African conditions there is the ethnic factor, which may induce considerable solidarity between exploitative rulers and their victims, some of whom may even consider themselves as rulers too by virtue of ethnic affinity to those in power.

How about the support for democratization? The people who have an objective interest in democratization are the ordinary people who stand to benefit from a more equitable redistribution of power. In the final analysis, they have to be the social base of any serious democracy movement, otherwise it will have no depth.

The rub is that the constituents of this base are the very people who are marginal economically and politically. Far from controlling the coercive resources of the state, they are the objects of the oppressive use of these resources. Their economic and political marginality and their cultural deprivation tend to reduce their self-esteem and their sense of efficacy and the feasibility of democratization. The weaknesses of their social position render some of them diffident, submissive and vulnerable to indoctrination into finding common cause with their oppressors and even to being too easily reconciled to minor and even nominal gains in democratization. All these factors make it extremely difficult to mount a challenge for democratization, especially in Africa where most of those in power are not inclined to make concessions to democratization even on grounds of enlightened self-interest.

While the objective situation of the subordinate classes means that they stand to gain the most from democratization and must be the vanguard of a democratization process that is to have any depth, they do not exhaust the democratic constituency. In all probability, some of the people who are in power but not in office will, because of the informality or nonofficial nature of their power, perceive themselves as not being in power. This may lead them to be hostile to the power structure of which they are part and to join the movement for democratization. In these instances this democratic commitment will come under pressure when the egalitarian import of democratization begins to be manifest in practical political arrangements and social and political behaviour. The democratization which they pursue is likely to be shallow or to be just a strategy of power.

These reflections are essential preliminaries for appreciating the problems and prospects of the process of democratization in Africa. Considering the difficulties of democratization even in the best of circumstances, the spread and the intensity of the struggle for democratization has been remarkable. The idea of democracy is seriously engaged in Africa in a manner which will not only be decisive for Africa but also for democracy. It is clear enough from these country experiences that democratization is not just a fad in the way that some development strategies have been, or a reaction to political liberalization in Eastern Europe, or an expression of the contradictions of westernization or the product of political conditionality. It is expressing a very deep need for self-realization, a need so deep as to elicit arduous effort and monumental risks. Without exceptions the democratization processes reviewed briefly here attest to this.

If there is no doubt about the commitment and the intensity of the struggle, the question of the achievement of this commitment is less clear. At first sight the achievement looks impressive. To begin with, while in assessing what the commitment has achieved in substantive democratization, it should not be forgotten that the very commitment itself is an achievement, not only because it is sustained in the face of formidable obstacles and dangers, but also because it contributes a great deal to the feasibility of democracy. Democratic behaviour does not come naturally to most people, and the existence of democracy can never be taken for granted; it has to be defended in daily struggles, at any rate, in 'eternal vigilance'.

The commitment has also yielded concrete results. The surge of democratization is changing the legacy of dictatorship, military regimes and single-party rule in Africa. These were the forms of governance which dominated Africa from the era of political independence in the early 1960s through the 1980s. In the 1990s these kinds of regimes are the exception rather than the rule. At the end of the 1980s, 35 of the 45 states of Africa were under military or one-party rule; the rest were under personal or monarchical rule and rather limited pluralistic systems. (Hadenius 1994). By the end of 1993, the distribution had been neatly reversed with at least 35 countries having accepted multiparty systems. By the end of 1994 virtually every country in Africa, except some like Sudan, Liberia and Sierra Leone which were fighting a civil war or virtually in a state of anarchy (Zaire) or just recovering from a civil war (Uganda), had held multi-party elections or were on the verge of doing so.

It is tempting to read too much into these developments. Welcome as they are, they suggest rather more progress towards democracy than the realities on the ground. To begin with, the democratization process in contemporary Africa is largely an urban phenomenon. It has hardly engaged the rural areas where 60 to 80 per cent of Africans live. This relative exclusion of the rural areas is not only due to the physical isolation and economic marginalization of the rural areas, it also has to do with the sociology of rural poverty. Democratic politics, indeed virtually any other national politics, is often inaccessible to rural people. The rigours of subsistence farming, of scavenging for water and firewood leave them very little time for politics. In any case they have so little access to education they cannot effectively participate in politics—all the more so because the prevailing political style hardly connects with their cultural experience.

It is problem enough that the new democratic politics is largely confined to the urban areas. But, worse, it has tended to be dominated by the Westernized elite, especially university teachers and students, labour leaders, business leaders, human rights lawyers and activists, and prominent politicians some of whom had collaborated with the rulers against whom they now agitate. The influence of this leadership is moving the democracy movement from its social base and to a shallow form of democratization. The tendency to reduce democratization to multi-party election is not so much an imposition of Western supporters of democratization in Africa as a reflection of the social base of the leadership of the democracy movement. It is disturbing that in too many countries in Africa, democratization is little more than an opening for elites who were previously excluded from power to compete for it.

Perhaps this accounts for another apparent weakness of democratization in Africa, namely, the fact that it is not being associated with the transformation of the African state whose form and content is anti-democratic from its legacy of colonial oppression and military and single-party rule. To all appearances democratization is not doing much about the democratic transformation of the state; attention is on who will control this state. But in so far as democratization is limited to the competitive selection by political society at large of those to control the state, what has been gained in the end is only the right to choose between oppressors, not the right to choose between liberty and oppression. Democratization should offer much more than what it appears to be offering now, namely, electoral competition which conceals the illusion of voting without choosing.

The fundamental changes which might have been expected from those countries that went to democratization through fairly open national conferences (for instance, Bénin) as opposed to those who went by way of stage-managed conferences such as Gabon, do not appear to have occurred. Fundamental changes might have been expected because these national conferences started by freeing themselves from the existing structuration of power and had the liberty to visit anew all the fundamental issues of political community and political obligation. And yet even in these cases, the national conference appears to be no more than a 'collective exorcism' (Semilinko

1991) unable to produce any captivating vision on how to proceed, or a surge of new energy:

> ... after convening national conferences, at least in Bénin and Gabon, people went on behaving as if the exercise had simply consisted of replacing the old battle horses or political key figures, with new ones. The real impact of these changes on the population has yet to be revealed. The elites still behave with the same condescension towards the illiterate population; their conquering hero mentality sticks in the throat and the order of priorities has not changed at all.... There is little or no far-reaching structural reform. The same old wooden legs are still in service; they have simply been put in plaster. All the effort has been cosmetic: a change of emblem of the coat of arms, a change of name, and incidentally, of administrative structures, are the most visible signs of democratic change (Semilinko 1991:12).

It would appear that Africa has not fully risen to the opportunities of the national conference. None of them has come up with strikingly original or incisive analysis of national problems, none has gone beyond seeking the replacement of the government in office to challenging the elite in power. They suffer from a dearth of original and interesting ideas on how society might proceed with progressive transformation. They have displayed a surprising predilection to bureaucratic solutions, including a taste for the leadership of bureaucrats. They have continued the legacy of copying Western political and economic institutions, and they show hardly an appreciation of the need to customize democracy to African conditions.

It is going to be extremely difficult to find political arrangements, values and practices which enable expression of the democratic will of the people in the African context. Existing political arrangements and their assumptions are quite alien to the cultural experience of rural Africa. For instance, a modern democratic polity is like a joint stock company which turns on common concerns and common interests, the very interests which make democratic participation meaningful in the first place, for there can be no question of having a legitimate right to participate in something in which one has no stake. But the social discontinuities of plural pre-capitalist societies where primary groups rather than secondary groups still predominate, do not offer the social conditions for this type of polity.

The democracy movement in Africa does not appear to reflect sufficiently the fact that for most people in rural Africa the national political society is really an incomprehensible abstraction. Their sense of political community tends to be localized, as does the focus of their primary political identity and loyalty. Having very little sense of affinity and the sharing of common concerns with the national political society, existing forms of democratic participation tend to make little sense.

Africa has come a long way with democratization but there is still a very long way to go.

3

Democracy and Development

Introduction

The feasibility of democracy in Africa will depend crucially on how it relates to the social experience of Africans and how far it serves their social needs. Accordingly, this chapter will explore the import of democratization for economic and political development in Africa. That entails treating democracy as an instrumental value rather than a consummatory one, as it is often regarded. There are many who fight for democracy because they believe that it ought to prevail whatever its utilitarian import; they think that without it human life is impoverished, vitiated even. Some are more interested in its instrumentality. Others, not so many perhaps, find democracy essentially dysfunctional.

The question of the feasibility of democracy in Africa cannot be dissociated from that of its utility in the African context. As is clear from the preceding pages, democratization in Africa has been approached rather obliquely from the need for economic and political incorporation and the demand for a second independence from a political class whose governance performance has been generally poor and, in some cases, disastrous. There is a strong instrumentalist element in the democracy movement in Africa. The utility of democracy, utility measured by the values, concerns and priorities of African peoples, will determine to a considerable extent how far they will accept democracy.

Part One

Democracy and Economic Development

By far the most debated aspect of the utility of democracy is the question of the relation between democracy and economic development. Is democratization conducive to economic development? Or could it be dysfunctional to development, at least in the short run? Are developing countries in general and Africa in particular better off seeking development with authoritarian regimes? Or is the prospect of development indifferent to the authoritarian or democratic character of regimes?

The scholarly literature on the relationship between democracy and development is somewhat misleading in that development and economic development or economic growth are often used as though they mean the same thing. More often than not, development is used where economic growth would be more appropriate. So what is being problematized? Is it the relationship between democracy and economic development or between democracy and development? Problematizing the latter will be a tautology because some element of democracy is an important aspect of what it means to be developed. Some components of democracy, especially the rule of law, the consent of the governed, accountability and transparency are now accepted universally as being defining elements of political development. That is why even those who find democracy inconvenient or threatening do not make an issue of being against democracy; everyone is for democracy even when their political behaviour belies their democratic claims.

It is the relationship between democracy and economic development which is problematic and pertinent. Unfortunately, knowledge of this relationship is quite limited and rather confused. Much of it is impressionistic, some of it is articulated in correlations which do not often point in the same direction and hardly any of it exists in the more rigorous form of causal relations. What exists is basically two broad contradictory trends. One side posits a correlation between democracy and economic growth, another sees a trade-off between democratization and economic development; a much smaller body of scholarship is ambivalent.

To begin with those who correlate democracy to economic growth, the position has a prima facie plausibility by virtue of the fact that the wealthiest countries in the world are democracies. One of the earliest instances for this point of view is Adam Smith's *The Wealth of Nations*. Adam Smith strongly argued for political liberalism as the necessary condition for effective operation of the market, which he considered the engine of efficiency and economic growth. For Adam Smith the government which governs least, governs best; minimal government is more conducive to individual freedom, competition, efficiency and the prospects of growth.

The most sustained and systematic schorlarly argument regarding the correlation between democracy and economic development is the Lipset thseis. This thesis was launched in 1959 with an article in the *American Political Science Review* entitled 'Some Social Requisites for Democracy: Economic Development and political Legitimacy'. In 1960 came the book, *Political Man*, perhaps the best-known work on the thesis. Lipset studied samples of countries from different regions of the world and found for each regional set, a correspondence between democracy and higher levels of economic development. The correspondence is the product of several sociological variables. Economic development is associated with more education, assertiveness and a push for participation, it tempers the tone of politics and creates cross-cutting interests and multiple affiliations which facilitate democratic consensus-building and political stability. Finally, economic development is associated with growth and vitality in associational life and civil society.

Lipset's studies started a trend of very capable quantitative scholarship which has, on balance, greatly enhanced his thesis (Coleman 1960; Dahl 1971; Cutright 1963; Olsen 1968; Powell 1982; Bollen 1979, 1983; Diamond 1992; Lipset, Seong and Torres 1991). To be sure, it also elicited criticism (Rustow 1970; Huntington and Nelson 1976; O'Donnell 1973).

Political Man is a great pioneering work which also reflects the rudimentary development of qualitative political sociology in its era. Thus there was nothing in its methodology that was truly a multivariate analysis with proper control for determining the precise significance of particular variables, much less multiple regression or dynamic analysis such as event history. Even though there is nothing in the study that establishes causality, it appears to assume that development is what has brought about democracy (Diamond 1992:451).

However, the thesis has been revisited from time to time with higher methodological sophistication. Cross-tabulations of very simple classifications of economies and regimes such as Coleman (1960) and Russet (1965) established a relationship of interdependence of democracy and development, although not causality. Cutright (1963), using multivariate analysis found a high correlation (0.81) between his index of 'democratic stability' and a set of four indicators of development, namely, communication development, urbanisation, education and industrialisation. Olsen (1968), using a larger sample of countries and an index of 14 socioeconomic development indicators, found a level of correlation similar to that of Cutright.

Attempts have also been made to assess the Lipset thesis in terms of causality. Winham (1970), using correlations over a long period, was able to establish a causal relation between economic development and democracy. So did Bollen and Jackman (1985), who used multiple regression models to examine the valency of a selection of factors which are usually regarded as determinants of democracy. Most significantly, they found that economic development was a more significant determinant than the other variables taken together. This has been confirmed in a later study in which Lipset, Seong and Torres (1991) revisited and extended the analysis of Bollen and Jackman.

This is only a small selection from a considerable body of work which has been testing the Lipset thesis and its varieties for over 30 years. Even though a correlation has been established between economic development and democracy, the Lipset thesis does not help us very much in resolving the question as to whether democratic or authoritarian regimes are more conducive to economic development. However, to hold this against the thesis will be to blame it for not accomplishing a task it did not set for itself. The thesis was meant to show that economically developed societies tendentially become democracies, which is a different question from whether democracies or authoritarian governments are more conducive to economic growth. Here economic development is the dependent variable, whereas in Lipset it is the independent variable while democracy is the dependent variable. Would a backward country such as Nigeria, seeking economic development and as yet undemocratic, be more likely to succeed if it becomes democratic rather than authoritarian? Is it better off remaining authoritarian, or does it not matter? The thesis does not illuminate these options very much.

There are new trends in arguing the conduciveness of democracy to economic development which are markedly different from Lipset's. One such new trend is represented by Grossman and Noh (1990). The thrust of their argument is that democracy ensures accountability of rulers to the ruled with the result that rulers are motivated to allocate resources efficiently and productively in order to be allowed to stay in power. In similar vein, Dahl (1971) had argued much earlier that democracy ensures that rulers limit their extraction of resources to what is optimal for growth and productivity. Another approach posits that democracy protects property, especially from the state and so encourages accumulation to the benefit of growth. Olson (1991) contends that democracy commits rulers to avoid pursuing selfish interests rather than policies which optimize growth and collective well-being. There is no need to go into the numerous problems of these arguments. It is enough to note that they say nothing definitive about the relation between democracy and development and are not as convincing as the quantitative elaboration of the Lipset thesis reviewed here.

Bhalla offers a different approach to the relationship between economic development and democracy. He argues that democracy is a form of government strongly associated with freedom, and proceeds to test the relationship between economic development and freedom (both political and economic) rather than the relationship between democracy and economic development. He contends that because they did not control for economic freedom, past studies may not have estimated appropriately the relation between economic development and political freedom (Bhalla 1994). This is a useful point; it sheds some light on the significance of the 'Asian Miracle' for the Lipset thesis. Indeed, one of the attractions of his study is that it addresses the 'unusual East Asian experience' rather productively.

Another useful refinement of this study is that Bhalla assumes the likelihood of simultaneous covariance between economic development and freedom. He hypothesizes that freedom is conducive to greater economic development, which in turn leads to greater freedom also, and he models statistically this simultaneous relationship. Bhalla concludes that 'no matter how freedom is measured, and no matter how welfare change is defined, there is a strong and positive relationship between the two' (Bhalla 1994:6).

There are studies about the relationship of economic development and democracy which are inconclusive. In a study conducted in 1993, Przeworski and Limongi conclude that they could not determine 'whether democracy fosters or hinders economic growth' (1993:64). Helliwell (1992) found that there is no significant relationship between democracy and economic growth. So did Alesina et al.(1992), who conclude that democracies and nondemocracies do not appear to have different growth paths.

Przeworski and Limongi (1994) have made another useful intervention in this debate. By using a classification of regimes as democratic or dictatorial and calculating average per capita growth rates, they found that on the average, democracies grew at 2.44 per annum while dictatorships grew at a rate of 1.88 per annum. When they ran regressions with their data they reached the same conclusion. But they proceed to give good reasons why their numbers are biased:

> they reflect that fact that these regimes existed under different conditions. Regimes are likely to be indigenous with regard to their performance. And if they are, then the observed world of institutions is not a random sample of the underlying population (Pudney 1989, Chapter 2). In turn, if observations are selected by non-random mechanism then inferences based on them are biased and inconsistent, even if we are dealing with the entire observable population, as we are (Przeworski and Limongi 1994:6).

After complexifying their analysis in several ways, the difference between democracies and dictatorships in terms of growth rates virtually disappeared. But they are not unhappy with this conclusion. They argue that if there is indeed no difference, the results are positive because they would imply 'that there is no trade-off between development and democracy: democracy need not generate slower growth' (Przeworski and Limongi 1994:13).

Another important conclusion which they reach is that at all income levels the prospects for democracy are better in so far as the economy is growing. They argue that poor countries can be democratic and that economic development can take place under democracy. For them 'the trade-off we face is not between democracy and development, but at most between consumption in rich countries and democracy in poor ones' (Przeworski and Limongi 1994:14).

The Case for Authoritarian Regimes

How about the case for authoritarian regimes? One line of argument which is made in terms of overconsumption and under investment has been advanced by Galenson (1959), DeSchweinitz (1959), and Huntington (1968). They argue that people who are not materially well off, which is the bulk of nonelites in developing countries, cannot afford to postpone consumption. To the extent that democracy gives the poor opportunity to shape public policy, it will be biased in favour of immediate consumption and against saving and investment, and this will make their influence prejudicial to growth.

Some suggest that it is desirable for governments to be shielded from unproductive consumption and even sometimes necessary to compel investment (Haggard 1990). Huntington and Nelson (1976:23) suggest that dictatorships are desirable for economic development, and political participation has to be limited if only temporarily in order to facilitate accumulation. La Palombara agrees (La Palombara 1963:57). So does a former leader of one of the most successful developing countries, Lee Kwan Yew (1992):

> I do not believe that democracy necessarily leads to development. I believe that what a country needs to develop is discipline more than democracy. The exuberance of democracy leads to indiscipline and disorderly conduct which are inimical to development.

More surprising perhaps is the fact that this view is encountered so frequently among elites in the industrialised countries. The East Asian miracle has apparently made a powerful impression on the West even on institutions like the *Economist* of London which are not so easily impressed. During the tenure of former Nigerian military ruler General Babangida, whose regime was reputedly corrupt, repressive and openly contemptuous of democracy, the *Economist* of London and the Government of Britain were very partial to him partly because he had embraced a structural adjustment programme.

In the same vein, on June 29, 1991, the Economist carried an article proclaiming that Asia has had the fastest-growing economies in the past 25 years without having 'the best' democracies and suggesting that authoritarian governments find it easier to get people out of poverty than democratic governments.

The case for authoritarian regimes in fostering democracy has not been studied with quite the same rigour as that of democratic regimes. Much of it is theoretical and impressionistic. And it gives even less room for firm conclusions than the case for democratic regimes. Quite often the case is rested on the experience of the East Asian economies. Here again it is rather loosely made, as Bhalla among others has shown. In the debate concerning the relation of democracy and growth, the empirical studies tend to test regime types and economic development. Often there is not enough attention to the specifics of the salient characteristics which constitute the regime types.

Should one be testing the relation between regime types and growth or between freedom and growth? Bhalla thinks that it should be freedom, in which case one is dealing with a composite index which has at least two important elements, political and economic. Part of our confusion over the East Asian experience is that describing these countries as simply authoritarian conceals, too much for in these countries relatively small amounts of political freedom have co-existed with relatively large amounts of economic freedom (Bhalla 1994:29).

But why should one privilege authoritarianism? Is it because it is common to a group of countries which have done extremely well economically? But then there are many other authoritarian countries, for instance, Zaire, Nigeria and North Korea, which have not done so well. Is it a special kind of authoritarianism that is at issue here? If so, what is it? And if it is a special kind of authoritarianism, why generalize about the relationship between authoritarian regimes and economic development rather than limiting focusing on the *differenfia specifica* of this particular authoritarianism? Should one still be talking about regime types instead of decomposing that category to identify a different variable?

Finally, what can be reasonably said about the relationship between democratic regimes, authoritarian regimes and economic development? By all indications, the debate is still unresolved. The scholarship on the covariance of democracy and development is more rigorous and more persuasive. Some of the best work on this side of the debate suggests with plausibility a causal relationship between economic development and democracy, but given the variations of the strength of the correlations and the disagreements and even confusion over the operationalization of democratic regimes, it cannot be said that the causal link has been conclusively established. Przeworski and Limongi (1994), whose intervention in this debate is among the most rigorous, may well be right in suggesting that one significant outcome of this side of the debate is to have shown that there is no trade-off between democracy and economic development.

The other side of the debate, which posits a positive correlation between authoritarianism and economic development, has not had the benefit of much theoretical or methodological rigour and it has not made a plausible case. Often resorting to reasoning by example, it has latched on to the East Asian experience, tendentially making easy assumptions in the interpretation of this experience. In the end, the support which this experience lends to the authoritarian thesis is more apparent than real.

What is the relevance of all this to Africa? This question may seem odd, given the fact that the debate is about the relation of the two issues which are an old and continuing preoccupation in Africa. Nonetheless the question remains pertinent. Africa is not economically developed. Rather it is struggling with a singularly severe and protracted crisis of underdevelopment. Most African countries have had over half a century of highly authoritarian regimes which are only just beginning to yield to a surge of demand for democratization. Very few even among the ones which are supposedly democratizing come anywhere close to being democratic, indeed, as suggested earlier, what is happening so far is the democratization of disempowerment. With minor exceptions, Africa is still struggling to overcome a legacy of political authoritarianism, a legacy which has been associated with growing poverty and immiserization.

In these circumstances debating the merits of authoritarianism for development and whatever value does not arise. It does not arise, not only because authoritarianism has been catastrophic politically and economically, but also because Africa is now racing to achieve a democratic political renewal in order to avoid compounding its economic marginality with stagnation in an outmoded political tradition, as well as becoming irrelevant and even unintelligible to the rest of the world.

No one, except the few who want to hang on to exploitative power, disagrees with this. Rather, interest is overwhelmingly on the side of democratization. The rigour, intensity and staying power of the democracy movement in Africa attests to this. So does the emerging consensus on the view that Africa cannot deal with the crisis of underdevelopment without embracing democracy, at any rate, abandoning the legacy of authoritarianism.

This position was best expressed by a conference of over 500 groups, mainly non-governmental organisations as well as grassroots organisations,

United Nations agencies and governments, which convened in Arusha, Tanzania under the auspices of the United Nations Economic Commission for Africa in February 1990. The meeting adopted an African Charter for Popular Participation in Development and Transformation, whose main argument is that the absence of democracy is the primary cause of the chronic crisis in Africa.

The emphasis is overwhelmingly on democratization. In a declaration entitled, 'The Political and Socio-Economic Situation in Africa and the Fundamental Changes Taking Place in the World' adopted by the Organization of African Unity in Addis Ababa on July 9-11, 1990, it was acknowledged that a political environment guaranteeing human rights and the rule of law would be more conducive to governmental accountability and probity, and that 'popular based political processes would ensure the involvement of all... in development effort'.

The Bretton Woods institutions are also espousing similar views. At the April 1990 Bretton Woods Committee meeting in Washington, the World Bank President Barber Conable listed better governance as the primary requirement for economic recovery in Africa. The World Bank's Long Term Perspective Study, *Sub-Saharan Africa: From Crisis to Sustainable Growth,* highlights the need for accountability, participation and consensus-building in order to achieve successful development. This view has been further developed in a World Bank discussion paper of August 29, 1991 entitled, 'Managing Development: The Governance Dimension'. In the light of these considerations, the developmental prospects of authoritarianism are hardly of interest to Africa.

Is the other side of the debate, which posits correlations between democracy and economic development, any more relevant? The case that has just been made against the opposition to it would appear to have answered in no uncertain terms the question of its relevance. But not quite. The thrust of the Lipset thesis and the numerous interventions through which it has been developed over the last three decades is that economic growth would eventually lead to political democracy. In so far as a causal relation is being sought, economic development is the independent variable. That is a problem for its relevance in Africa which is not already economically developed. Strictly speaking, none of the dependent or the independent variables currently prevails in Africa. Africa is not economically developed and it is not democratic yet, nor simply authoritarian.

On all three variables Africa is at some stage of transition. But the debate under review is not about transitions and does not shed light on it. Without prejudice to the need to take interest in the scientific achievements of the debate on regimes and development, it is more appropriate to take Africa on its own terms and to address the realities on the ground, including the concerns of Africans. One of these realities is that whatever social scientists may be finding about the interface of economic development with democratic and authoritarian regimes, Africans are struggling with some success for democratization against a legacy of authoritarianism that has been decidedly disastrous.

The African situation is extremely complex, for at issue is the transitionality of the critical elements of the political system and the economic system and also the simultaneity of democratization and economic development. This problem is all the more interesting, because there is no experience to draw on since these elements developed sequentially in the West, taking economic development before democratization. It is more interesting still because it not just an academic problem but an important practical matter.

How can this simultaneity be realized in conception and practical policy given the complications of transitionality, the stress and strain of unrelenting underdevelopment and the political and social contradictions which plague many African countries?

This complex problem sheds light on the considerable limitations of prevailing development strategies in Africa. They do not reflect the dynamics of social forces and the consciousness which have constituted the option that gives rise to this problem. They pay no heed to democracy, hence the people are marginalized in the quest for their development. They assume that the people and their 'backward ways' are a problem for their own development, they pay little attention to the realities of Africa, and tend to look at it not as it is but as it might be according to their values; they implicitly assume the separation of the economic and the political in development despite assertions to the contrary; they think of the prerogative of democracy in political terms and abstractly, and never bother about the material conditions for their realization, and so on.

The problem of simultaneity cannot be solved without addressing these shortcomings of prevailing development strategies; and addressing them adequately will lead us to a radically different type of development strategy. This is not the first time that the problem of simultaneity is being identified. It is in fact identified in the familiar talk about trade-offs between development and democratization and in the search for ways of accelerating economic development while democratizing. It is instructive to see how this problem is usually solved in orthodox development thinking. Orthodox thinking attempts to solve the problem without synthesizing the elements that constitute the dilemma. This is associated with thinking of the prerogative of democracy in political terms and abstractly, and never caring about the material conditions for its realization. Development and democratization are taken to relate in externality and their mutual impact is assumed to be dysfunctional unless appropriate compensation is in place.

To illustrate, in the last decade, development strategy has been virtually reduced to structural adjustment programmes (SAPS). The unique feature of African SAPS is their rigorous austerity: outright ban on some essential commodities, even where no local substitute exists; precipitate rollback of subsidies; massive privatisation usually associated with a steep rise in prices and unemployment; massive devaluation and phenomenal inflation; steep cut in government expenditure, often disastrous for the social sector. For instance, when Gabon started its 1989 SAP, its government expenditure was cut by 50 per cent with devastating effects on the social sector. It is not difficult to imagine the effects of these draconian SAPS in countries where as many as 40 per cent of the population might be living below the poverty level. African SAPS are not merely inconvenient, they generally cause deep despair, widespread malnutrition and premature death.

In most cases the regimes implementing SAPS have been in power for some time and were bitterly resented for creating the conditions which necessitated a SAP in the first place. Often the vehement opposition to SAPS in Africa, which is much misunderstood by the international community, was directed not against the rationale of SAP, but against a political leadership which could no longer inspire any confidence in its ability to make things better. This was certainly the case in Nigeria, where SAP was debated and overwhelmingly rejected on the basis that the loans for the programme would be corruptly appropriated. The necessity of SAP itself, a conspicuous acknowledgement of failure, further eroded regime legitimacy and increased the alienation of the political leadership.

These circumstances did not encourage consensus-building by African leaders. Besides, for the most part, the international development agencies did not encourage them to do so. Instead, they urged political will, which is a euphemism for ruthless persistence. It was not simply that the circumstances were unfavourable for consultation and consensus-building, there was a strong presumption to the effect that it was undesirable to debate SAP or to seek a democratic mandate for it because the people would not presumably be willing to accept its hardships. Thus it came about that policy reform was put beyond democratic legitimacy and regarded as something which had to be imposed. And so it was. The very instantiation of SAP was a setback for democracy. Its hardships even more so. The African SAPS often break down existing social consensus partly because they invariably require a strong dose of authoritarianism.

This is why there is so much concern about compensation, especially giving international financial support to reforming countries. This is the means of reconciling policy reform with democratization, the point being that reforming regimes should be generously supported with aid so that austerity can be cushioned and prevented from causing popular revolt against the reforming regime. Presumably in conditions of shrinking surplus and economic austerity democracy is unlikely to thrive; people are more prone to hostility against the regime and to seek authoritarian solutions.

But this assumes too much and underrates democracy. How people react to economic austerity will depend on how the austerity came about, how its burdens are shared, and the political context of its management, including the legitimacy of the managers of state power and so on. Thus austerity is unlikely to lead to revolt against the regime, if it is imposed through a democratic mandate, if its burdens are seen to be shared with equity, if public opinion does not hold those in power responsible for causing it and if the managers of state power and the austerity programme enjoy the confidence of the people.

It is reasonable to expect that in Africa, severe austerity programmes will be bitterly resented and that people would revolt against the regimes responsible for the programme if they could. But that is mainly because austerity programmes are imposed by fiat rather than adopted by democratic mandate and because the managers of the state lack legitimacy and are held responsible for causing the conditions which produced austerity in the first place. While poverty is decidedly undesirable, neither poverty nor economic hardship is necessarily the enemy of democracy, but they are dangerous enemies of regimes which lack legitimacy.

This conventional way of solving the problem of simultaneity is a non solution. It brings into clearer relief some of the most serious problems of development thinking and development practice, especially the separation of the political and the economic, and often the opposition of development and democracy, which betrays a superficial understanding of both. In the context of this conventional thinking it is not really possible to deal with the question of the utility of democracy for the bias in this approach towards trivializing democracy and rendering it a value essentially competitive to development is too strong. How is the dilemma of simultaneity to be approached so that it brings into clear relief the relation of democracy and development in the African context and also the question of the instrumentality of democracy?

To begin with, it is necessary to abandon the parallel paths of movement and think of these two values as dialectical moments amenable to a synthesis, a synthesis which is genuine in the sense of creating a new totality. This synthesis is achieved by combining two concepts to which the development community pays lip service but studiously shuns: the democratization of development and the development of democracy, that is the deepening of the democratic experience in every sphere. This produces a development strategy which is radically different and entirely more appropriate than the development strategies which the development community and most African leaders have been using to little effect. It is this that underscores the functionality of democracy. The matter of instrumentality of democracy, especially in regard to development in Africa, is so important that it will be given some close attention here.

Why Democratization of Development Matters

What does the democratization of development mean and what difference does it make? It means that the people 'possess' their own development, which becomes something the people do about themselves and their circumstances rather than something done for them. Most importantly, it means that development becomes a lived experience instead of a received one. In operational terms, it means that the people now become the agents of development as well as its means and its end. If the people are to be the agent of development, that is, those responsible for deciding what development is and what values it is to maximize, they must also have ultimate control of public policy.

They must not only participate in the conventional sense, they must have the responsibility of deciding how to proceed with social transformation and every other major common concern. The people become the means of development when their energy and resourcefulness is the engine that drives development. For the people to be the means of development means taking the idea of self-reliance and its onerous responsibilities very seriously. Finally, if the people are the end of development, then their interest and wellbeing is the measure of all things, the supreme law of development.

Mainly because of its undemocratic character, development in Africa has largely been an exercise in alienation What is happening now tends to be development against the people: assault on their culture in a misconceived battle against backwardness; draconian measures such as SAPS which traumatise people and break down social consensus; rationalistic policies insensitive, to the social condition of the people; and paternalism which undermines the people's self-esteem even when it is benign. Prevailing strategies tend to assume that the people and their way of life is 'a problem' but when the people rather than the process of development are problematized, development is derailed and becomes an exercise in alienation. Democratic development will take the people as they are, not as they ought to be in someone else's image of the world, and try to determine how the people might move forward on their own steam in accordance with their values.

To illustrate these principles briefly, in as much as development is democratized so that the people become its agents, its means and end, then development will be construed initially as rural development and more precisely as agricultural development. This is because over 70 per cent of the people of Africa are rural dwellers who get their livelihood predominantly from agricultural activities. It is agriculture which gives them the opportunity to participate in economic life. This is the sphere of economic activity in which they have skills to offer and to receive enhancement. Also as a World Bank study points out, 'agricultural production will remain the most important element for addressing food security and poverty, since most of the poor and the food insecure are rural people' (Cleaver 1993:3).

In Africa agriculture accounts for about 40 per cent of exports and 75 per cent of employment (Jaycox 1992:29). By 1978, after almost two decades of independence, agriculture in sub-Saharan Africa was getting only 9 per cent of government expenditure, less than defence which got 10.5 per cent (World Bank 1981). And yet as the World Bank vice-president for Africa, Kim Jaycox says, 'if agriculture is in trouble, Africa is in trouble'.

The combination of relative indifference and poor policies caused food production per capita to fall by 0.1 per cent per annum in the 1960s and by 1.4 per cent per annum between 1970 and 1974. The World Bank reports that in 30 years, agricultural exports declined steadily while food imports rose at 7 per cent per annum. But 'despite the rapid growth in food imports, an average of about 100 million people in the early 1980s were undernourished—many more in years of poor harvest' (World Bank 1989). It was not until the tragic food crisis of 1983-1985 that the neglect of agriculture finally hit home. It was then agreed that investment in agriculture should be raised to between 20 and 25 per cent of total public investment. Even this modest target proved difficult for some African countries.

The demise of agriculture expresses the undemocratic character of development strategy: agricultural development in Africa has largely been a struggle between the state and the elite on the one hand and peasants on the other for control of production and the appropriation of the surplus. It is caught in a contradiction between its manifest and latent functions. The manifest function of policy demands increase in agricultural productivity, but the latent function tends to prioritize control of what the peasant produces. This contradiction is evident in reforms such as Nigeria's Land Use Decree of 1978, the Settlement Schemes in Kenya, extension services such as the World Bank's Agricultural Development Projects (ADPS), especially in Nigeria, the marketing of products through marketing boards and quality control schemes.

The dialectics of development and control is well illustrated by the Sudanese irrigation scheme of Wad Abbas (Bernal 1988). This scheme was an attempt to increase the productivity of cotton farmers by providing irrigation, tractors, advisory services, pesticide, transport facilities, grading, ginning and marketing. But this largesse effectively turned farmers into wage labourers.

The scheme did not separate farmers from all means of production; however, it introduced insecurity of tenure and dependence. Farmers could lose their land if deemed negligent in cotton production. Between 1980 and 1982 alone, at least a dozen Wad al Abbas farmers lost land this way. Farmers' ownership of means of production was further weakened by the introduction of pumps and other technology needed for production, which was controlled by the management.

> With the establishment of the scheme, control over the production process was transferred from farmers to managers and policy-makers. The household remains the basic unit of production in that each household determines and organises its own labour inputs and contract independently with any hired labourers or sharecroppers it employs. Each household also controls production on the sorghum plot. But farmers have no choice in the decision to grow cotton. And all inputs to cotton beyond labour are determined by management. Farmers cannot limit inputs such as fertiliser and aerial pesticide spraying or the prices at which they are supplied although they bear much of the cost. Farmers are also locked into a schedule as they receive water in succession along canal lines. Each must perform operations on time. Some observers of the Gezira Scheme have likened it to an assembly line (Bernal 1998:95).

The latent function of agricultural policy which expresses the interests of the political elite is able to prevail over its manifest function because of highly asymmetrical relations of power between the managers of state power and the peasantry. Political parties and political formations and interests groups representing the interests of peasants are rare in Africa. Rarer still are political formations with a peasant base strong enough to threaten the political elite or even muster sufficient resources to place the interests of the peasantry on the national agenda. Political parties or social movements with a peasant base have not been allowed to function. In Kenya a splinter faction of the ruling Kenya African National Union (KANU) which opposed the privatisation of land was systematically persecuted; when it joined the opposition Kenya People's Union (KPU), that party was persecuted out of existence. In Ghana, President Kwame Nkrumah's ruling Convention People's Party (CPP) severely repressed the National Liberation Movement (NLM) which was affiliated to cocoa farmers when the NLM opposed the government's cocoa pricing policy. After constant persecution, including assassinations, the NLM was proscribed.

Instead of coercing the peasants to control their production and surplus, a democratic development will make the rural dweller, especially the peasant producer, the centre of development strategy. One significant implication of this is that development will become primarily rural development; it will prioritize agriculture and rural industrialisation. The failure of African development strategies to proceed in this manner has been a serious impediment to agriculture as well as industrial development. Past development strategies have been concerned with import substitution, export promotion and huge basic industrial projects such as iron and steel and petrochemicals.

For the most part, they have failed to achieve any tangible degree of industrialisation and have succeeded only in increasing indebtedness and the disarticulation of African economies. A policy of rural industrialisation integrated with agricultural development as part of a strategy of rural development would have stood a much better chance. For industrialisation would be pursued mainly in self-reliance fuelled primarily from the incomes of farmers and the multiplier effect of the linkages between farm and nonfarm activities.

This strategy taps into the immense potential for the improvement of agricultural technology. For centuries, African agriculture has been dominated by hoes, wooden paddles for threshing and machetes. Immense opportunities exist for improved agricultural technologies such as seeders, ox-ploughs and inter-row weeders. Being scale-neutral, they could be manufactured in small lots locally, to the advantage of farmers and rural industrialisation.

There are forward linkages, for example, food processing, brewing and packaging. The untapped potential here is immense. Finally, there are considerable opportunities in consumer demand linkages. Rises in farm incomes increase the demand for consumer goods such as shoes, clothes, furniture, building materials, and new kinds of food. This demand at once promotes industrialisation and the availability of the consumer goods provides a strong incentive for increased agricultural productivity.

With the expansion of these forward, backward and consumer demand linkages, there will be greater integration of rural and urban development. Urban development will initially be primarily about the informal sector, which employs the vast majority of urban dwellers in Africa. As in the case of rural industrialisation, the concern is to enable people to be more productive in what they are doing, to encourage movement to higher technological levels eventually. Rural industries and the informal sector will be producing similar goods under roughly similar conditions for the same market.

Clearly, this approach will improve the prospects of development considerably. It proceeds in daily response to the practical needs of the people, it is endogenous and self-reliant, it is not driven by foreign loans and foreign technology primarily, or foreign investment and foreign trade. It relies on an assured and gradually expanding domestic market; it obliterates the dichotomy between industry and agriculture, urban and rural and promotes internal balance and autocentrism. The democratization of development is functional in a manner that matters a great deal.

This is only part of the case for the utility of democracy for development. It can also be approached from the point of view of the peculiar political problems of development in Africa which are not captured by the general debate about authoritarianism and economic development. Colonialism gave Africa a legacy of a state which had near-absolute control of society, polity and economy and yet remained the private property of the rulers. By virtue of being appropriated by particular interests instead of rising above all interests in society, this state became the negation of the very essence of the state and its civilizing element namely its 'relative autonomy'. It could not express the corporate identity of its subjects or engender it. It could not effectively mediate social conflict between contending private interests because it is also a private interest. Far from mediating conflict, it became a theatre of war, a war for the appropriation of its vast power resources.

Like the state, politics in much of post-colonial Africa tendentially negates its essence. For instead of being the occasion in which disparate interests are aggregated to define common interests and to pursue collective goals, politics is perverted into a relentless war of all against all. As politics degenerates into warfare, it also throws up governmental forms and leaders appropriate to its character, hence the high incidence of military and authoritarian rule. The consequences of this for economic development in Africa have been disastrous. To begin with, it means that there is no national community, only groups competing to capture and to appropriate the state. That condition virtually nullifies any prospect of evolving and carrying through a national project; including development. Where attempts are made to seek development, policies tend to be hampered by social and political contradictions such as the divorce of public policy from social needs.

The lawless struggle for power and the coercive use of power by those who control the state against other interests leads to endemic political instability which has been highly detrimental to economic development. For example, it has led to considerable exodus of highly capable people who are sorely needed and whose training represents substantial public investment for countries with scarce resources. It has led to considerable flight of capital, including the capital of those in power such as Mobutu, Eyadéma and Omar

Bongo who worry that their wealth in their own country will not be secure once they lose power. By these effects, the form and content of the post-colonial state in Africa and the politics associated with it are perpetuating underdevelopment in Africa. Democratization will reduce these dysfunctionalities.

Part Two

Democratization and Ethnicity

In assessing the instrumentality of democracy, it is essential to review the interface of democratization and ethnic conflict in Africa. As Africa democratizes there is considerable concern that the liberties of democracy will unleash ethnic rivalries whose embers are forever smouldering in African conditions and destroy the fragile unity of African countries. Several African leaders such as Arap Moi of Kenya, Kenneth Kaunda of Zambia and Paul Biya of Cameroon have encouraged this thinking. Struggling to remain in power against a strong tide for democratization, Kenneth Kaunda argued that the adoption of the multi-party system would bring 'chaos, bloodshed and death'. Paul Biya, another holdout on democratization, defended the power monopoly of his Cameroon People's Democratic Movement by arguing that it ensured' a united Cameroon devoid of ethnic, linguistic and religious cleavages'.

Concern that democratization might cause ethnic violence and political disintegration is shared by many who are committed to democracy, Africans and non-Africans alike, scholars and politicians, development agents and business people. Carol Lancaster, an astute student of Africa and a committed democrat, fears that with democratization, ethnic strife may be rampant:

> ... political divisions would increasingly fall along ethnic or regional lines, heightening tensions and, ultimately, threatening national unity. The volcano of ethnic or clan strife remains dormant throughout much of sub-Saharan Africa. But it could erupt—as it has in recent years in Ethiopia, Liberia, Somalia, and Sudan— should ethnicity became the leading factor in the struggle for power (Lancaster 1991:158).

There is a prima facie plausibility to this expectation. For instance, if one regards the process of decolonization as democratization, which it was, the peak of the process was associated with a rise in ethnic particularism, if not ethnic conflict. The surge of nationalism was liberating not only for those who led the nationalist movement, it also created an atmosphere in which social groups become more self-conscious, more politically oriented and more assertive. Some of these were groups which had defined themselves as ethnic groups. As political independence began to look inevitable, these groups worried about their stake in the new order and how they would cope with its uncertainties. They began to position themselves for access to power resources and sometimes got quite aggressive in this process, with the result that in most polyethnic countries in Africa, such as Nigeria, Sierra Leone, Kenya, Ivory Coast, Ghana, Togo and Uganda, ethnic competition tended to intensify on the eve of independence.

There are instances in which the struggle for democracy has been associated with what is generally believed to be ethnic conflict. In Kenya, demands for democratization were associated with rising conflict between Luo and Kikuyu, especially during the events leading up to the incarceration of Oginga Odinga by the Kenyatta government. Again, when the pressure for democratization in Kenya escalated under President Arap Moi there were violent clashes between Kalenjins, Arap Moi's ethnic group, and Luos and Kikuyus.

In Cameroon, the bitter struggle for multinational elections to end Paul Biya's grip on power has been fuelled by Anglophone separatist movement. After Burundi's first democratic election in June 1993, which brought the Hutu majority to power under the umbrella of the Front for Democracy in Burundi (FRODEBU), ethnic consciousness rose again. In less than seven months there was a coup against democracy. Tutsi extremists sacked the democratically elected Hutu government in a violent coup on October 21, 1993, setting off another orgy of killings between Hutus and Tutsis which some have blamed on democratization. In neighbouring Rwanda some of the extremist Hutus who incited the genocide against the Tutsi in 1994 after the death of Juvénal Habyarimana on April 6 1994 had blamed the democratization wave of 1990 for what they perceived as the unacceptable softening of Habyarimana to the benefit of the Tutsi and also for the Arusha Accord of 1993 which they considered humiliating.

The Concept of Ethnicity

Nonetheless, the link between democratization and ethnic conflict remains problematic. It is not clear that ethnic groups exist. Nor is it clear that there is anything that can properly be called a specifically ethnic conflict. Much depends on how one understands ethnicity. There are essentially two schools of thought on the meaning and nature of ethnicity—the primordialists and instrumentalists (Stavenhagen 1994; Van de Goor 1994). Primordialists may be defined as those who hold that 'members of the same ethnic group have a common primordial bond that determines their personal identity and turns the group into a natural community of a type that is older than the modern nation or modern class systems' (Van de Goor 1994:18). Instrumentalists, on the other hand, are those who see ethnicity essentially as a means for people, especially leaders, to pursue their own purpose such as 'forming, mobilizing and manipulating groups of people for political ends' (Van de Goor 1994:18).

This division of the ethnic discourse may be misleading; it is preferable to think in terms of objectivists and constructionsts. To begin with, the traditional distinction between primordialists and instrumentalists segments the discourse in a manner that obstructs interlocution; one side is positing what ethnic groups are, while the other posits how ethnic groups or ethnicity might be used. They are not comparable.

The problem is not only in relationality. Even on its own terms, each of the categories is misleading. Now, the original problem to which the two schools of thought are responding is what ethnic groups are and if indeed they are. Increasingly in the last 15 years, scholarship has been concerned with the 'if.' The primordialist categorization is misleading in that it grosses over the question of the reality of ethnic groups. It takes their existence for granted and suggests that their very essence is precisely the timelessness of their existence. But this really begs the issue of their existence, which has become increasingly the important issue in the discourse.

The instrumentalist categorization is misleading in so far as it prioritizes an element in the discourse which is of secondary importance. It suggests that the ethnic group is an ephemeral phenomenon conjured up at will as an exploitable resource. It is misleading by virtue of the emphasis it places on the manipulative and exploitable aspect of ethnic construction, for the simple reason that manipulability or exploitability is not and cannot be a useful definition of ethnicity. Whatever it is, ethnicity is not always exploited or always exploitable. More importantly, for the ethnic discourse, the thorny issue is not the instrumentalization of ethnicity (no one denies that ethnicity is often manipulated) but its construction, the assertion that it is contrived, a mere ideological representation, or, as some prefer to put it, imagined rather than real. In the light of these considerations, it is more useful to think in terms of objectivists who objectify the ethnic group, insist that it is real, and the constructionists who insisting that the ethnic group is contrived, imagined or a social construction.

Within the objectionist literature, there is a wide range of objective characteristics of ethnic groups. It does not make the understanding of ethnicity easier that white the objectivists agree that the ethnic group is defined by putative commonalties, they differ what these commonalties are. Clifford Geertz emphasizes 'the congruities of blood, speech, custom (Geertz 1963:109). Smith emphasizes 'myths, memories, values and symbols' (Smith 1986:15). Horowitz argues that the defining characteristics of the ethnic group are birth and blood, belief in a common ancestry, a common history with common heroes and enemies and historical attachment to a particular territory (Horowitz 1985:139-40). Some definitions such as the *Harvard Encyclopaedia* (Thernsttom et al. 1980:iv) list as many as 14 indicators of ethnicity without saying which one, or which combination, must apply before a group can be said to be an ethnic group.

The constructionist view is somewhat easier (Barth 1969; Anderson 1983). The constructionists do not have to posit and justify the concrete existence of ethnic groups. They mainly have to deny it. They say that ethnicity is a figment of the imagination and support it by showing how ethnic identities wax and wane, how ethnic boundaries are porous, shifting and unsustainable, how ethnic markings are arbitrary and how the common past and the traditional values on which members of ethnic groups anchor their identity may have very little to do with historical realities and much more with invention.

Perhaps it is unnecessary to settle the question whether ethnic groups are real or imagined. To be sure, it is very difficult to prove their reality, for all we can see is some evidence of shared consciousness which rises and falls, often as a result of manipulation, sometimes constituting the primary group identity of those who share it, sometimes receding behind other identities, sometimes disappearing altogether.

On the other hand, it is not very useful to conclude from this that ethnic groups are merely imagined and have no reality. Strictly speaking, ethnic groups are no less real for existing intermittently, for having subjective or even arbitrary standards of membership, for opportunitistic use of tradition or even for lacking a proprietary claim over a local space. Ethnic groups are real, at least in the limited sense of a solidarity of consciousness, however misguided or spurious. This may be called a transitive or proxy reality for it is not so much the ethnic group that is real as the consciousness through its varying spread and intensity. To think of ethnicity in this way entails breaking away from associating it with primordiality, the fossilized precipitate of a long historical process. It means treating ethnicity and ethnic consciousness as a living presence produced and driven by material and historical forces. It begins, becomes and passes away, and it can only be understood and interpreted through the complex dialectics of its being, dissolution and reconstitution.

Ethnicity and Conflict

There is a tendency which goes back a long way to assume that ethnic relations are very conflict-prone. This presumption has become stronger still in the contemporary world in the face of the bloody phenomenon of ethnic cleansing attendant on the disintegration of parts of the collapsed Soviet Empire, especially Yugoslavia, as well as the violent implosions in Sudan, Liberia, Burundi and Rwanda. This underlies the fear that democratic openings in Africa would trigger conflict and political instability in the region. Are ethnic relations inherently conflictual?

This question is easy enough. There is nothing inherently conflictual about ethnic relations, that is relations between social groups who respond to different ethnic interpellations. In this sense they are no different from any other social group. Social groups do not get embroiled in conflict just because they are different. They get into conflict only because of what people make of these differences in specific historical situations, because of how the differences are understood, interpreted and represented in particular circumstances. How social differences are interpreted, represented and used depends on how the actors are socially situated, how they perceive and the demands of their interests in the competition for economic goods, status and power.

The view that ethnicity causes conflict is widely held. This can be seen from the popularity of the phrase 'ethnic conflict'. This phrase forecloses the correlation between ethnicity and conflict by its very meaning. But it does not seem so, because having characterized conflict as ethnic, we still wallow in the confusion and the tautology of trying to explain it. The presupposition of the correlation between ethnicity and conflict thrives, despite that fact that this correlation has never been demonstrated. Scholars like Singer who have been conducting quantitative studies of conflict discount the correlation and suggest that its presumption is a prejudice:

> First, in a study now under way at Michigan, we find that ethnic, religious and linguistic differences between states show virtually no correlation with either the onset of rivalries or war between them. Similarly, we find that such cultural cleavages within the society have little discernible effect on the frequency of civil war. Then, in an ongoing study of inter-state disputes 'over territory', Huth (1994) again finds that ethnic differences play only the most modest role in the onset of these disputes as well as their resolution. Moreover, these patterns hold not only for the 175 years since the Congress of Vienna, but for the more recent period beginning with the establishment of all the newly independent states after 1960 as well. Second, to so label the conflicts within and between these states is not only to ignore the quantitative evidence, but also to manifest an embarrassing degree of cultural provincialism. That is, we recognize that the more developed industrial states get into disputes over such 'reasonable' issues as threats to spheres of influence, control of and access to markets, resources, investment and trade opportunities, and territorial integrity, while suggesting that people of colour do so merely because of long-standing tribal, religious, and ethnic rivalries. Of course 'we' used to do so, but that was before we in the western world became more 'civilized', ethnic conflict is, we imply, quite pejorative (Singer 1994:10).

The presumption about the conflictual nature of ethnicity may not be unconnected to the tendency to regard ethnic differences as being particularly exclusive partly because they lack the flexibility to be negotiated. There is also the assumption that ethnic differences are differences which people care about, are partial to and alert to, hence ethnocentrism. But, as Smith and other anthropologists have argued, the ethnocentrism of African traditional societies was markedly benign. While people may have preferred their own way of life and used its standards to judge others, and stressed their difference from 'strangers', this invariable 'involves no denigration, but implies parity even for groups regarded as hostile' (Smith 1993:56). There are good reasons for this benign ethnocentrism and they are not merely subjective:

> Given the social organization of these peoples and their neighbours, neither is capable of conceiving, much less achieving the forcible domination of any other. Indeed none of these populations has yet developed the necessary institutional basis for its inclusive organisation as a political unit under effective central direction. In effect their common fragmentation excludes both the need and the incentive for negative ethic stereotypes of one another. Despite pride in their tribal identities and commitment to their cultures and communities, the neutral ethnocentrism of these tribesmen is especially significant since it enjoins corresponding tolerance and recognition of other peoples and cultures, though unfamiliar (Smith 1993:57).

If this is correct it is not enough to say, in the African context at least, that ethnic consciousness is not inherently conflictual; it is has to be said also that it is improbable for it to be conflictual. The question then arises, under what circumstances might ethnic consciousness lead to conflict? Is the process of democratization one of these circumstances? To take the first question first, it is easily answered on the level of generality:

> Conflicts between ethnic groups are not inevitable nor are they eternal. They arise out of specific historical situations, are moulded by particular and unique circumstances, and they are constructed to serve certain interests by idealists and ideologues, visionaries and opportunists, political leaders and 'ethnic power brokers' of various kinds (Stavenhagen 1994:2).

But not much is learned by remaining on the level of generality. It is useful to try to answer the question more concretely by looking at a case study of the interface of ethnicity with democratization.

The Case of Nigeria

Nigeria is a complex plural society which is popularly perceived as being ridden with ethnic conflict so serious as to cause systemic breakdowns and civil war, and amid the ethnic conflict it has been struggling with limited success at democratization. The Nigeria experience shows that ethnicity has indeed to be understood in the complex dialectics of imagination and reality, of construction, dissolution and reconstitution. It also illustrates the difficulty of positing a specifically ethnic conflict, and it sheds some light on the relationship of ethnic consciousness and the process of democratization.

The disparate peoples of this richly plural society were forcibly brought together by British colonialists under one government in 1914. Nigeria was and still is a project rather than a reality. Paradoxically the policies which the colonial government adopted to turn project into reality were self-defeating because, among other things, they engendered centrifuge tendencies. Because the colonial state relied heavily on force to subjugate the indigenous peoples and to carry out its mission it projected a threatening image and induced some of its subjects to regard it as a hostile force. Many of them were driven to traditional solidarity groups such as ethnic or national groups, and even some hastily contrived ones such as literacy clubs or community development associations. These solidarity groups became centres of resistance and means of self-affirmation against the colonizer's integrative policies and acculturation as well as networks for survival. Even in the urban areas, which should have been the melting pot of parochial identities, colonial rule was recreating traditional solidarity groups and ethnocentrism.

This tendency was accentuated by the fact that colonial rule was cheap rule with little commitment to a social welfare system. The lack of a social welfare system was hard on lonely first-generation urbanites who had to cope with the notorious problems of colonial cities. In the pressure of the cities they sought the companionship of people of their kind, people who came from the same rural community or spoke the same language. Every colonial city quickly spawned a rich harvest of 'improvement' or urban associations of people from the same rural background, ethnicity or nationality. Most of these associations provided for their members a rudimentary social welfare system. They gave scholarships for education, assistance for people in difficulty with the law, for those wanting to set up small businesses, the sick, the bereaved and the needy. By virtue of this role, these solidarity groups overrode the state as the primary focus of political allegiance.

It is interesting that while Nigeria was being ethnicized in this way, it was nonetheless possible to forge a country-wide solidarity to struggle against colonialism. Indeed the traditionalization of modernity under colonialism contributed directly to the provenance and strength of the nationalist movement. The urban associations brought development to the rural communities as well as political consciousness; they became a vehicle for participating in the struggle against the imposition of an arbitrary and coercive state. They threw up a political leadership by giving scholarships for higher studies. The first generation nationalist leaders in Nigeria, such as Nnamdi Azikiwe, were largely beneficiaries of these scholarship programmes.

Not surprisingly, the nationalist movement in Nigeria first emerged as a network of 'ethnic associations' and mass organisations. When the Nigeria National Council, which heralded the coming of age of the nationalist movement in Nigeria, was launched on August 28, 1944, it was a coalition of eight professional bodies, eleven social clubs, two trade unions, two fledgling political parties, four literary societies and a hundred and one urban ethnic associations which constituted the bulk of the membership (Coleman 1958, 1986).

Despite the social heterogeneity of Nigeria, the council became a truly national force, winning supporters from every part of the country, despite the ethnicizing tendencies of colonial policies. It was because of its national following that the council stoutly opposed a colonial transition programme which effectively regionalized and ethnicized the nationalist movement and the nationalist leadership. However, in the end, the opposition of the nationalists in general and the NNC in particular, was not enough to stop the process of regionalization and the rise of political ethnicity. One can already begin to see how ethnic consciousness and political ethnicity wax and wane. At one historical conjuncture, a nationalist solidarity holds in the face of policies which were encouraging ethnic political identities. At another, political ethnicity grows strong and defeat a nationalist outlook.

It is useful to explore this dialectics of ethnic consciousness in Nigeria by looking at the responses of colonial policies to nationalist pressures, responses which effectively defined the path to independence. By the policy of indirect rule which the British adopted in Nigeria, the stage for the regionalization of the nationalist leadership was already set when the main administrative and political units of Nigeria were made to coincide with the spatial locations of the major nationalities of Nigeria, the Hausa-Fulani, the Yoruba and the Ibo.

The regionalization got firmer when the British colonial government decided to devolve power to the regions, especially by the Constitution of 1954, which is often described as the 'regionalist constitution'. Residual power accrued to the regional governments which were also granted self-government under regional prime ministers, the leader of the majority party in each regional legislature. As was to be expected, the three leading nationalist leaders, Ahmadu Bello in the Northern Region, Nnamdi Azikiwe in the Eastern Region and Obafemi Awolowo in the Western Region, opted for power in the region instead of remaining in the central government which was still under British control.

Each of them won control of the government in his own region in the ensuing election. They not only won, but they won with a substantial majority derived mainly from the majority nationality of the region, which also happened to be the nationality of the leader of the dominant party. The National Council of Nigeria and the Cameroons (NCNC), now down to a predominantly Ibo base, was dominant in the Eastern Region, the Action Group (AG), with a predominantly Yoruba social base, was dominant in the Western Region, and the Northern People's Congress (NPC), with a Hausa-Fulani base, was dominant in the Northern Region.

This was the context of the rising tide of ethnonationalism which marked Nigeria's march to independence. In the Constitutional Conference of 1953, it had been decided that Nigeria should be a federation of the three states, North, East and West, with residual powers in the federating units. This set up a structure which was antithetical to federalism. The problem was that one of the federating units, the Northern Region, was bigger than the two other units put together. And within each region, one nationality was so dominant that it was virtually guaranteed the monopoly of power.

Thus there was widespread anxiety about domination. Eastern and Western politicians feared Northern domination. More important still, the smaller nationalities within each region were greatly fearful of being subordinated and marginalized by the dominant nationality. Soon these fears became so obsessive and dominated political life so much that the Secretary of State for the Colonies appointed a commission of inquiry to 'ascertain the facts about the fears of minorities in any part of Nigeria and to propose means of allaying those fears, whether well or ill founded' (Minorities Commission 1959:2).

In its report, the commission determined the causes of the fears of the minorities as follows:

> The fears of the minorities in Nigeria arise from two circumstances, first the division of the whole country into three powerful Regions, in each of which one group is numerically preponderant, and secondly, the approach of independence and the removal of the restraints which have operated so far. Reference to these restraints was in some areas explicit in others implicit; it was everywhere the essence of the case put before us that the fears and grievances of which we heard today were indications only of trends likely to become much more serious when independence was attained (Report of the Minorities Commission 1959:2).

Was the minorities movement merely a surge of ethnocentrism and ethnic conflict? Only on the surface. It was a product of decolonization, which is in the general direction of democratization. Its aspirations and demands were largely democratic. The minorities were looking for incorporation, for participation and for the guarantee of their rights. A small proportion of those involved in these movements demanded secession. But the majority were demanding federation to give them more local autonomy, to secure human rights and to improve their access to political participation.

The minorities movement also contributed directly to the process of democratization. For instance, on the tour of the commission through the country between 1957 and 1958, the open hearings and the campaigns of the affected groups and the lively debates heightened political consciousness of the issues of human rights, minority rights and the balance of power. Remote parts of the country which had been relatively apathetic politically came alive; many of the smaller nationalities which had been quiescent came alive, became organized and assertive. Political pluralism was increased as some of these smaller groups formed political parties, for example, the Niger Delta Congress founded in 1959 by the Rivers Chiefs and Peoples Conference. The process of democratization gained some depth from the minority people's parties which emerged in each region to protect the interests of the minority nationalities and to resist the domination of the ruling party and the national group which formed its social base.

These new parties effectively challenged the dominant party and the nationality behind it because they were highly motivated and able to exploit the rivalry between the major parties. The most notable of these parties were the Northern Elements Progressive Union (NEPU) of Mallam Aminu Kano which was resisting the Northern People's Congress and Hausa-Fulani domination in the North; the United Middle Belt Congress (UMBC) of Joseph Tarka which was resisting Fulani domination in North Central Nigeria; the United National Independence Party (UNIP) which was challenging the National Council of Nigeria and the Cameroons (NCNC) and Ibo domination; and the Mid-West State Movement which was formed to resist the Action Group (AG) and the domination of the Yoruba nation.

While the minorities movement developed democratic politics, this politics degenerated into a rather lawless struggle as the colonial masters began to disengage, exposing a serious structural weakness which they had created but which their role as the midwives of political independence concealed, namely the state's lack of autonomy and inability to rise above the conflicts and struggles among particularistic interests. As expected in the pre-independence election of 1959, each of the three major parties had won decisively in its own regional base. The standing of the parties in the House of Representatives was the NPC, 148, NCNC, 89 and AG 75. The performance of the parties reflected their domination of their regional base and, more significantly, the fading prospect of a national party which the NCNC had represented.

However, since no party was strong enough to rule alone, the NPC and the NCNC formed a coalition government while the Action Group went into opposition. But the polity was soon in crisis arising from the state's lack of autonomy and its immense and untamed power which rendered the quest for power intense and prone to lawlessness. The party in opposition was narrowly fixated on power and apparently determined to get it by whatever means. The government was equally determined to keep it by whatever means it could. Eventually the government used its powers to harass the Action Group, which in turn remained confrontational as Nigeria quickly headed towards a deep political crisis.

The government capitalized on factional strife in the Action Group-controlled Western House of Assembly to go for the liquidation of the Action Group. A state of emergency was declared, and an administrator whose powers were virtually limitless was appointed by the Federal Government to run the government. The administrator came down heavily on the Action Group and its supporters. The Western Regional government was subjected to a relentless punitive investigation. Awolowo and the elite of the party, called the Tactical Committee, were arrested and charged for treason. He was given 10 years' imprisonment, and the machinery for the dismemberment of his political domain through the creation of a new state was quickly set in motion. In the face of this persecution, members of the embattled party defected en masse, its strength in the House of Representatives fell rapidly from 75 to 13.

Once the battle was joined, it spread. The NPC, the dominant party in the Federal coalition, had grown in confidence from its ruthless routing of the Action Group, especially after gaining seven additional Federal seats in the House of Representatives as a result of the amalgamation of Northern Cameroon. This gave the NPC an absolute majority in the legislature. The political crisis and the growing confidence of the NPC caused a great deal of tension between the NPC and its coalition partner, the NCNC, and a confrontation seemed inevitable.

It came quickly as a result of a controversy over the outcome of a national census. The census was bound to be a problem in a situation in which the premium on power was so high, because it had serious implications for the distribution of power. The census of 1952-53 conducted by the colonial government was the 'basis for the allocation of seats to the regions in the federal legislature. The Action Group and the NCNC had been hoping that the projected census of 1962-63 would give the regions they controlled a much higher population increase relative to the North and lead to a redistribution of the seats in the Federal legislature to their advantage and to the mitigation of what they considered the

Northern domination of the Federation. The census returns released in July 1962 gave the North a 30 per cent population increase from 17.3 million to 22.5 million; that of the East increased by 71 per cent and that of the Western region by 70 per cent.

The NPC-controlled government decided that the increase in the Western and the Eastern regions were too unrealistic to validate the census much to the anger of the Action Group and the NCNC. Once more, Nigeria was plunged into deep political crisis. Another census was conducted in 1963-64. The new census gave the North and the East a population increase of 67 per cent each over the 1952-53 census results, while the Western region got a percentage increase of 100 per cent. By this result the new population distribution was as follows: the Northern Region– 29, 777, 986; the Eastern Region–12, 388, 646; the Western Region–12, 811, 837. The political leaders of the Eastern and the Western Region were disappointed that the census would reinforce the preeminence of the North by maintaining the old distribution of parliamentary seats, and angrily rejected the result. By now the political crisis had become so deep that the viability of Nigeria began to look doubtful, and it did not help matters that this crisis was presented to the popular consciousness as a struggle over ethnic domination.

In this highly charged atmosphere, Nigeria entered a campaign for the general election scheduled for January 11, 1965. As was to be expected, the electoral campaign virtually degenerated into warfare: thugs intimidated people, property was looted, candidates were abducted, some were killed, pitched battles were fought between political supporters of the contending coalitions. In the end Michael Okpara, leader of the opposition coalition, the United Progressive Grand Alliance (UPGA), decided that there was no chance of a fair election and pulled out his alliance. The governing political alliance using the powers of incumbency went ahead with the election and won.

Dr Nnamdi Azikiwe, the president of the country, who was the a founder of the NCNC, the leading party in UPGA, and Okpara's mentor and kinsman, refused to invite Tafawa Balewa of the NPC, the incumbent prime minister, whose political formation had supposedly won the election, to form a government. In the deadlock ethnic antipathies grew to alarming proportions, and civil war and political disintegration looked increasingly likely. Somehow a face-saving formula for forming a government was worked out on May 4, 1965.

On October 11, 1965, the elections to the Western House of Assembly were conducted. Against the background of the declaration of the state of emergency in the Western region, the imposition of a federal administrator on the region and the attempt to liquidate the Action Group by persecuting its leaders and supporters, this election was more violent than the Federal election. It was a hard-fought war in which many party supporters, politicians, electoral candidates, policemen and electoral officers lost their lives and a great deal of property was destroyed. At the end of the election, both sides claimed victory. The leader of the Action Group/NCNC alliance, Adegbenro, whose coalition appeared to have won over the Federal government-supported NNDP, formed a government to displace the incumbent NNDP government. But he was promptly arrested and incarcerated and this led to riots, looting and considerable loss of life.

The Nigerian political system, which had never functioned well since independence, had clearly broken down. On January 15, 1966, the military intervened. However, the intervention was indecisive and messy, and the pattern of killings in this bloody coup touched off suspicions and anger regarding an ethnically motivated coup. A counter-coup took place, followed by what was perceived as ethnocide against Ibos resident in the Northern region, and a mass exodus of Ibos from the North to the South began, signalling the disintegration of Nigeria. The Eastern Region, feeling that in the light of the killings of the Ibo, the conditions for political association no longer existed, opted for secession. On July 6, 1967, fighting broke out between Biafra, the new name which the seceding East had assumed, and the Nigerian government. It turned out to be a long and bloody civil war.

After the civil war, military rule continued for a decade, finally terminating in 1979 when elections were held and the Second Republic inaugurated. Military rule was rationalized as the inevitable consequence of a political system that had already broken down, the means to neutralise political ethnicity, to get the state-building project back on course and to crystallize collective purpose to the benefit of development. But far from enhancing state-building, military rule has undermined it.

The military's turn at the state-building project has been self-defeating, rather like that of Nigeria's colonial rulers. The military has ruled Nigeria like a unitary state and exacerbated the fears of domination partly because it was generally perceived as lacking objectivity, a replay of the problem which the Minorities Commission had identified as the bane of political integration and democratic political stability in Nigeria. This time the lack of objectivity is singularly problematic because the concentration of power under the military and the inherent lack of legitimacy and accountability of its power causes a lot more anxiety and increases the premium on power as well as the motivation of subordinated groups and classes to overturn the prevailing political order. But while exacerbating tensions and nurturing destabilizing tendencies in this way, the military was able to maintain a surface stability by its repressive capabilities. But beneath the surface, the state project regressed, as did democratization.

Military rule did not curb ethnic consciousness but its conflictual manifestations, and only to a limited extent. By all indications its failure to stem the tide of ethnic consciousness was due at least in part to its blockage of democracy. The coercive ecumenicism of military rule and its arbitrary power alienated people from the state and drove them to traditional solidarities. Ever a chain of command even in government, the military was unable to comprehend the need for negotiated consensus. It could not mediate pluralism but rather accentuated the divisive potentialities of social pluralism. It appears that the addiction of the Nigerian military to power and its poor performance while in power may well be the main contribution of the military to the political development of Nigeria. For it led to strong demand for democratization amid strong antipathies for military rule. The antipathy of Nigerians to military rule became strong and the objective of ending military rule so compelling that they became more united; attention shifted from religious, nationalist and ethnic solidarity. Particularly interesting for our purposes here is the dialectic of military rule in first giving impetus to ethnic consciousness and then helping to create the conditions for transcending it.

The 1993 presidential election in Nigeria illustrates this dialectic. In this election the country voted against the National Republican Convention (NRC), the party reputedly preferred by the military and the conservative wing of the political class in alliance with it.

But it is the circumstances surrounding the defeat of the NRC by the Social Democratic Party (SDP) that are significant. To understand its significance we should begin by noting that the basic dichotomy of political life in Nigeria is that between North and South, now that a potentially more important dichotomy, that between the dominant and the subordinate classes, has been largely depoliticized.

The North, which is predominantly Moslem, is much more populous and more backward economically and educationally, but it has had virtual monopoly of power at the centre. It is usually expected that the North would use its numerical strength to ensure the election of a Northerner and a Moslem as the President of Nigeria in order not to compound its economic and educational disadvantages with the loss of political power. However, this time the North voted for Moshood Abiola, the Southern candidate in the 1993 presidential election. Not only did Abiola take more states than Bashir Tofa, the Northern candidate of the purportedly Northern party, the NRC, Abiola even defeated Tofa in his home state of Kano.

It is also highly significant that Abiola won decisively in the South. Going by trends in Nigeria's political history, it was assumed that Abiola would perform very poorly in the South, especially the South Eastern states, Abia,

Imo, Enugu and Anambra, because the Ibo are considered to be traditional ethnic foes of the Yoruba, Abiola's ethnic group. But Abiola made a very strong showing in the Eastern states, and it is widely believed that the use of the machines of the state cost him outright victory in these states.

Another remarkable aspect of this election and the performance of Abiola is that owing to some confusion in his party, the SDP, Abiola, who is a Moslem, was obliged to take Babagana Kingibe, another Moslem, as his running mate. By conventional expectations and political behaviour, it would have been unthinkable to have a Moslem-Moslem ticket because in a country in which religious differences are highly politically charged, it would be courting certain defeat.

But in this election, the South voted overwhelmingly for Abiola. Even the Christian Association of Nigeria (CAN), which is ever on the alert for signs of Moslem domination, supported the all-Moslem ticket. It is no wonder that the Nigerian mass media has proclaimed the 1993 presidential election a peaceful revolution. But what exactly is revolutionary about this? What is revolutionary about it is the demonstrated capacity of democracy to override the parochial identities, especially ethnic, religious and regional identities, which the Nigerian political class had inculcated studiously for nearly half a century to divide and exploit ordinary Nigerians. More often than not students of democratizing plural societies in the Third World worry about democratization giving impetus to ethnocentrism and ethnic conflict. In this instance at least, democracy overrode ethnic identities.

The significance of this election was well understood not only by the military regime but by the Nigerian political class at large. On the eve of the election, the Nigerian government, sensing the mood of the electorate, had got nervous and made a clumsy attempt to stop the election, but the attempt failed and the election took place. When the results became available, it was clear that not only was it not a 'hung' election, but that the NRC candidate, Bashir Tofa, had been soundly beaten by the Moshood Abiola, the SDP candidate. President Ibrahim Babangida, the military ruler, suspended the result and then nullified the election altogether, despite the fact that it was generally regarded as free and fair, and indeed the fairest election Nigeria ever had by the government's own agencies, the National Electoral Commission (NEC), the Centre for Democratic Studies (CDS) and international observer teams. As was to be expected, the annulment caused a monumental crisis which nearly led to civil war and political disintegration.

Some were surprised that any government in a complex country such as Nigeria, even a military government, would have the temerity to take that decision and to have done so without being sacked immediately. However, this perception does not reckon with the fact that the decision was not unpopular with a considerable slice of the political class. To begin with, apart from a few exceptions, the leaders of the defeated party supported it, and some of them, especially the members of the national executive of the party, the state executive and the serving governors of the NRC, supported the annulment vociferously. And they did so for the simple reason that it gave them another opportunity to win power instead of waiting another four or eight years.

More interesting still, some of the politicians of the winning SDP and their followers even supported, tacitly at any rate, the annulment of their own victory. They did so because annulment opened the contest again, offering another opportunity for themselves or their preferred candidates to win the party presidential nomination. Some politicians from both parties were worried that the voting pattern of the election did not augur well for the preservation of their political base, invariably shored up by regional, national, ethnic or religious identities. Within the political class the annulment of the election was not as unpopular as it seemed. That is why the struggle to reverse the decision was so difficult. The ambiguities and contradictions of the political class regarding the annulment brought into clear relief one of the major problems of democratization in Nigeria, namely, that for significant numbers within this class, democracy is primarily just a strategy of power.

Following the annulment there was an attempt to re-ethnicize Nigerian politics. The government tried to cope with the threatening crisis by isolating the winning SDP candidate and his close supporters. It did so by pointing out that military regimes in Nigeria had disqualified candidates before and cancelled elections and they had been taken in good faith. It was only the recalcitrance of the Yoruba (the nationality to which Abiola belongs) which was creating the crisis. Some Northern politicians took this line of reasoning and suggested that if Abiola's insistence on claiming his mandate was allowed, then previous Northern rulers, namely Tafawa Balewa and Shehu Shagari, whose electoral mandate had been aborted by coups d'état, could also reclaim their mandate.

As was to be expected, opposition to the annulment was particularly strong among the Yoruba nation, Abiola's home base. But government propaganda capitalized on this and tried to represent the ensuing unrest as something which was fomented mainly by the Yoruba and largely confined to their region. Some of the politicians who collaborated in the betrayal of the popular mandate suddenly remembered that the Yoruba had victimized their people in the past or had declined to support their people when they were in distress. Some of those who lost property in Lagos during the political unrest blamed not the government who cancelled the election, but Yoruba radicalism. By such attitudes and tactics, the democracy movement was weakened and ethnicity regained some of the ground which it had lost in the election.

However, the resurgence of ethnicity was short-lived. Ethnicity was being exploited by the military rulers to maintain themselves in power, but the very continuity of military rule became a formidable problem for the military. For it had the effect of de-ethnicizing politics and expanding the opposition to military rule. After the annulment popular outrage was so strong that it was simply impossible for General Bagangida to remain in office. Eventually he concocted a civilian interim government headed by Ernest Shonekan and handed over office to him. But Shonekan was widely seen as a surrogate for General Babangida, so the democracy movement continued to put pressure on the new government, effectively making it impossible for it to rule.

The power behind him, the Minister for Defence and the of General Staff, General Abacha, stepped forward and ousted Shonekan in a bloodless coup. But Abacha had to face the fact that Nigerians were adamantly opposed to military rule. Indeed, opposition to the continuation of military rule had become the one factor over which all the politicians could unite. He tried to buy time by proposing a constitutional conference, a watered-down version of the national conference which the democracy movement had been demanding. The constitutional conference, which was made up of elected and government-appointed representatives, was to draw up a new constitution after reviewing the fundamental issues of political association in Nigeria, such as revenue allocation, the distribution of power, minority rights, the conditions of tenure of public offices, the form of government, the creation of states and local governments and the balance of power between local governments, states and the Federal government.

If the review had been taken seriously and conducted by a more credible body, it could have been a point of entry for the Abacha regime to win some legitimacy and make a real contribution to the political development of Nigeria, because these were issues which many Nigerians including the democracy movement were eager to rethink in order to forge a collective identity and enhance democratic stability. However, the procedures, instruments and personnel which the government chose to realize the conference sent the wrong signals, namely that the conference was not taken seriously by the government which set it up, that it would not change anything and that it was a ruse for extending military rule as much as possible.

Paradoxically, the conference that was supposed to redeem the government threatened it. Some were frustrated because it promised the opportunity for revising the fundamental issues of the Nigerian polity which they had always wanted to do and then backed off. Most importantly, many were surprised and outraged that the military still wanted to stay in power after nearly three decades of dismal governance performance and an eight-year political transition that nearly ended in civil war. Even the fractions of the political class who had given overt and tacit support to the annulment of the 1993 presidential election were outraged that Abacha was stalling and delaying, if not denying their chance at power. However, the Abacha regime managed to contain this challenge.

These circumstances have forged massive opposition against the ruling military government. In the face of the agitation to bring down the Abacha regime, General Abacha became suspicious of civilians and reorganized his government radically by eliminating civilians from the all-powerful Supreme Military Council. That was a watershed in the de-ethnicization of the crisis. The move lent the struggle a much broader appeal by giving it the face of contest between military rule and democratic rule. It is interesting that those who led the opposition to a protracted transition process included the influential Northern politicians such as Shehu Yar Ardua who had supported or acquiesced in the annulment of the Presidential election.

In November 1994, the conference decided to give the government just one year to wind up its constitutional conference, set up the machinery for transition to civilian rule, conduct elections and hand over to a democratically elected government, forcing an astonished government to resort to stratagems such as long and unnecessary postponements of the constitutional conference, for instance a two month postponement for Ramadan. From December 1994 through January 1995, Nigerian newspapers and tabloids such as *Tell Magazine, The News, Tempo* and *Vanguard* were full of reports of attempts to sway the constitutional conference with financial inducements to support a protracted political transition. In April 1995, however, under heavy pressure from a military regime that had become extremely repressive, the conference rescinded its decision on a 1996 handover deadline. The military prevailed over the conference by being more repressive, but this has only brought the clash between military rule and democratization into sharper focus and reduced the regime's ability to survive by exploiting primordial loyalties.

The Salience of Ethnic Consciousness

This discussion of the dynamics of ethnic consciousness in the general context of political struggles which were essentially about democratization has been useful in showing the complex dialectics of the ethnic phenomenon, especially its precarious bestriding of the real and imagined, its power and impotence.

But that is not enough. It is necessary to look at the content of what we have called ethnic consciousness. For our failure to be specific and concrete about the content of ethnic consciousness is a source of misunderstanding and confusion, especially confusion of phenomenon and subject. For instance, quite often some posit the saliency of the subject, ethnic group when it is not salient—a group which is construed loosely as sharing the same ethnic markings is seen determinedly making some political demands and we immediately posit ethnicity. But the subject, that is, the ethnic identity, may just be conjunctural and insignificant relative to the political demand, which could be a highly significant emancipatory project. There is a tendency to privilege the subject ethnicity rather than the phenomenon emancipatory project without even problematizing our choice. That is why ethnicity and ethnic conflict are seen so ubiquitously and why so much is attributed to ethnicity and why its relationship with other phenomena is so often misrepresented.

To do this, there is need to return once more to the minority movement in Nigeria. Following the decisions of the Constitutional Conference of 1953 and the rash of minority movements demanding special protection and separate states, the colonial government set up a Minorities Commission in September 1957, amid fears that the movements would delay, abort or mar Nigeria's march to independence. This seemed to be a good example of the belief that democratic openings might lead to a surge of ethnic consciousness and ethnic conflict. The immediate cause of this movement was the decision that Nigeria should be a federation of three states, North, East and West, with residual powers accruing to the regions. In this unique federation, one of the federating states was more populous than the other two together. And in each of the two smaller states, one nationality is approximately two-thirds of the state's population while the rest is a scattering of smaller nationalities. The minorities feared that voting strength would make them a permanent minority subject to the arbitrary will of a permanent majority assuming, of course, that voting would follow nationality.

This fear of domination had regional specificities. The fear expressed in the Northern Region was that after independence the more conservative tendencies in 'the Northern system' would gain the upper hand, while recent moves in the direction of democracy would be abandoned, together with tolerance of non-Muslims and all minorities which were a part of the NPC's political philosophy. What was feared, in short, was a swing back towards Islamic conservatism and the autocratic rule of the Emirs (Report of the Minorities Commission, *Daily Times*, August 1958):

In the Western Region the minorities feared that they would be dominated by the Yoruba with their secure majority which could not be changed. They also feared the Yoruba intention of 'obliterating' their culture or encouraging tendencies to that effect (Minorities Commission 1958:5). The Commission found that they were concerned about domination by the Ibo majority which could never be challenged. According to the Commission there was almost no concern with cultural domination as was the case in the North. But the fear of political domination was very strong, so strong that 'the minorities were prepared even to reject the hope of independence, asserting that colonial dependence had been preferable to what was now before them' (Minorities Commission 1958:12).

It is useful to consider the context of these fears. To begin with, the state had no autonomy and so could not rise above and mediate social conflicts. The colonial state had looked superficially objective in the dying days of colonialism because the colonial authorities had become referees in the competition between the indigenous political class for access to power. But the referee was soon to disappear before anything could be put in place to give the state autonomy and objectivity. The federal structure chosen for Nigeria was a contradiction of federalism. Instead of reconciling social pluralism, stability and democracy, it merely tried to affirm stability while denying pluralism and threatening democracy and stability.

Against this background, the fears of the minorities which the Minorities Commission catalogued were obviously democratic concerns. What is salient about the movement is the phenomenon of democracy not the subject of ethnic identity. If one looks at the minorities movement in Nigeria from this perspective—that is, assigns saliency to democracy or democratization rather than ethnicity—the relationship of ethnicity and democracy now looks different. Ethnicity is not threatening democracy but facilitating it. In fact, what the Nigerian experience shows is that if indeed ethnic consciousness is a problem, especially for peaceful coexistence and political stability, then democracy is the answer.

The findings of the Minorities Commission are interesting in this respect. The smaller nationalities, afraid of being a permanent minority in a state with no autonomy, had demanded the creation of new states to give minorities some local autonomy. In considering this request, the commission ran into the practical difficulty of demarcating such states. It found that 'it is seldom possible to draw a clean boundary which does not create a fresh minority: the proposed state had in each case become very small by the time it had been pared down to an area in which it was possible to assert with confidence that it was desired' (Minorities Commission 1958:26). More important still, they had to face up to the elusive nature of the ethnic group and the ebb and flow of ethnic consciousness:

Until the last few years when the prospect of independence came close, the tendency within Nigeria (as in other parts of Africa) was for tribal differences to become less acute; this was beginning to happen to some extent even among the uneducated in the big towns, much more in the secondary and higher places of education and in general among those who had reached a higher level of education.

With the approach of independence, the tendency has been reversed and there has been a sharp recrudescence of tribal feelings. But it does not necessarily follow that this will continue; in a few years' time, a Nigeria which has to face the outer world may find within herself forces working strongly for unity. It would be a pity if, at the moment when Nigerian achieved independence, separate states had been created which enshrined tribal separation in a political form that was designed to be permanent (Ibid., 26).

There for, the commission decided that the creation of more states was not the best response to the fears of the minorities. It agreed with the minorities movement that ideally what was needed was a fulcrum, 'a fixed point outside and above politics from which absolute impartiality can be exercised' (Ibid.) Since the colonial masters could not play this role after independence, the commission came down to the view that what was really required was a functioning democracy, especially 'to distribute powers in such a that it may be to the interest of the party in power to pay due attention to the interests of others'. The commission questioned the assumptions of minority rights leaders that voting would always be along ethnic lines. It argued that the point of the political transition was to establish a liberal democracy in which voting would be a matter of choosing between competing political parties and that once the party system was established none of the parties could afford to neglect the minorities.

As to the assumption that power will only be used to the exclusive advantage of the party in office, it would be a rash commission that made prophecies. But as we have said, there are possibilities in the political scene that would make it to the interest of any party to woo the minorities, and there is one further point. The whole structure of the proceedings leading to independence is based on the belief that Nigeria means to follow the road of liberal democracy and parliamentary government, to base parts of the structure on the opposite assumption is to invite government to do their worst. But if that road is followed, votes will count and in the last resort it is the votes that will win fair treatment for minorities (Ibid.).

In the light of these reflections one may conclude that there is no reason why ethnic consciousness or ethnic identity, if it exists, should necessarily engender conflict under any conditions, including the conditions of democratization. Indeed, ethnicity is hardly a problem for democratization. A fruitful entry to the relationship between democratization and ethnicity must begin with recognition of the fact that democratization is inherently conflictual because it entails a radical redistribution of power as well as the acceptance of a political culture of equality. Since it involves a radical redistribution of power, it is generally strongly resisted by those, in power and often has to be achieved with violence.

More significantly, the process of democratization aims to bring an entirely different political order, and so motivates politically conscious persons, groups and interests to strive to maximize their power resources in the new order. This repositioning could mean very intense and conflictual competition because a great deal is at stake; a great deal is at stake because power resources lost or gained at the beginning of the process may determine political status and access to power and other resources for a long time. The conflict may conceivably involve nationalities or ethnicities as well. But how do identities and groups, especially ethnic groups, get involved in democratization?

They may be involved in resisting democratization and keeping the status quo. Typically this occurs because the ruling elite or dictator has resorted to a strategy of defending the old order by use of ethnic ideology, as was the case of Arap Moi in Kenya, Paul Biya in Cameroon, Eyadéma in Togo and Babangida in Nigeria. The propagation of the ethnic ideology may be effective enough for a good part of the membership.of an ethnic group to internalize the belief that the ethnic group is collectively in power, as seems to have been the case with the Kalenjins during the Presidency of Arap Moi in Kenya, and with Samuel Doe in Liberia and Diori in Niger.

But an ethnic group cannot properly be said to be collectively in office or in power whatever the level of solidarity. Only a ruling elite can be said to be in office or power. So the two instances can be collapsed into one, namely a ruling elite mobilizing ethnic ideology to defend its power. If one can resist the temptation of privileging ethnicity in everything to which it is remotely relevant, it is readily seen that what is important here is the defence of power against threat by those who hold it. Ethnicity is just one possible means among many others for accomplishing this task. Even if those in power succeed in getting some support from part of their ethnic group to defend their power against democratization, we cannot infer from this that ethnicity or the ethnic group is a problem for democracy; it is still unyielding power holders that are the problem for democracy. And what do we make of the ethnic groups in the same polity who are not involved in this defence of the status quo but are interested rather in its radical transformation so that their interests can be better accommodated?

The second and more usual entry of ethnicity and ethnic groups into the democratization process is through the struggle for incorporation from marginalization or exclusion. The vast majority of ethnic groups in Africa would be involved with democratization in this way because, if we accept for the purposes of argument the implausible idea of an ethnic group being in power, the ethnic groups that are actually in power as opposed to those who are out of power and marginalized and oppressed will be very small. The marginalized and oppressed ethnic groups struggling for democratic incorporation are de facto supporters of democratization although their support is not without ambiguity.

By these considerations, the presupposition that ethnic groups are a problem for democratization is untenable. But is that not evasive? For in the discourse about the interface of democratization and ethnicity, the main point is that democratization tends to engender ethnic conflict. What if an ethnic group successfully mobilized by ethnic ideology to support the ruling elite against democratization now gets into a fight with the ethnic groups seeking incorporation? Does this not underscore the conduciveness of democratization to ethnic conflict?

Actually it does not. It only seems so because we are once more privileging ethnicity rather arbitrarily. What is known logically and empirically and the issue that is primary here is that democratization tendentially engenders conflict. It is not known that it generates a high or a low incidence of ethnic conflict or that it generates a higher incidence of ethnic conflict than any other type of conflict.

A more important question is whether one can properly talk of ethnic conflict in this instance. Such characterization is misleading for what is being described is not so much an ethnic conflict but a 'democratic conflict', a democratic struggle in which some of the contestants happen to have got involved by the pull of ethnic ideology. It makes a great deal of difference whether one is seeing ethnic conflict or an emancipatory struggle, and the magnitude of this difference underscores the dangers of the habit of privileging ethnicity wherever it happens to be relevant and doing so negatively.

Finally, far from being prone to generating ethnic conflict, democratization is actually the antidote to those things which promote ethnic identity and what passes for ethnic conflict in Africa. What are these causes? The most important is the character of the post-colonial state in Africa. As was suggested earlier, the post-colonial state in Africa is very much like its colonial predecessor; its power over economy and society is enormous, arbitrary and it is largely privatized. For all but a few of its citizens, it is alien and remote, uncaring and oppressive. They encounter it as ruthless tax collectors, boorish policemen and bullying soldiers, corrupt judges cynically operating a system of injustice, a maze of regulations through which they have to beg, bribe or cheat their way every day. Accordingly, many of them have turned away from the state and given their loyalty to subnational social formations such as the community, the subnationality or ethnic group. The appeal of such social formations is not, as is sometimes imagined, owing to regressive consciousness, but vigorous rationality bent on maximizing utilities.

In a truly democratic African state where there is the rule of law, equal opportunity, accountability of power, a leadership which must be caring because its power derives from the consent of the governed and a firm commitment to sharing the burdens and the rewards of citizenship with equity, the ethnic group would be far less attractive. The Minorities Commission in Nigeria was right in insisting that the best solution to the problem of ethnic conflict was a democratic dispensation.

Part Three

Democratization and Political Instability

The concern that democratization might engender ethnic conflict is part of a general concern about political instability. In assessing the instrumentality of the process of democratization, it is essential to address also the implications of this process for political stability. This is a complex issue which cannot be treated in the depth that it requires here. It will only be treated partially in some of its African specificities.

To understand the relation between democratization and the prospects of political stability in the African context the point of departure again has to be the form and content of the post-colonial state. This is because in the context of nation-states, political competition is ultimately about the control of state power. And, contrary to popular notions, the character of political competition, especially its intensity, lawfulness or otherwise, is determined less by the subjective qualities of the competitors than the form and function of the state as the expression of the equation of power among social forces.

Following the classical theories of political liberalism, we tend to regard the state as a public force which is objective, that is, largely impartial, especially as regards the rule of law. Consequently, we usually dissociate the state from politics, regarding it as a legal institution or as an ensemble of public institutions related to politics only in so far as the political process selects those who manage the state in the public interest or mobilizes pressure for particular policy outputs. While the state can be and has to be susceptible to the pressures and influences from political society, it must nonetheless be substantially independent of every group in political society. The state is a public force brought into being and sustained by political society but independent of it.

The post-colonial state in Africa is markedly different from this. For the most part, at independence the colonial state was inherited by the indigenous elite rather than being liquidated or transformed. As was the case with the colonial state, the distinguishing characteristic of the post-colonial state in Africa is its lack of autonomy; power was highly fused and used by those in control of the state simply as the instrument for serving their own interests. Lack of autonomy has been compounded by the enormous power of the state over economy and society and the lack of institutional checks on this power, all of which have raised enormously the premium on political power.

Politics in much of post-colonial Africa puts an unusually high premium on power. In this type of politics violence and instability are endemic. Despite the enormous power of the state, a political order does not really emerge. Anarchy lurks below a mere semblance of order, the political system is as disarticulated as the economy.

A significant feature of this politics is that it militates against the crystallization of the political class as well as the transition from power to hegemony. The generally intense and often lawless political competition is even more so on the level of elites because they are more focused on power and they have more to lose in a situation where power tends to be coextensive with right, including the right to property. The faction of the political elite in power uses state power to accumulate in order to strengthen their characteristically weak material base and by doing so renders the capture of state power more attractive still. The lure of power is further increased by the general insecurity caused by the rudimentary development of the rule of law and the balance of power, as well as the lack of a basic consensus on how to seek and use power.

In a context in which the premium on power is so high and the competition for power is effectively an anarchy of self-seeking, a political class is not easily crystallized—nor a political order. From time to time, a faction of the fragmented political class gains ascendancy and may have the accumulated power to repress the others or even to exterminate some of them. But this ascendancy remains a matter of pure force. The triumphant faction hangs on desperately wielding power in a siege mentality until it is overthrown, usually by violence or systemic breakdown, and the cycle of repression and struggle starts again.

What is prevailing in much of post-colonial Africa is a peculiarly dynamic political instability which reproduces itself constantly. It not only reproduces itself, it often does so on an extended scale.

The State-Building Project

To understand the problem of political instability in Africa, it is not enough to look at the form and function of the state and the politics which it engenders. It is necessary to place this in the context of the state-building project. In most of Africa, the state is not so much a reality as a hope or, less subjectively, a project. It is still in the process of becoming. The process may well not be consummated but there is a discernible and persistent impetus to this effect. This impetus comes from the faction of the political elite in power who must act out, in whatever way, the reality of the state—the reality which brings for them a seat in the United Nations, the pomp of state visits, armies, navies and air force to control, foreign aid to administer, taxes to collect, public services to run, and development plans to produce and implement. The chances are that they know that the state is a project rather than a reality. But their interests compel them to create the illusion of the existence of the reality while they hurriedly coerce it into being.

That is how the state-building project invariable translates into programmes of coercive integration including ideological indoctrination, villagization programmes, cultural assimilation, single-party systems and the like. It seeks political integration in a threatening way, which throws up a multiplicity of communities and social groups who in their common subordination grow more conscious of their separateness and mutual alienation.

The top-down integrative policies that are projections of power aimed at eliciting integrative behaviour or gestures may be called vertical articulations. In vertical articulations the public force impacts on indigenous society to transform harness or control it, for instance, to fractionalize pre-capitalist social relations of production and to extract taxes, loyalty and obedience, to curb destabilizing behaviour, to elicit submission and so on. In the face of this threat, the subjects of the state try to appropriate state power or to limit it to doing the least harm. Since appropriation is the most appealing option, vertical articulations valorize political power immensely and spark off intense competition for it.

Vertical articulations trigger adjustments in the relations between the disparate social and political formations that are being forcefully integrated. These may be called horizontal articulations. These adjustments include the strengthening of traditional solidarity groups as a defence against the state, alliances to appropriate state power, intense competition between the leaders of the disparate social and political formations, rivalries among the formations themselves and the denomination of rival social formations. Essentially, horizontal articulations dynamize traditional solidarities while increasing their mutual alienation and their proneness to conflict.

The embrace of traditional solidarity groups as a means of coping with vertical articulations is something of a default option. The social formations and production relations in most of rural Africa are pre-capitalist and civil society is not much developed. That reduces drastically the options for organizing to deal with the challenge of vertical articulations. Ideological mobilization is difficult given cultural and linguistic diversities and the limited literacy in the common colonial language. The development of secondary groups is still very rudimentary in what are still essentially societies of mechanical solidarity. Thus primary consciousness and traditional solidarity groups, especially nationalities, ethnicities and subnationalities, are dynamized and politicized in the process of horizontal articulations. In some cases, as in the Yoruba Kingdoms of Western Nigeria, and the Emirates of the North, the process of state-building rehabilitated traditional political formations that had been slowly disintegrating. It gave some traditional political formations more coherence than they had (Smith 1966). As these political formations struggled and collided with other groups, their solidarity was enhanced.

In this light, the state-building project is initially self-defeating in throwing up, organizing and invigorating social formations in competition with each other for power and with the state for political allegiance. These social formations, whose identities are often defined in cultural terms, are essentially strangers to each other, and their relation is largely based on an amoral calculus of power and characterized by intense competition.

Even in the most favourable circumstances, state-building is a difficult and violent process (Tilly 1975; Callaghy 1984). It entails the initiation and protection of a new definition of authority in opposition to those that already exist. It is a struggle for dominance with internal societal groups and external groups, organizations and forces, for compliance, resources and the fulfilment of ideal and material interests; it is a struggle for internal control, political unification and external security (Callaghy 1984:81). Machiavelli argued this persuasively in the *The Discourses on Livy* and in *The Prince*, where he also tries to show that state-building even requires a different political morality. More recently the violence of the state-building project has been argued by Charles Tilly (1975, 1990). In Africa the process has been rendered harder and more violent still by its tendency to initially reinforce the factors which potentially resist it.

In the contemporary world, Africa has become notorious for political instability and violent conflict. In recent times the spread and intensity of political instability and violence, especially in Burundi, Rwanda, Mozambique, Liberia, Sierra Leone, Sudan, Somalia, Djibouti, Zaire, Central African Republic, Togo, and Cameroon has been such that some are now projecting Africa's collapse in an orgy of violence. As a result of this escalating violence, Africa has become the continent of refugees and internally displaced persons.

About 7 million of the world's estimated refugee population of 17 million are Africans, and approximately 16 million of the 25 million internally displaced persons worldwide are Africans (Deng 1994).

It is instructive that this violence is not, as might have been expected, due primarily to interstate conflict. It is predominantly state violence; that is, violence perpetrated by the state on its subjects to bring them into conformity with its conception of how they ought to be. This trend is by no means unique to Africa. It is decidedly universal, as a study, *Death by Government* (Rummel 1994), clearly shows. The statistical analysis in this work show that in the period 1900 to 1987, about 30 million people were killed in international wars as opposed to 130 million killed in genocide by their own governments.

These reflections bring the question of the relation of democratization to political instability in clearer relief. The question is usually presented as though there is an existing state of political stability which democratization may jeopardize. In most of Africa, however, the norm is a situation so inherently unstable that it is difficult to imagine it being more so. Admittedly, it can be argued that the African condition can conceivably be more unstable still. There is no need to contest this point. It is enough if it is granted that it is highly unstable. The point of entry of democratization is a situation in which political instability is a serious problem urgently demanding solution and not an absence which could become a presence. What difference would democratization make in these circumstances?

To answer this question, it is useful to take note of the nature of the political instability in question here. First, it is instability arising mainly from the use of force to project power and to shape people into acquiescence in new power relations, status distributions, new forms of material and cultural production which these people find extremely threatening and resist determinedly. It is associated with the relative absence of any adequate system of justice and rule of law capable of inspiring confidence. Finally, it is associated with the relative absence of prospects for transforming domination to hegemony.

Having taken note of this, there is still the need to relate this threatening coercive authoritarianism to the historical memory of Africans. As is well known, rural Africa where the vast majority of Africans live is still predominantly pre-capitalist in social relations as well as production relations. Traditional political practices and culture, although highly distorted and assimilated into a new hybrid totality, are still influential. While the coercive presence of the state is conspicuous and its extractive capacity considerable, it coerces in externality, its penetrative capacity is comparatively limited.

The violent authoritarianism associated with the state-building project in the colonial and the post-colonial era was a new and traumatic experience for Africa. The traditional political systems of Africa (and that excludes the Sultanic regimes from the Arab invasions) were not democratic. But they were a far cry from the coercive authoritarianism of the typical post-colonial state in Africa. In most cases the material base of the state, including the relations of production and the mode of production, could not sustain political autocracy, and patrimonialism could not be reconciled to the violent repression that post-colonial Africa experienced. Most of the traditional systems were small and egalitarian, although severely limited by the oppression of women.

In almost all cases, there was a profound distrust of the coercive hierarchization of power as fixed positions of command and obedience as is clear in the ethnographies of the Ibo, Ewe, Masai, Luo, Makonde, Kikuyu, Tallensi, and Tiv among others. In some cases, for instance, the Lozi and the Tallensi, so strong was the ideological commitment to egalitarianism that they feared and avoided war and sought peace avidly in order to avoid the risk of the concentration of power needed to wage war. The monarchies of traditional Africa were usually constitutional monarchies. For instance, the Barotse of Central Africa balanced the power of the monarch carefully with a council of ministers and then segmented the council of ministers into units carefully balanced against each other. The king was bound by strict rules of conduct and could be deposed if he failed to conform to the constraints on his power.

One recurrent feature of African traditional political systems which mediates authoritarianism is kinship. Political society was typically a family writ large. This is reflected in a political discourse replete with kinship idiom and imagery. For instance, the Ekie call the ritual tshize, the king's wife (Fairley 1987; Murphy and Bledsoe 1987). Relations of equality, subordination, clientage, patronage, competition and conflict may be expressed in the metaphor and idiom of kinship. The perception of political society as kinship would tend to exclude the violent repression of regimes such as those of Amin, Bokassa, Mengistu, Siad Barré and Banda.

Another mediating factor is that in traditional political systems, political dominion was tendentially constituted as an essentially noncoercive hierarchy based primarily on the differential distribution of status, which became only incidentally an asymmetrical relationship of political power. This occurs through the entire range of traditional systems from the monarchies such as the Baganda and the Yoruba to the more typical acephalous societies such as the Tallensi and the Tiv. The hierarchy is based on criteria such as age, gender, chronology of origin, proximity in genealogy to the royal house, order of initiation into cults or age-grade, order of marriage in polygamous marriages, athletic prowess, artistic talent, knowledge of history, oratorical ability and reputation.

These criteria are not in themselves a hierarchy of power but of status, even though they may eventually be perceived as power. Still the relation of status and power never comes to identity because claims to seniority or competition for seniority are not necessarily focused directly on power but on access to roles of social recognition, and political power is not appropriated directly but rather in a highly oblique and ritualized manner through complex mediations in an ascent of status.

Somewhat paradoxically, the power of those at the top of the hierarchy was checked rather than absolutized by the tendency to regard them as the incarnation of both polity and society. Usually all the leaders, personal qualities become inseparable from the welfare of the community (Young 1966). If he is ill, weak, strong, virile and dynamic, so is society. He was actually controlled meticulously in regard to what he could see, where he could be and when and how he could mate, if, when and how he could show emotions.

There was a daunting array of taboos to observe. It was taken for granted that the leader would act in the collective interest of the community. This assumption was not questioned when the community was at peace, prosperous and healthy. But once things began to go wrong, the leader was accountable. It was a unique and rigorous kind of accountability which effectively transformed the leader into a scapegoat for everything, even things he could not control, such as epidemic, drought and external aggression. Thus the Junkun King was expected 'to die' in the event of famine, or drought or if he fell seriously ill (Young 1966).

Implicit in all this is an unusual domestication of power. The leader, answerable for everything even fortuitous events and acts of nature becomes essentially a scapegoat, the role of the weakest which not only lacks power but entails subjection to oppression. As if to underline this, some of the taboos and ritual control of the behaviour of the leader deny him values. In all cases, they make the point that the leader is not subject but object, controlled in the public interest in an infinite variety of ways, not free to live or even to die. Even at the top, power and dominance become very paradoxical and elusive.

To summarize the salient features at the point of entry of democracy: a situation of endemic political instability which seems to feed on the repression that is supposed to remove it and gets ever more intractable. The process of state-building, violent enough in the best of circumstances, has been particularly difficult and violent in Africa because it initially reinforced the very obstacles that it was supposed to remove, such as primary group loyalties. As if this was not enough, the problem was compounded by the fact that the severe repression to which most of Africa was subjected in the post-colonial era was so contrary to traditional African political culture that it was not only painful but immensely disorienting and traumatic. African polities have become so disoriented and incoherent that they are unable to crystallize political order even with all the repression.

It would appear that there is no other way of stemming the violence, achieving some coherence and also a minimum of political legitimacy without democracy, especially in the sense that democracy boils down to striving to move forward together by negotiated consensus.

But this is too easy. To begin with, granted that democracy has some merit, why should we chose it over the prevailing conventional model of state-building which assumes coercive instrumentality? Even though nearly a century of state-building spanning the colonial and the post-colonial era has achieved very little, some may still argue that there is no alternative to coercion and violence in the project of state a building and that Africa needs persistence rather than a democratic alternative.

There are good reasons to reject this argument. Coercive nation-building in Africa is not only not achieving much, it is in deep crisis. After the experience of intra-state violence in Africa between 1985 and 1995 especially in Djibouti, Central African Republic, Zaire, Sierra Leone, Rwanda, Ethiopia, Sudan, Burundi, Somalia, Liberia, Mozambique and Angola, there is consensus in both Africa and the international community that this level of violence is unacceptable for whatever reason, including state-building.

To put an end to the continuation of such violence there is now an earnest debate and a small crop of concrete proposals both in Africa and the world community about the need to find ways of preventing such violent outbursts or ending them as soon as they start. What is interesting about this debate is an implicit assumption that respecting the sovereignty of states does not necessarily override humanitarian intervention, including peace-making. Proposals by the Organization of African Unity and the governments of the Netherlands, Britain and France are already on the table. It would appear that the decision against pressing on with the violent ways of the past has already been taken.

There is a related consideration which is equally important. It used to be assumed that the nation-state is the inevitable political organization of humankind. However, several developments in the contemporary world have brought into question not only the organizational salience of the nation-state but also its survival. We are witnessing the emergence of new regional and functional formations such as the North American Free trade Agreement (NAFTA) and the European Economic Community that are claiming with increasing success some of the rights and prerogatives previously conceded only to states. Since the end of the Cold War, the international community seems increasingly unimpressed by the claims of the state and the principle of its inviolability. As the cases of Yugoslavia,

Ethiopia, Czechoslovakia and the Soviet Union have demonstrated, there is a remarkably easy tolerance of the disintegration of well-established states. Only a decade ago this would have seemed inconceivable.

These circumstances have made the search for alternatives to the old violent ways of state-building, as well as to alternative forms of political organisation of humankind, highly desirable if not compelling. We have already suggested that in African conditions the one real alternative to the escalating violence growing out of political incoherence and resort to primary group loyalties and identities is democratization. And democratization is the alternative because more than anything else what is needed is negotiated consensus.

But how about the familiar concern that the opening of democratic spaces will throw up more groups pulling in different directions, demand overload, possibly anarchy and more violence? The logic of this argument is uneasy; indeed, it is upside down. It is not the opening of democratic spaces that brings out more groups to demand rights, roles, and autonomy. It is the making of demands, especially the demand for rights, justice, incorporation and the like, which brings about the opening of democratic spaces. What is feared has already happened, and it has produced an entirely desirable outcome, an outcome which we falsely perceive as leading to the things (assertiveness and demands) that in fact produced it.

What accounts for this reversal? What produces this logic that makes the opening of democratic space the cause of demands rather than its effect? It would appear that this is no careless mistake. It is a misrepresentation which arises from the tendency to ignore and devalue the democratic struggles which had been raging in Africa. It is actually in Africa and not in the collapsed Soviet Empire that the struggle for democratization in the second half of this century has been most intense, most demanding and most heroic. And it is also here that the struggle was saddled with the greatest difficulties. The resistance of the forces against democracy was rigorous, ruthless and violent, and those resisting forces included some of the Western governments which were not concerned about the democratic credentials of their African allies. By all indications, the struggle cost more suffering, more destruction and more lives in Africa than in Eastern Europe.

The concern about the effects of opening up democratic spaces on political stability typically devalues the struggle by denying implicitly that a considerable amount of democratic spaces have already been opened—democratic processes started, of course, not necessarily democratic outcomes. It devalues implicitly the suffering and sacrifices of those who have struggled for democracy in Africa by relocating the contradictions, conflicts and violence to the future when democratic spaces have supposedly been opened.

However, the contestation and its agonies lie in challenging for the opening, which is what Africans have been doing with remarkable courage for several decades. In the case of Africa the challenge was rigorously met by those in power, and the struggle was waged bitterly at immense cost. Some of its tragic effects are all too evident. The conflict and violence belong to the past, so to speak, the moment of challenge and engagement which pre-dates and determines eventually the possibility of the opening of democratic space.

That is not to say that there will be no conflict and violence in the future. There will be because the challenge and the contest are not a once-and-for-all event; the challenge is made in different ways over time to advance the struggle and to deepen democratization. But however protracted this process may be, it does not affect the distinction we are making between challenge and contestation on the one hand and the opening up of democratic space on the other. The challenge and the contestation bring about the opening of the space, that is, when they are successful. And it is in the course of the contestation following the challenge that the much-feared political instability, conflict and possible violence occur.

The move from challenge and struggle to the opening of democratic space or democratization is a qualitative leap. It is a qualitative leap from a situation in which democracy is absent or waiting in the wings while its fate is being determined on the battlefield to a situation in which democracy is present, albeit partially and with worrying fragility. It is also a qualitative leap from the state of war to civility, from conflict to better prospects of peaceful coexistence.

The fears about democratization causing anarchy, conflict and violence miss the significance of this change, and in doing so misrepresent the import of democratization. In so far as democratization occurs, a political practice is operationalized which tendentially prevents these fears from materializing. In so far as democracy is being practised, people are articulating their interests, and these interests are being aggregated along with other interests in the emergence of a negotiated consensus. In so far as democracy is being practised every vote counts; everyone is incorporated in what is, at the very least, a form of consumer sovereignty; everyone's consent is solicited, even if it is not always so clear what is being consented to. Finally, in so far as democracy is being practised no one is subject to arbitrary power, for there is the rule of law and accountability of power.

To be sure, in any historical practice of democracy, some of these values may not be realized or even realizable. However, that does not disprove the point that the practice of democracy entails the realization of these values. If any of them are not realized, then to that extent democracy is not being practised. Indeed, the democratization going on in Africa is superficial in various respects.

Considerable confusion has been caused by claiming democratization for what is really still the conjuncture of challenge and contestation or something even before that. For instance, in some of the emerging democracies of Africa, the consent of the governed is largely a farce: people are voting without choosing, and despite multi-party elections, state power remains arbitrary and the rule of law does not exist any more than accountability of power to the governed.

All this is admitted. Nonetheless, they say nothing against the proposition regarding what it means to practise democracy and how that meaning really excludes the prospect of democracy causing the kind of social disorganization, conflict and violence which is occurring in some parts of contemporary Africa. Far from causing these problems, democracy is their only answer.

Conclusion

This chapter has examined the import of democratization for the economic and political development of Africa on the understanding that the feasibility of democracy in Africa depends crucially on how it relates to the social experience of Africans and how it serves their social needs. At this historical conjuncture, democratization will be a great asset to the economic and political viability of Africa although its contribution in this respect is not without ambiguities.

4

The Feasibility of Democracy in Africa

Part One

Introduction

Is democracy feasible in Africa? This raises another question: what democracy? However, it will not be useful to select one type of democracy and focus on its feasibility for there are several democracies vying for preferment in a struggle whose outcome is as yet uncertain. For this reason it is more useful to start with the complex sociology of the democracy movement in Africa.

The democracy movement in contemporary Africa is not a single homogenous movement with a coherent doctrine and an agenda. It is typically a loose coalition of groups sharing rather vague notions about an emancipatory project and a common enemy, notions which remain common only because they are so vague that everyone can give them whatever content they want. There are variations from one country to another but the groups which make up the democracy movement usually include:

- Political elites who have been denied access to power.
- Social groups which have been excluded from power and often from the mere prerogatives of citizenship by religious, national, regional or ethnic discrimination.
- Business people who deplore prevailing governance practices, especially corruption, lack of transparency and the rule of law.
- Elements of civil society such as students, teachers, lawyers' groups, trade union groups, women's rights advocates and minority groups.

- Workers and peasants, sometimes in mass organisations and sometimes not.
- The international community, especially the industrialized Western countries, development agencies and the international financial institutions, especially the World Bank and the International Monetary Fund.

The International Community

The international community, especially the West and its development agencies, support democratization in Africa partly as a hegemonic project but mainly for its instrumentality. Supporting democratization as a hegemonic project is a carry-over from the Cold War, which was itself a hegemonic project not only for the West but for the Soviet Union also. With the winding down of the Cold War, the hegemonic element in the Western support of democracy is more conspicuous, especially for the triumphalists who see the globalization of capitalism and democracy as the last event of history.

To some extent, the triumph of these values is now being conflated with their desirability. The old hesitations about their imperfections at least in practice have largely disappeared, as has concern with customizing them to the requirements of different historical settings. To all appearances, there is very little patience with those who hesitate to accept them or those who are fussy about what versions to accept; it is as if such hesitation devalues the triumph, and puts them on trial again.

Apart from concern with the tidy consummation of a hegemonic project, Western support for democratization in Africa is also motivated by the practical concern that democracy will improve economic performance in Africa, which could translate into less internal and regional conflict, less aid and less humanitarian intervention. Disillusioned Western aid donors had independently come to the conclusion 'that economic development could not be pursued in isolation from concern for accountable and responsive governance, and that development assistance to African dictatorships had generally proved a disastrous failure' (Diamond 1993:5).

These are among the practical considerations at the root of political conditionality. This new matrix has been much criticized by many, especially Africans, some of whom suspect a new imperialism. Nonetheless, the logic of political conditionality is impeccable. Although there has been a tendency to apply it selectively and even opportunistically, political conditionality has been useful to those at the forefront of the democratic struggles in Africa who have generally welcomed it. When Nigeria's military dictator Ibrahim Babangida attempted to renege on his pledge to conduct presidential elections on June 12, 1993, the United States Embassy in Lagos reacted very strongly. It is widely believed in Nigeria that fear of sanctions may have been a factor in saving the election. Just as the Babangida government had feared, the election did not go the way it had hoped it would. When it cancelled the election on June 23, 1993, the United States and most of its allies condemned the move very strongly and imposed limited sanctions, a reaction which greatly encouraged and emboldened the pro-democracy movement in Nigeria and contributed to the retirement of Babangida from office.

In Malawi, Western pressure was decisive in forcing President Banda to hold a referendum on the adoption of a multi-party system as well as compelling him to accept the result of the referendum. He only reluctantly agreed to the referendum after donor countries suspended an aid package of $174 million. In the Central African Republic President Kolingba refused to recognize the result of the multi-party election of August 22, 1993. When he realized he had been soundly beaten to fourth place with only 11.46 per cent of the vote, Kolingba backed down only after the France on which the Central African Republic was highly dependent halted all bilateral cooperation. External pressures contributed to multi-party elections in Ghana, Ivory Coast, Benin, Zambia, Kenya, Togo and Cameroon, among others.

But what kind of democracy is the international community, especially the West, actually supporting? By all indications it is electoral democracy of limited depth which tends to see political pluralism and free and fair elections rather too ubiquitously. For instance, while the West has indicated its firmness in the application of political conditionality, it was not concerned that Jerry Rawlings used state power to get himself elected civilian President of Ghana at the end of highly manipulated transition programme which gave his opponents little chance of challenging him. It was much the same thing in Burkina Faso, in Kenya, Cameroon and the Ivory Coast.

The rejection of the reelection of Eyadéma on August 25, 1993 in Togo was the rare exception. But Eyadéma had overplayed his hand crudely and had given no leverage whatever for upholding his election by contriving to contest only against himself. Of the three strong opponents, Gilchrist Olympio was arbitrarily disqualified by the Supreme Court on the orders of Eyadéma. Edem Kodjo, former Secretary-General of the Organization of African Unity (OAU), and Yao Aghoyibo were obliged to withdraw from an election whose outcome was completely predetermined. Eyadéma unleashed his special army of 15,000, mainly drawn from his own Kabye kinsmen, on Lomé, a hostile but critical constituency, and sent about one-third of its residents fleeing into neighbouring countries, especially Ghana. In a country of young people he managed a voter registration of 2.7 million, out of a total population of 3.7 million.

Taking their cue from the Western countries, the Bretton Woods institutions have begun to show interest in governance issues. Since they are virtually the monopoly agents of Western multilateralism in Africa, they are also the main implementing agents of political conditionality. When the concept of political conditionality was introduced, the Bank and the Fund were quite concerned that it may have been misguided and pointed repeatedly to their legal instruments, which do not allow them to act politically. They eventually acquiesced, but only after replacing democracy with governance and further reducing governance to the administrative requirements salient to the operationlization of the market and to effective structural adjustment programmes, namely, the rule of law, accountability and transparency. The Fund and the Bank think that this route will take care of the pressing problems of economy and polity, though not of democratization, make the polity less corrupt and arbitrary, the economy more competitive and efficient, and both more pluralistic.

By replacing democracy with governance the Bretton Woods institutions partly circumvented political conditionality. They are focused mainly on SAP, convinced that it is the only way out of the African crisis. They are inclined to embrace African leaders willing to submit to SAP and to forgive virtually everything else, including human rights performance and rejection of democratization. Thus military dictators such as Jerry Rawlings of Ghana and Ibrahim Babangida of Nigeria found favour with the development agencies and the Bretton Woods institutions anxious to find willing pupils of SAP. African leaders soon caught on to the fact that they could, within limits, trade SAP for democratization. Some of them, for instance, Arap Moi of Kenya, Houphouët Boigny of Ivory Coast, Eyadéma of Togo and Paul Biya of Cameroon, tried to do just that. But this evasion was not always successful because of public opinion in the West and the democracy movement in Africa.

The Bretton Woods institutions are really not promoting democracy but economic liberalization. But they think that they are supporting democracy by doing just that, since economic liberalization will, they believe, reduce the role of the state and enhance pluralism.

The Business Class

There is no strong business lobby for democratization in Africa. The business, class is very small to begin with because of the rudimentary development of capitalism. There is also the legacy of statism and accumulation with state power, which tends to draw potential business people into politics. Those who remain in business are usually obliged to seek the cooperation of the state; it is certainly much easier to do business that way and often extremely lucrative. Some part of what remains of the business class is actually hooked to statism and not inclined to support destatization.

However, there are pockets of a real bourgeoisie in Africa, especially South Africa, Nigeria, Egypt, Algeria, Kenya, Ivory Coast, Senegal, Morocco and Tunisia. That section of the business class which is relatively independent of the state tends to be critical of economic mismanagement and political authoritarianism, a tendency well illustrated by the Manufacturers Association of Nigeria (MAN). They have been singularly critical of the inefficiencies which led to SAP in the first place as well as the character of the SAP regimes, especially their tendency to cause inflation, flagging demand, low capacity utilisation and the exposure of local producers to foreign competition. Like the multilateral development agencies, they tend to support the rule of law, accountability and transparency. Like them, they support economic liberalization but mainly in the domestic sphere. The thrust of their support for democratization is in the direction of the minimalist pluralism of electoral competition. Some of them worry that democratization may embolden the masses to demand redistribution and even larger investment in the social sector.

This fear certainly existed in South Africa and Nigeria. In preparing for Nigeria's return to civilian rule in 1979, the military government set up a political bureau to recommend what type of government the country should have. To everyone's surprise this government-appointed body recommended socialism, on the plea of reflecting popular opinion. This caused a great deal of concern in conservative circles and in the business class and led to strong intervention of the business community in the transition programme. The intervention contributed to a high level of corruption in the electoral process and to the making of electoral rules which limited eligibility for election to public office to the affluent self-employed. In South Africa, the intervention of the business class in the process of democratization appears to have been more benign; the initiatives of the business class played an important part in the thaw of Apartheid and facilitated the earlier contacts between the liberation movement and the white elite.

Counter-Elites

Elites out of power are ostensibly among the most enthusiastic supporters of democratization in Africa, but it is not always clear that they are supporting democracy. There are interesting affinities between most of those holding office in Africa today and many of the leaders of the democracy movement who are challenging them. They are usually factions of the same elite, some of whom had shared state power in the past.

Most of the leading figures in the agitation for multi-partism in Africa had been previously associated with power either in the party or in the government; some of them were quite comfortable with the one-party state as long as they were associated with power. For instance, the prominent members in the democracy movement in Kenya, especially the Kikuyu leaders such as Kibaki, were quite content to serve in Jomo Kenyatta's government. But when the shift of the ethnic base of power to the minority Kalenjin ethnic group occurred on the succession of Arap Moi, they became advocates of multi-partism. Others such as the Luo leader, Oginga Odinga, the late President of Forum for the Restoration of Democracy (FORD), were reacting to what seems even by Kenya standards the extreme ethnocentrism of the Moi regime.

In the Central African Republic, some of those who led the movement for pluralism which ended the 12-year rule of Andre Kolingba had served under him or under previous dictatorships. For instance, Ange Patassé, leader of the Movement for the Liberation of the Central African People (MLPC), had served under Bokassa as the minister for agriculture as well as health. The major opposition group to Kamuzu Banda and the single-party rule of his Malawi Congress Party (MCP), the United Democratic Front (UDF), were formerly government ministers under Banda and members of MLPC. The UDF was led by Aleke Banda, Edward Bwanali and Bakili Muluzi. Aleke Banda, a popular and highly respected youth leader of the 1960s and 1970s; fell into disfavour when he was being mentioned as a likely successor to Kamuzu Banda. Edward Bwanali was a regional minister who fell out of favour because he was suspected of being an advocate of reform.

One of the most important pro-democracy groups in Nigeria, the Association for Democracy and Good Governance in Nigeria (ADGN), had a core leadership of senior officials of previous military dictatorships, beginning with its overall leader, Olusegun Obasanjo, who was head of a military government. Other notable members of the core group were: Major Muhammadu Buhari, the head of state in what is arguably the most rigorous of Nigeria's military dictatorships; his deputy, Major Tunde Idiagbon; Lt Alani Akinrinde, another prominent member of a former military regime; Major Joseph Garba, who had served in Babangida's military regime as Ambassador to the United Nations; Commodore Ebitu Ukiwe, formerly Chief of Staff in Babangida's regime; and Major Theophilus Danjuma, who had served in the government. The civilian members of ADGN also included people who had served in military regimes. Similarly, of the leaders of the National Coalition for Democracy (NADECO), which is leading the opposition against Abacha's military dictatorship in Nigeria, for example, Dr Bolaji Akinyemi had served with Abacha in the cabinet of Babangida.

For the most part, the politicians and former public officials who are so conspicuous in the leadership of the democracy movement have no previous history of democratic commitment. It is entirely possible that some of them are new and genuine converts to the cause of democracy. However, by all indications their commitment to democracy and political pluralism has come by way of specific grievances, notably, loss of status in the political hierarchy, diminishing access to government officials and government contracts, personal disagreement with colleagues in power, reaction to perceived marginalization of one's region, ethnic group or religion, and so forth. A major factor motivating politicians and officials to join the democracy movement is frustrated ambition. For many who have been denied access to power in the monolithic political systems, the resurgence of pluralism offers a welcome opportunity to get back into power, or to compete for it.

These considerations suggest that for African elites, support for democratization is highly instrumental. Political pluralism nurtures hope of access to status, values and a chance to overcome regional, ethnic or religious marginalization. Focussing on these prospects, these elites find themselves supporting democracy, sometimes without seeming to know what it entails and what obligations it enjoins. Sometimes they find themselves acting against democracy. In democratic politics they give the highest priority to the goals for which they joined democratization. Thus in Kenya, the leaders of the democracy movement opposing Arap Moi were so focused on ascending to power that they neutralized themselves and allowed Moi to prevail.

For much the same reasons, they sometimes refuse to accept the discipline of democracy and invariably subvert it in the end. In seeking office, they are just as likely to violate the rule of law as the dictators whom they oppose. One of the most revealing experiences of Nigeria's programme of transition to democracy in the period of 1990 to 1993 was how little those politicians who insist on being called pro-democracy seemed to care about democracy. Party nominations for public office at the primaries went to the highest bidder, votes were purchased openly, thugs were hired to destroy unfavourable results or to kidnap and put away the militants of opposing parties, facilities for voters' registration were denied those who looked as if they might vote for the opposition. For the political elite, democracy is not about winning a popular mandate, but rather about access to power by every means possible.

The influence of the members of the political class, especially the opposition on the democracy movement, is not salutary. Their commitment to democracy is thin when it exists at all, for they tend to see democracy as a means, especially a strategy of power. That inclined them to a highly trivialized version of liberal democracy, a version which makes democracy the institutionalization of multi-party elections, elections significant mainly as the allocation of power rather than an exercise in democracy.

On these considerations one may conclude that Western governments, the multilateral development agencies, the business class and the fractions of the political class without access to power essentially have the same vision of democracy in Africa. They tend to limit democratization to the achievement of multi-party electoral competition. Since these groups are very powerful in Africa, they have been a decisive influence on the democracy movement. Even a cursory reading of the world press and the African press readily shows that issues of democratization of every country in Africa eventually reduce to the prospects of moving from political monolithism to pluralism and the derivation of the mandate to govern from multi-party elections.

Activist Elements of Civil Society

One of the most important groups in the democracy movement is the activist elements in civil society, which include the human rights lobby, minority rights groups, movements for the empowerment and participation of marginalized groups such as women and youth, students and labour. The activist elements may be organisations or individuals. Examples of such organisations are the Congress of South African Trade Unions (COSATU), the Zambia Congress of Trade Unions (ZCTU), the Committee for Democracy (CD) and the Civil Liberties Organization (CLO) and the Constitutional Rights Project (CPR) in Nigeria. The activist individuals are usually people who believe in human rights, equal opportunity and democracy and who, by virtue of these values so grossly neglected in post-colonial Africa, have always been outsiders to power. Examples are Gani Fawehinmi, Femi Falana, Balarabe Musa, Bala Usman and Ransome-Kuti in Nigeria, Peter Anyang Nyong'o in Kenya, the late Emmanuel Hansen in Ghana and Tipotch in Liberia.

Professionals and intellectuals, especially lawyers and university teachers, tend to feature prominently in this group. It is from here that the intelligentsia and the theories of the democracy movement tend to emanate. This group supports the institutions of liberal democracy, namely, multi-party elections, accountability and the rule of law not only in principle but also as a practical project of securing rights, overcoming economic and political marginalization, and exploitation and empowering those who are weak and making public policy responsive to social needs. The democracy that this group supports is qualitatively different in that it has more depth, although there is still a tendency to focus on multi-party elections and very little sign of any understanding of the radical social transformation and the creativity which it will take to make democracy empowering for the African peasant.

The Masses and Peasants

The masses and peasants are the ones asking for a second independence from an indigenous leadership that lost faith with the nationalist movement and became unacceptably exploitative and oppressive. They are the ones who have put their lives on the line in demonstrations and every form of defiance, but they do not control the democracy movement, which does not appear, now at least, to express their interests. That is a major reason why the movement lacks depth. These people have to be the social base of the democracy movement and its decisive influence if it is to have any depth, because they are the ones with the greatest stake in the democratic redistribution of power.

However, they are not often very conscious politically. When they are, they may direct their political consciousness to the support of the political elite who exploit them. Sometimes they are profoundly radical. Now and then, some of them challenge the state and its coercive machinery with extraordinary courage.

They come at democracy differently. They come at it from the dialectics of economic and political oppression and the struggle for survival at the extremities of social existence. Democratization operationalizes their call for a second independence. The first independence, from the colonial masters, has clearly not worked. In the post-independence era, most of Africa found itself in a situation in which the only thing which was developing was underdevelopment. sub-Saharan Africa has been recording negative growth rates for nearly two decades; on several critical indicators, the average African is worse off today than 20 years ago. Economic stagnation, the fiscal crisis of the state and intensifying poverty have led to large-scale collapse of social and physical infrastructures, caused a great deal of stress and a proliferation of violent conflicts, chronic malnutrition for many and death by starvation for some.

Accordingly, all over Africa, ordinary people are in revolt against a leadership whose performance has, in some cases, become life-threatening. As all the national conferences have shown, they link their increasing immiserization to leadership performance, and they are convinced that their economic plight will not improve until the politics changes, until they empower themselves to intervene in public life for the improvement of their own lives. That is how they have come to call for a second independence from their own leaders.

They are now asserting the need for the colonial revolution to be followed by a democratic revolution. Clearly, they are not demanding a minimalist liberal democracy. They have not been theoretically articulate about what democracy they want, but by all indications, it will be markedly different from the electoral democracy which the elite and the international community favour. They want a democracy which will translate to empowerment, upliftment and concrete rights. As yet, the process of democratization in Africa shows no sign of getting there.

Conclusion

The sociology of the democracy movement in Africa shows that two distinct and ultimately incompatible democracies are incubating in the same movement. One is a minimalist liberal democracy focused on multi-party elections. This is the kind of democracy that the disaffected politicians and business people and some of the urban intelligentsia want. It is the kind of democracy that the Western governments and their development agencies, including the Bretton Woods institutions, are supporting in Africa. Those who support this kind of democracy are basically in control of the leadership of the democracy movement in Africa, and so far the democratization of Africa appears to be moving in this direction.

The democracy which the masses and peasants and human rights activists demand is markedly different. It is essentially a social democracy with emphasis on concrete rights and concrete equality; it presupposes substantial investment in the upliftment and the empowerment of ordinary people. Those who are demanding this kind of democracy are the social base of the democracy movement; they are the ones who are demonstrating and taking bullets to bring down dictators in Kenya, Cameroon, Malawi, Egypt, Morocco, Algeria, Nigeria, Niger, Central African Republic, Congo, Togo, Bénin, Ivory Coast, Zaire, Chad, Zambia and Senegal.

The differences between these two democracies are not, for now, conspicuous in the democracy movement, and it does not appear that many of those who are attached to these divergent views of democracy are aware that they are in conflict. Differences have been largely submerged because the movement is still at a rudimentary stage when the focus is on raising consciousness, attacking the prevailing dictatorship and pushing for pluralism, objectives that readily appeal to virtually every faction of the movement.

But as the movement matures and starts to move towards more rigorous self-definition the differences will emerge, and it will be clear that the two kinds of democracy are irreconcilable. In the end, any attempt to confine the process of democratization to multi-party elections will not meet the democratic aspirations of the masses who want material betterment, equal opportunity and cultural upliftment, and concrete rights. At the same time, any attempt to move beyond multi-party elections to social democracy will be resisted by the bourgeoisie who see multi-party electoral democracy as merely a strategy of power. Eventually these two positions will clash and allies will become enemies. The dynamics of this contradiction and its resolution will determine importantly the feasibility of democracy in Africa. For the time being, a trivialized liberal democracy prevails.

Part Two

The International Environment

The global environment is highly pertinent to the feasibility of democracy in Africa. In the past, its hostility was highly detrimental to the democratization of Africa; a more favourable environment could enhance the impetus of the process of democratization in contemporary Africa.

Through its decades of involvement in Africa, the West's attitude has been that democracy is not for Africa. That attitude was an important component of the ideology of colonisation which held that Africans were unfit to govern themselves, that they needed the civilisation of colonial tutelage, which was their one hope of eventually achieving self-determination and development.

Even in the era of political independence in Africa, the West remained indifferent to issues of democracy on the continent, alienated by the nationalist onslaught on its presumptions and quite concerned that the self-government which Africans had so 'hastily' demanded would fail. Western governments were happy to cooperate with the newly independent African governments in a 'partnership in development'. They gave indulgent support to authoritarian African regimes in order to maintain some influence in the ex-colony and to protect their interests. This support was all too readily given because the authoritarian tendencies of the post-colonial era only confirmed their prejudices against the political maturity of Africa. In their quest for allies for the Cold War, the great powers ignored considerations of human rights performance in Africa and sought clients wherever they could. All this crystallized a climate of opinion against democracy in Africa.

The prejudice was so strong that the question of democracy in Africa was hardly ever raised as an issue. From time to time, for instance, during the Carter administration in the United States, human rights became an issue, but never democracy. On the rare occasions when democracy was discussed, it was mainly to raise doubts about its feasibility.

From the early 1990s issues of democratization and human rights began to dominate the West's interest in Africa. This is due mainly to the 'capitalist' revolution in Eastern Europe and the winding down of the Cold War. The Soviet empire was, in Western eyes, the very antithesis of democracy, and the spectacle of the long dramatic and largely successful democratic struggles which took place there convinced the West that liberal democracy was feasible everywhere, and it began to be sensitive to its possibilities everywhere, including Africa.

Thus democratic struggles which had been waged in Africa for decades but which in the prevailing prejudice had been dismissed as ethnic strife, political chaos and teething problems of nation-building began to be recognized for what they are, emancipatory projects. At the same time, encouraged by developments in Eastern Europe, the West turned from the Cold War to a mission of democratization, a mission which it believed would consummate the hegemony of Western political values all over the world, including Africa. Thus the West began to regard democracy as a significant item on the African agenda.

This change in attitude was reinforced by the fact that the winding down of the Cold War occurred at a time when the long struggle for democracy in Africa was beginning to show results, such as the popular opposition to military rule in Nigeria and the move to civilian rule, the demise of Apartheid in South Africa, of Samuel Doe in Liberia, Kérékou in Benin Republic, Siad Barré in Somalia and Moussa Traoré in Mali. There were also the modest gains for pluralism and multi-partism in Niger, Togo, Madagascar, Cameroon, Gabon, Ivory Coast, Guinea, Mozambique, Angola, Sao Tomé and Principe, and the Congo, and the deepening crisis of democratization in Kenya, Somalia, Sudan, Cameroon, Ghana, Sierra Leone, Ethiopia and Zimbabwe.

The change in the West's attitude to democracy in Africa drew additional impetus from the marginalization of Africa caused by changes in the world economy. The world economy is now driven less by trade than by capital movements; there 'is a massive movement from the production of goods to the production of services and a shift from industries of material intensity to those of knowledge intensity. Advances in science and technology are producing more synthetic products, which are more flexible and more versatile. These changes have made Africa's primary economies far less relevant to the economic needs of the West.

Now, with the winding down of the Cold War, the strategic significance of Africa to the West is greatly diminished also. As Europe draws closer to unification, even the former colonial powers, notably France, are finding it necessary to downgrade their special relations with their former colonies, relations which are far less useful now than they used to be. The marginalization of Africa has given the West more scope for dealing in a principled way in its relations with Africa. In the past, the West had affected a posture of indifference to issues of human rights and democracy in Africa in order not to jeopardize its economic and strategic interests and on account of its obsessive search for allies against communism. Now that these concerns are not so important, it is free to allow its African policies to be more consonant with its value commitments.

The decisive factor in changing Western policies towards Africa, including those affecting democratization, is the end of the Cold War. Western policy makers readily acknowledge that while it raged, the Cold War determined their policies towards Africa. James Bishop, a former US Ambassador to Somalia, said in a policy review that Africa was just 'another playing field on which the struggle between the Soviets and ourselves was to be waged' (Bishop 1992:1). The American Secretary of State, Warren Christopher, put it just as bluntly:

> During the long Cold War period, policies toward Africa were often determined not by how they affected Africa, but by whether they brought advantage or disadvantage to Washington or Moscow. Thankfully, we have moved beyond the point of adopting policies based on how they might affect the shipping lanes next to Africa rather than the people in Africa (Christopher 1993:2).

The consequences of the Cold War focus were unfortunate for Africa. The most autocratic and corrupt regimes in Africa tended to be the most willing Cold War allies for the simple reason that they needed external support to make up for their lack of legitimacy at home. These were the regimes that the West gave the most support. From 1962 to 1988, the highest recipients of United States aid to Africa were Ethiopia, Kenya, Somalia, Liberia, Sudan and Zaire. For three decades, 1960 to 1990, Zaire was the highest recipient of United States aid. Within a few years in office, Samuel Doe of Liberia received more aid than Liberia had got from the United States in the previous half century.

Cold War concerns also led the West to intervene against emancipatory projects in Africa. For instance, the United States lavishly supported Portuguese dictator Salazar against the liberation struggle of Mozambique and Angola for access to the Azores. In the same vein military and strategic considerations led the United States into supporting Apartheid South Africa.

By 1990 a decisive shift had occurred. Western leaders were insisting that support for democracy would be a central concern of their relation to Africa. They had apparently reached a consensus to the effect that they would use their leverage in development assistance and trade and investment to support human rights and democracy in Africa.

For instance, the United States Congress indicated that aid would go to aspiring democracies and not to autocratic regimes. The US Assistant Secretary of State for African Affairs, Herman Cohen, speaking at the Bretton Woods Committee meeting in Washington in April 1990, announced that in addition to economic policy reform and human rights, democratization would be added as a third condition for US assistance. On May 8, 1990, upon his return to Nairobi from a Chiefs of African Missions meeting in Washington, the US Ambassador to Kenya said that 'there is a strong tide flowing in our Congress, which controls the purse strings to concentrate our economic assistance on those of the world's nations that nourish democratic institutions, defend human rights and practice multi-party politics. He went on to suggest that this would be a 'fact of political life in other donor countries tomorrow'.

Speaking at the meeting of the Overseas Development Institute on June 6, 1990, the British Foreign Secretary, Douglas Hurd, said that Britain's assistance would favour 'countries tending towards pluralism, public accountability, respect for the rule of law, human rights, and market principles'. President Mitterrand, addressing the French-African conference at La Baule in June 1990, served notice that in the future, French aid would flow 'more enthusiastically' to countries moving towards democracy, as evidenced by free elections held under universal suffrage, freedom of the press, independence of the judiciary, multi-partism and the abolition of censorship'.

Even before these formal declarations of the new line, it was already being implemented. France had discontinued aid to the bankrupt regime of Mathieu Kérékou, thereby putting pressure on him to summon a national conference. Kenya was perhaps the compelling example of the new Western line. President Arap Moi's record on human rights and democracy had worsened steadily despite pressures from the human rights movement in Kenya and the US Ambassador to Kenya, Smith Hempstone; the regime was widely believed to be abusing, torturing and murdering opponents as well as being very corrupt. In September 1991, the Consultative Group for Kenya (a consortium of Western aid donors to Kenya) meeting in Paris decided to suspend aid to Kenya until the Moi regime met some clearly stated political conditions, which included action against corruption, improved human rights performance, political reform in the direction of pluralism and the rule of law. Against this threat, Arap Moi reluctantly and bitterly gave in. A special meeting of the Kenya African National Union (KANU), the ruling party was convened to authorize repeal of the ban on opposition parties and to enable Kenya to move towards multi-party elections.

Western donors used the same tactic with success in Malawi. In May 1992, following a mass demonstration against President Banda's brutal repression, Malawi's donors suspended $74 million in aid to Malawi. President Banda was obliged to release political prisoners and to legalize opposition. From here the country moved quickly towards multi-partism, which was formally sanctioned in a referendum of June 1993 with a sizeable majority of 63 per cent, a remarkable figure in the face of the opposition of President Banda and his use of state power to influence the referendum.

Among some donor countries, such as Sweden and the United States, the new political conditionality is looking less like an occasional posture and more like a policy. The Clinton Administration in the United States has spoken clearly and repeatedly about allowing aid to flow with governance performance, and policies are moving in that direction. In this spirit, the United States stopped its active support of Jonas Savimbi, the head of UNITA, and extended diplomatic recognition to the Government of Angola on May 19, 1993. Ibrahim Babangida was pointedly denied his wish for a state visit to the United States. Instead the Clinton Administration chose to receive the first elected president of independent Namibia, Sam Nujoma.

The allocation of United States aid to Africa has changed in accordance with the new conditionality. The favoured clients are the democratizing countries such as South Africa, Ethiopia and Mozambique. The old favourites, Liberia, Zaire and Sudan, are not getting aid. The United States has been steadfast in supporting pro-democracy elements in Nigeria in their struggle against the attempt by the Nigerian military through Generals Babangida and Abacha to perpetuate military rule.

But the evidence of political conditionality is mixed. There are instances of inconsistency, ambiguity and even some hints of reversal. For instance, the policies of France in Djibouti, Gabon, Rwanda and Togo, Ivory Coast and even Nigeria have not been examples of enlightened support for democracy. Of particular note is the French government's role in Cameroon. Amid universal condemnation of President Paul Biya for using violence to steal an election in which it is agreed by international observer teams and the diplomatic community in Cameroon that he was defeated by John Fru Ndi, and despite the fact that Biya's armed forces killed hundreds of people after the election to keep him in power, France continues to give him indulgent support. France upheld the election and, while the slaughter was going, loaned Cameroon about $110 million which gave the Biya government the leverage to reschedule with the World Bank and the IMF and to avert the freezing of all international aid.

France is an extreme case of ambiguities and inconsistencies that are quite widespread. These ambiguities and limitations are perhaps inevitable given the competing objectives driving the foreign policies of the Western countries:

... support for democratization is just one of several objectives that form the basis of the foreign policies of the established democracies that now share this concern maintaining peace and security, halting the spread of nuclear weapons, promoting and protecting a nation's former colonial empire, controlling drugs, conserving the environment—all compete to varying degrees and, depending on the locale, with democratization as foreign policy objectives (Barkan 1994:17).

Even a cursory look at this list of competing objectives shows that expectations regarding political conditionality have to be modest, that the commitment of the Western countries to the democratization of the Third World cannot be very compelling for the simple reason that it is more difficult to rationalize this support in terms of the national interest of the Western countries than it is to rationalize the control of drugs, the defence of markets and raw materials, and the security of investment. This is even more so in the case of Africa because the strategic and economic significance of Africa for the industrialized countries is relatively marginal and because Africa has failed to inspire any confidence in its ability to deal with its crisis of underdevelopment.

In considering the prospects of strong intervention for democracy, it is useful to consider essential differentiations within Western countries, especially the differences between civil society, the executive arm of government and the legislature. Politically conscious elements in civil society in the West have been more inclined to support strong intervention for democracy than the governments. But this has to be weighed against the reality of 'the silent majority' who are not inclined to be concerned with benevolent gestures of uncertain national benefit in foreign lands.

As regards the government there is usually a division between the executive arm and the legislative arm. The legislative arm of government tends to be more supportive of political conditionality except in cases where the ideological colouration of the legislature is very conservative, as in the Republican-controlled Senate under the Bill Clinton Administration. Usually the executive arm tends to be much more cautious about intervention to promote causes abroad whose benefit are not concrete, visible and relevant to the immediate needs of voters. It fears, with some justification, that such adventurism is unlikely to do the Administration a great deal of good and may do it considerable harm in an ideological climate in which the Third World is mainly perceived by the North as 'a problem'.

The differences between the executive and the legislature and the cautious disposition of the former came out very clearly during the George Bush Presidency in the United States. During his tenure, influential members of Congress supported strong intervention to promote democracy, notably: Foreign Relations Committee Chairman Clairborne Pell, House Foreign Affairs Chairman Dante Fascell, House Majority Whip

William Gray, Chairman of the House Subcommittee on Human Rights Gus Yatron, Chairman of the Senate Subcommittee on Africa Paul Simon, and Chairman of the House Subcommittee on Africa Howard Wolpe.

Despite substantial support for sanctions in pursuit of democratization during the George Bush Presidency, the Administration was very circumspect about taking action, preoccupied as it was with keeping options open, causing no offence to friendly governments and avoiding conflicts in pursuit of seemingly intangible objectives. Thus against the tide of public and Congressional pressure, the Administration moved very slowly and reluctantly on sanctions in South Africa, Zaire, Liberia and Haiti. Congressional calls for sanctions against President Arap Moi, who had promised to kill the opposition 'like rats', elicited only a visit from Herman Cohen, the Assistant Secretary of State for Africa, to Kenya, at the end of which a delighted President Moi declared that relations between Kenya and the United States were back to normal. Since it is the executive which has to effect the intervention for democracy, its inherent disposition to caution is an additional obstacle to the promotion of democracy abroad.

Intervention through Multilateralism

How about political conditionality through multilateralism, especially through the International Monetary Fund and the World Bank, which do not have to worry about national interest and electoral popularity? These institutions certainly have considerable leverage. The Western countries tend to take their cue from the IMF and the World Bank in their dealings with Africa. Thus an African country which cannot obtain an IMF certificate of aid-worthiness is unlikely to get cooperation from the West. This prompted a former Executive Secretary of the United Nations Economic Commission for Africa, Adebayo Adedeji, to say that the IMF and the World Bank are now more powerful in Africa than the former colonial masters. These agencies used to think of development as being nonpolitical, a view that has been a major stumbling block to the development effort in Africa. But they now admit the relevance of political factors to development; they are especially concerned that poor governance performance has been a major constraint to development particularly in Africa.

While admitting that political factors are constraining the development effort including their own, the Bretton Woods institutions still appear to believe that they can seek development without being involved in politics. They usually assume that political variables can be treated as an engineering problem and factored in to improve the effectiveness of the structural adjustment programmes without changing their approach to development. At the same time they insist that they are not turning their backs on democratization because the cause of democracy is best served by simply pressing on with adjustment programmes which strengthen the market against the state.

In their view, privatisation will enhance pluralism and a freer market will decentralize decision-making, pluralize the locus of power and strengthen civil society. This view is widely held in Western government circles and also among intellectuals. Writing in the *Washington Post* on May 24, 1990, Chester Crocker, the former US Assistant Secretary of State for African Affairs, argued that structural adjustment programmes 'are vital to the liberation of market forces, which in turn, represent the building blocks of pluralist democracy'.

Without meaning to do so, the multilateral agencies collaborate in political authoritarianism. In *Sub-Saharan Africa: From Crisis to Sustainable Growth*, the Bank had argued quite correctly that 'programmes of action can be sustained only if they arise out of consensus built on dialogue within each country'. And yet there is not one instance in which the Fund or the Bank seriously encouraged discussion and consensus-building in regard to the introduction of their structural adjustment programmes. In every case, they were quite content to settle the issues with the presidents of the client countries or their economic or finance minister. Having done so, they constantly urge the necessity of political will, which is a euphemism for coercive imposition of the programme.

The indications are that neither in the context of bilateralism nor in that of multilateralism is political conditionality likely to be pushed hard enough to be a major source of impetus to democratization in Africa. For one thing the economic leverage for political conditionality is getting weaker, with diminishing interest in Africa and decreasing investment and aid flows. It is likely that things will get worse in the prevailing ideological atmosphere, where the market is the quintessential panacea and where major donors want to revert to being countries pursuing their own interests rather than being a cause. The chances are that there will continue to be humanitarian aid and little else.

Nowhere is this more evident than in the United States, especially since the 1994 Congressional election which gave the Republicans control of the Senate and the House of Representatives. Senator Jesse Helms, the Chairman of the Senate Foreign Relations Committee, and Senator Mitch McConnell, Chairman of the Senate Appropriations Subcommittee, and the majority of Congress have indicated their strong commitment to a drastic reduction in foreign aid, in the case of Africa, as much as 30 per cent. And what is left of foreign aid is not going to the promotion of democracy but will be spent according to three new guiding principles which they have enunciated:

1. Foreign aid must protect American security interests;
2. Foreign aid must promote American economic interests;
3. Foreign aid must preserve political and regional stability.

These tendencies threaten to render political conditionality irrelevant.

Political Conditionality and Armament

It is odd that little is said or done about a potentially critical conditionality for leveraging democracy and development in Africa, namely armament and militarism, which are among the greatest threats to development and democracy in Africa. To begin with the obvious, military expenditure allocates resources wastefully and destructively at a time when Africa is in deep crisis, when the intensity of poverty has reached a level that threatens all prospects of well-being for ordinary people and even civilization.

Table
Military expenditure in Sub-Saharan Africa

	as % of GDP	as % of combined expenditure on education and health
1960	0.7	27
1990-91	3.0	43

Source: Adapted from UNDP, *Human Development Report,* 1994:171.

Military spending means that millions of people do not get access to education, clean water or to doctors. It means loss of opportunity to rescue disappearing social services and disintegrating infrastructures. The human cost of military expenditures in very poor countries is very high. The *World Development Report* 1994 captures this with poignant simplicity in a brief discussion of just one military transaction that Nigeria made recently:

> Nigeria purchased 80 battle tanks from the United Kingdom at a cost that could immunize all of the two million unimmunized children and provide family planning services to nearly 17 million of the more than 20 million couples who lack such services (*World Development Report* 1994:54).

By denying human development in this way, military expenditure also denies democracy. For the problem of democratization in Africa is complicated by the fact that Africa also has to produce its potential democrats, by a massive programme of upliftment from poverty, from ignorance and superstition, from poor health and cultural deprivation, from diffidence and submissiveness to higher self-esteem.

The level of poverty in Africa is such that the struggle of social existence is waged on a level of physical immediacy so absorbing and debilitating that it is hostile to the conditions of democratic citizenship. The chronically ill cannot adequately participate politically, nor can the uneducated, for there is no choice in ignorance. Military expenditure represents a lost opportunity for this much-needed investment in human development and the enabling social environment for democracy. And in the African context it has hardly any redeeming features.

Military expenditure in Africa cannot be justified on the need for security against external threat. For the incidence of war between African states is so low that threat to security is negligible. In this respect, Africa conforms to a global trend. The trend is the diminishing incidence of war between countries. This is giving way, especially in the developing countries, to war within countries. Between 1989 and 1992 there were 82 armed conflicts of which only three were between countries (*World Development Report* 1994:47). This trend holds for Africa even more strongly than most other parts of the world. Prospects of inter-state conflict in Africa are less likely still under prevailing conditions.

But that is not as comforting as it might seem. The wars within countries have been notable for their frequency and violent intensity, causing the death of millions of people and leaving many more suffering from injuries, displacement and loss of property. But it is worse than that because Africa has a very low incidence of war between countries in the sense that a war presupposes serious conflict between two social groups.

What is claiming these millions of lives in Africa and spreading so much misery is not war between groups but state violence, the state making war against its people. This war may be made in the name of maintaining unity, protecting cultural integrity, in the name of religious ideology or an ethnic or nationalist ideology, but that is only its latent function. Its manifest function is power, the maintenance and projection of power for domination and exploitation. It is the misfortune of Africa that so many of its leaders have nursed these ambitions. All too often leaders in Africa insist on keeping power by force, with the result that their people are often traumatized and made hostile to the state and its projects.

There is considerable concern in the international community with preventing these conflicts or managing them effectively. Efforts to deal with them have suffered from failure to recognize that they are not so much conflicts as state violence, usually violence without conflict. More relevant to our purpose here is that not enough attention has been given to the practical matter of the armaments which the African state uses to perpetrate this violence. There is not enough recognition of the fact that the arms industry, the arms trade and military assistance are a major part of the monumental tragedy which is unfolding in Africa. The rest of the world watches with horror and disbelief the suffering and the mounting death toll, and debates humanitarian intervention.

But it may be more productive to address the issue of human responsibility at a more fundamental level, namely the level of everyone's real and potential contribution to the remote and immediate causes of these conflicts, a matter of some distaste because at this level very few can pass as innocent or humane. The humanitarian intervention of France in Rwanda was very useful—it may well have saved many lives. But it has to be seen against the contribution of France to the conflict, which includes, among other things, a clumsy attempt to establish Hutu domination by arming the Hutu and raising the Hutu army of President Habyarimana from 5,000 to 30,000.

It is paradoxical that some countries of the North which are in the forefront of development and democratization are also implicated in the armament and militarism which has become a formidable obstacle, arguably the most formidable obstacle to development and democratization in Africa. Perhaps the greatest contribution that the North can make to development and democratization in the African context is to canvass and impose a total arms embargo in Africa and tie aid strictly to the reduction of military expenditures in relation to social expenditure and also in absolute terms. To its credit the World Bank and the United Nations Development Programme are already moving in this direction.

If it is feasible to do so, this process can be pressed to the point when African armies are abolished altogether. With few exceptions, African armies are useless against plausible external threats, and in the role of internal security they are disastrous. The real security need for Africans is not military security but social security, security against poverty, ignorance, anxiety and fear, disease and famine, against arbitrary power and exploitation; security against those things which render democracy improbable in Africa.

Positive Incentives

Political conditionality is essentially a threat and a negative incentive. What about positive incentives to support the democratization of Africa? The collapse of the Soviet Empire and the surge of democratization which gathered momentum after that singular event took the West and the world by surprise. The question of supporting the fledgling democracies all over the world had not previously arisen, and there was not enough advanced thinking or adequate institutional framework to deal with the new wave of democratization.

The world community was obliged to improvise with existing institutions largely developed in the context of the Cold War: the Human Rights Development Center, the Human Rights Watch and its subsidiary, Africa Watch, the National Democratic Institute (NDI), the National Endowment for Democracy (NED), the International Republican Institute (IRI), the Friedrich Ebert Foundation, the Friedrich Naumann Foundation, the Konrad Adenauer Foundation, United States Agency for International Development (USAID), Swedish International Development Agency (SIDA), Canadian International Development Agency (CIDA), Overseas Development Administration (ODA), Danish International Development Agency (DANIDA), the Norwegian Agency for Development (NORAD), Finnish International Development Agency (FINIDA), Center for International Private Enterprise (CIPE) and the Free Trade Union Institute (FTUI).

While these established institutions were being pressed into the business of promoting democracy to meet urgent demands, some new institutions were gradually being created. These may well be more effective because they are designed specifically to deal with the new challenges. One of these new institutions is Britain's newly established Westminster Foundation for Democracy which is very similar to the National Endowment for Democracy. The United Nations has recently created an Electoral Assistance Unit in its Secretariat to render assistance in the preparation, conduct and monitoring of elections. Another major institution for the promotion of democracy came into being on February 27, 1995 in Stockholm. Named the International Institute for Democracy and Electoral Assistance (IIDEA), this new body is sponsored by a consortium of 14 countries, namely, Australia, Barbados, Chile, Costa Rica, Denmark, Finland, India, The Netherlands, Norway, Portugal, South Africa, Spain, and Sweden. According to the agreement establishing it, the objective of the Institute is 'to promote and advance sustainable democracy worldwide', 'to improve and consolidate democratic electoral processes worldwide' and 'to provide a meeting-place for exchange between all those involved in electoral processes in the context of democratic institution-building' (*IIEDA Newsletter* March 1995).

By grants, training, conferences, technical assistance and special programmes these organisations support political parties, democracy and human rights activist organisations, judicial reform, empowerment projects, civil society enhancement activities, administrative reform, community survival projects, policy dialogue, the conduct and the monitoring of elections and many more.

These organisations have made useful interventions regarding the democratization of Africa. Notable in this respect is the support of the National Endowment for Democracy (NED) to the Civil Liberties Organization, which has been at the forefront of the struggle for human rights and democracy in Nigeria. Also notable is NED's support of Group d'Etudes et de Recherches sur la Démocratie et le Développement Economique et Social (GERDDES), which is concerned with strengthening democracy through, training, dialogue, research and education. NDI and IRI have made notable contributions in the area of elections. IRI has been involved in the training of political party officials and election monitors and has been involved in organizing and monitory elections, notably in Kenya and Angola. NDI's election training and monitoring assistance is acknowledged all round to have made a considerable contribution to the successful elections in Bénin, Zambia and Namibia. The Friedrich Ebert Foundation, Friedrich Naumann Foundation and the Hans Seidel Stiftungen as well as the Konrad Adenauer Foundation have been carrying out similar support programmes with levels of funding and success that match the American organizations.

Most of these support programmes have consisted of ad-hoc interventions, and short-term projects, which though successful in their immediate objective raise questions about sustainable development. But there are some long-term support projects. For instance, in 1992 USAID launched a three-year programme of $5 million to support democratic transition in Ethiopia. This money was to support, among other things, the election commission, the constitutional commission, the development of an independent press and the ministry of justice. But it is not clear that this programme has been successful. The Election Commission, which was the biggest beneficiary from the grant, failed to conduct a free and fair election. USAID has a similar long-time project for the support of democratization in Zambia. This programme was funded to the tune of $15 million and was to last for five years. The elements of this project include support of the constitutional commission, an institute to train journalists and to develop the mass media, and improve the administrative and professional support for the Zambian National Assembly.

Perhaps the most successful of the long-term projects for supporting the development of democracy was the USAID programme launched after the Comprehensive Anti-Apartheid Act of 1985 which was passed over the veto of President Ronald Reagan. Arising from this Act, USAID was instructed to help the victims of Apartheid to end it. This was to be achieved by developing civil society through support of NGOs, training, education, legal assistance and through community-based organisations, the 'civics'.

This programme played a major role in giving South Africa a vibrant civil society which was significant for the struggle to end Apartheid. Some of the NGOs which the programme supported, especially the Institute for Democratic South Africa (IDASA), played a major role in bringing about a democratic, nonracial South Africa.

Reflecting the Western view of the content of democracy in Africa, the Western support programmes are heavily concentrated on elections and related issues. It is not clear why the United States appears so fixated on elections, but here is one possible explanation:

> American policy-makers have long regarded the holding of 'free and fair' multiparty elections as the litmus test of democratic transitions. According to this view, a respect for human rights, the establishment of the rule of law, a vibrant civil society, a free press, and increased transparency and accountability of government, etc., all critical ingredients of any democracy; are not as important as the opportunity of the governed to choose between alternative groups of leaders to serve as their rulers. As a result, initial American efforts to promote democratic transitions consisted mainly of support for transitional elections (Barkan 1994:6).

It is not Americans alone who see democratization primarily in terms of multi-party elections. All its Western allies do to varying degrees. This may reflect the problems of democracy in the West, the Cold War legacy of defining the main threat to democracy as the communist institution of a single-party system, the fact that electoral competition makes democracy much more visible than accountability, the rule of law, the balance of power, transparency and so on. Whatever the reason for the emphasis on multi-party elections, it is misleading and threatening to the process of democratization in Africa because it trivializes democracy much more in African conditions than it does in the 'established democracies', and following this notion of democratization may lead to the democratization of disempowerment in Africa.

Even in the best of circumstances, it is easy enough for people to be voting without choosing. For instance, approximately 85 per cent of the Congressional Districts in the United States are effectively one-party districts (Barkan 1994:6). Choice mainly applies at the primaries, that is in intra-party competition; at the level of inter-party competition, the contest is predetermined. Multi-partism offers even less choice in Africa because of oligopolistic tendencies, the abuse of the powers of incumbency, the poverty and ignorance of the electorate.

To illustrate, in the Kenya election held in December 1992, President Moi manipulated the electoral rules and the delimitation of constituencies in such as a way that he was able to win the Presidency with only 33.3 per cent of the votes, and that is not taking account of other irregularities such as making 44 constituencies inaccessible to the opposition. In the National

Assembly elections, the opposition got nearly 70 per cent of the votes but only 86 of the 200 National Assembly seats. By all indications, voting without choosing is the rule rather than the exception in Africa.

Difficult Assumptions

The emphasis on multi-party elections is not the only problem associated with Western support for democracy in Africa. There are many others. In the following pages, some of them will be discussed briefly.

Homology of Economic and Political Liberalization

The assumption that economic liberalization and democratization go hand in hand in African conditions and that the cause of democracy in Africa is best served by supporting economic liberalization in the form of structural adjustment is a problem. The policies of the Bretton Woods institutions and Western governments towards Africa tend to make these assumptions. This is surprising because one of the interesting aspects of the South East Asian countries, which has elicited considerable interest from the West, precisely questions this assumption.

The experience of China is a case in point. China is arguably the quintessential East Asian miracle with a population of 1.2 billion (in 1994) and annual GNP growth rate of 9.4 per cent between 1979 and 1989, 11.4 per cent between 1982 and 1988 and a surge to 12 per cent in 1992. China achieved its high growth rate partly by economic liberalization reflecting the change of leadership from Mao Tse Tung to Deng. But while embracing economic liberalization, China resisted political liberalization, a resistance which came to be epitomized in the Tiananmen Square drama of 1989. The rest of the successful East Asian countries were also highly authoritarian 'developmental states' like China. They were able to fuel growth with liberalization combined with well-conceived and well-targeted intervention while maintaining an authoritarian political framework.

A great deal is made nowadays of the democratization of the East Asian Newly Industrializing Countries (NICs). Their democratization is presumed by some to show that economic liberalization goes hand in hand with democratization. Others see it as vindication of the Lipset thesis that economic growth is positively correlated to democratization. However, the pressure for democratization and the achievement of considerable democratization in the NICs, especially South Korea, does not say anything about a necessary connection between economic liberalization and democratization for the simple reason that similar pressures have led to democratization in other places which were not economically liberalized, for instance, the democratizing countries in Africa.

In the case of Africa, the pressure for democratization preceded SAPs and economic liberalization, although these events did lend it new impetus. Africans wanted a 'second independence' from a political leadership whose mismanagement of public affairs was spreading and entrenching underdevelopment. They had convinced themselves that their lot could not improve without their empowerment. In the Soviet Union and the Communist bloc, the struggle for democracy was caused by decades of political oppression increasingly associated with escalating poverty. It has led to economic liberalization, but this is mainly because of the logic of the Cold War and the way it had structured the world. It could quite easily have led to social democracy.

The Lipset argument, first fully developed in *Political Man* and carried through a series of books and essays, is really beside the point of this debate, for what Lipset and his disciples are saying is that the wealthier a country gets, the more democratic it is likely to be. Presumably a country can be wealthy without being economically liberal, as the NICs' experience suggests.

It may well be that the Lipset thesis implicitly assumes that a highly economically developed or wealthy country would also be a capitalist economy, and it may be that the thesis conflates democracy with liberal democracy. In that case, since the values of the market economy are the same as those of liberal democracy, the thesis may look like a circular argument. It is difficult to do justice to the Lipset thesis in this context.

The Opposition of State to Civil Society

Orthodox thinking on democratization in Africa tends to posit opposition between the state and civil society and the need to strengthen civil society against the state through privatisation and the development of associational life. Because of these presuppositions, the process of democratization in Africa has been linked with the survival strategies which the African crisis has engendered. It has been repeatedly said that the crisis has led to tremendous vitality at the grassroots where the people are organizing themselves to limit their vulnerability to a predatory state, to improvise through community effort rudimentary social welfare networks and to improve their material well-being. This thriving of associational life, this turning away from the state and establishing a local space of some self-government, has been seen as a significant element of democratization.

However, the democratic potential of these developments at the grassroots is limited, as the case of Kenya indicates. Kenya is one of the African countries in which rural grassroots organisations are most developed;

it is also one of the places where they have had immense success in grassroots economic development. And yet Kenya is anything but democratic. These grassroots organisations do not appear to represent, as of now, any substantial pluralization of centres of power, and they have not diminished the state's arbitrary and coercive powers.

Part of the problem is that they are isolated and are not usually aggregated at higher organizational levels where they may have some potential for influencing policy. With few exceptions, such as Senegal, grassroots organisations in Africa are not yet contributing much to democracy. In fact, they are not, in their political effects, so different from the local government systems which African governments have been setting up to make government cheaper and to deflect participative pressures. That is the kind of reform that Rawlings made in Ghana under the pretext of democratization. People are given some local political space, not to integrate them into a democratic polity but to separate them from participation; the granting of local space is not a liberty but a constraint. It signifies the confinement of local people and their disenfranchisement. This is clear from the fact that initiatives and directives flow from the central to the local government in what is strictly a one-way traffic.

Democratization as Destatization

A related confusion about the process of democratization in Africa is beginning to emerge. This is the view that democratization entails destatization. This view is finding fertile ground in the North, particularly in International Financial Institutions (IFIs) because it ties in with the liberal commitment to the primacy of the market (over the state) and the notion that democracy is associated with minimal government. Having now agreed, as suggested in the World Bank's blueprint on Africa, *Sub-Saharan Africa: From Crisis to Sustainable Growth*, that quality of governance can be a serious obstacle to development, the Bretton Woods institutions want to improve governance performance, especially the element of accountability, transparency and predictability. They are also concerned about the interventionism of government in economic life, interventionism which is often counter-productive. They see the necessity to reduce the role of the state, its expenditures, powers and controls. Sometimes the reduction of the role of the state is seen as an element of democratization, because it gives civil society, the market and individuals more scope. In the context of SAP politics, aspects of democratization have been debated in terms of the dialectics of the state and the market.

The coercive monolithism of most African political systems readily gives the impression of strong states with immense penetrative capacity, a state which is everywhere and doing everything. For all that, African states are actually very weak in that they have very limited penetrative and interventionist capacity. In Nigeria, for instance, the state has very little reach into the lives of the rural people. Much of the development that has taken place in rural communities occurred not because of the state but in spite of it. To many rural dwellers, the state is mainly a nuisance to be taken account of in their struggle for survival. In most other countries, the situation is worse. In Zaire, for instance, President Mobutu does not effectively control more than 15 per cent of Zairian territory. The state delivers so little service, it is all but irrelevant to the citizens except when they encounter it as a predatory force on the rampage.

It is the violent arbitrariness of states like Zaire that makes them seem so powerful.

By contrast, in the Western countries such as the United States, the state is very strong. It penetrates the lives of its citizens far more deeply partly because pervasive commoditization has created a society which is relatively homogeneous, interdependent and cohesive. And more amenable to control. The quintessential development of bureaucratic organisation backed by modern science and technology has given the state extraordinary powers of intervention, penetration and control, and the state may well be in danger of becoming what Foucault would call a threatening panoptic project. But the threat is hardly perceived. What is perceived is a benign aloofness suggested by lawful use of state-power and, more important, by the virtual automation of control and conformity. Democracy is not and cannot be a matter of weakening the state.

Conclusion

To recapitulate, the international environment has become more positive for democratization in Africa in the following sense: Issues of democratization are increasingly dominating the world's interest in Africa, breaking a legacy of indifference to the prospects of democracy. The West, seeing in the revolution in Eastern Europe the possibility of universalizing its values, particularly liberal democracy, has included the promotion of democracy as a condition for economic cooperation and assistance to African countries. This intervention for democracy in Africa will lead to economic sanctions against the more notorious African autocrats, and that will be some help to the democratic forces struggling in Africa. Even more helpful is the admission that democracy is applicable to Africa and the falling out of fashion of support for autocrats.

But Africa is so marginal now that it is very difficult for non-Africans, especially the North, to bring themselves to care about what happens in Africa, including democratization, especially when such interest entails some cost. The North says it cares about the democratization of Africa but, it would appear, not nearly enough. Clearly, it is more interested in economic policy reform and better governance performance rather than democracy, and it is promoting structural adjustment, in ways that tend to reinforce political authoritarianism. And some countries in the North continued to collude, often profitably, in making arms available to African governments, arms which are used for repression rather than defence and which facilitate the violent implosions that have immensely compounded Africa's problems. To the extent that the North is interested in democracy, it promotes a kind of democracy whose relevance to Africa is problematic.

Still, on balance, the international environment is more favourable to democratization than it was during the Cold War. At least everyone agrees now on the desirability, if not the necessity of democratization. However limited the international support for democratization, whatever its contradictions, it exists and it is helping to sustain democracy firmly on the African and global agenda.

Part Three

The Internal Situation

The prospects of democratization in Africa depend less on the international environment than on internal conditions. On balance these prospects are good because in the internal situation, the obstacles in the way of democratization are getting weaker, although they are still very strong; democratic forces are getting stronger but they are still quite fragile.

One of the underlying causes of this change is the vanishing legitimacy of the African political class and its international partners. The now familiar statistics of collapsing infrastructures, rising debt burdens, declining investment, exacerbated balance of payments problems, growing malnutrition, falling real wages and negative growth rates underline the failures of the African political class. These are not leadership and management failures in any ordinary sense. They are failures which have brought with them untold suffering, deep despair, malnutrition and, in some cases, premature death. All this has brought into clear relief the problem of the legitimacy of those in power. For most countries in Africa, the question is no longer how the performance of the political class might improve but how to do away with them or disconnect from them in some sort of exit option.

The standing of the political elite suffers not only from evident management failure but also from its appearance of neither knowing what to do about the mounting crisis nor being in control of events. It appears exhausted, defeated and bewildered, and it has ceded initiative to the international development community, which has also been beaten by 'the African problem', although it manages to keep up the appearance of self-assurance through ideological dogmatism.

The African political elite has been further weakened by the sheer visibility of its lack of control, its poverty of ideas and its humiliation. Everyone can see the tragic consequences of a grossly mismanaged economy, and everyone can see that those responsible for it do not know how to make amends. Every one can see how agents of the IFIs take over highly significant functions of government, approving tariff regimes, decreeing the level of social services, deciding on subsidies, privatisation, issues of trade, wage levels, the locations of industry, the choice of consultants for government projects and so on.

In some countries poorly paid policeoffcers are out of control, and openly extort money from citizens. Poorly paid soldiers have become bandits sealing off isolated country roads and mounting illegal checkpoints to extort money. As if it is not enough to cede control of the economy to foreigners and to lose control of its armed forces to indiscipline, Africa's ruling elites are also losing control of their cities to collapsing infrastructures, and their countryside to unserviceable roads and the encroachment of the forest. The evident helplessness and humiliation of African leaders has emboldened people to defiance.

The weakness of the ruling elite reflects and compounds the weakness of the state. All but a few African states are in deep fiscal crisis and indebted well beyond their capacity to pay. As they struggle with bankruptcy, these states are less able to buy support, dispense patronage and marshal and deploy coercive resources or inspire confidence. The weaknesses are compounded by a decreasing level of international economic support. For the most part, they are getting lower levels of technical assistance, foreign aid and investment.

The structural adjustment programmes which African countries have been obliged to adopt are compounding the weakness of the state in Africa with their one-sided emphasis on privatisation, destatization and reliance on market forces. These problems are usually so drastic and so severe in their impact that they engender hostility to the state and undermine its limited legitimacy. In some cases, as in Zambia, Gabon and Nigeria, they have led to popular insurrections against the state.

Finally, the rigours of the African crisis have forced the masses in Africa to turn away from states which seem helpless in the face of a persistent and deepening crisis, states whose ability to maintain social services and infrastructures is visibly declining or nonexistent. For the most part, people are turning to community organisations and special interest groups and self-help projects to survive and to arrest the erosion of social services and the collapse of social infrastructures.

[...] By 1989 authoritarian regimes were, being challenged all over Africa, and popular demonstrations for political liberalization and democracy were commonplace.

By 1990 there was no doubt that a watershed in the democratization had been reached. In that year alone there were popular uprisings in 14 countries for liberalization and democracy. In the Ivory Coast, demonstrations in February and May 1990 demanded a multi-party system. In Zaire, an innocuous forum for political dialogue, which Mobutu had allowed as a way of defusing political frustration, criticized him and his government vehemently. By May there were violent demonstrations for a multi-party system.

In Zambia, riots broke out as people demanded an end to one-party rule, prompting the government to promise a referendum on the issue. In August 1990, the Mozambique government was obliged to promise multi-party elections in 1991; Angola had been obliged to accede to a similar demand under pressure in June. In Kenya riots also occurred in June in protest against one-party rule and President Arap Moi's disregard of the rule of law. In July, Kenya endured four days of rioting following the arrest of two prominent opposition figures, Matiba and Rubia. When Yondo Black, the former head of the Cameroon Bar, was arrested for allegedly forming an opposition party in February 1990, people began to agitate openly for a multi-party election.

The majority of African leaders initially tried to ignore these pressures or to contain them by minimal reforms by which they hoped to deradicalize the democracy movement. The reforms usually entailed changing the style of the prevailing dictatorship but not its substance, or changing the form of the ruling party to make it look more inclusive or amenable to internal democracy. Among others were Moi's commission on the reform of the ruling party, the Kenya African National Union; Eyadéma's restructuring of the ruling party in Togo in January 1990; Rawlings' decentralization reform in Ghana; the resignation of Mobutu as head of the ruling Movement of the Revolution (MPR) and the revocation of the ban on opposition political parties in April 1990; the abandonment of the doctrine of the supremacy of the ruling party in Benin, in December 1989 and in the Congo in July 1990. But such measures failed to contain the surge of the demand for democratization.

Invariably the demands intensified and African leaders were forced to go beyond token gestures to more substantial reform. In Benin Republic, President Kérékou who had hoped to contain the democracy movement lost control after initiating the 'National Conference of the Active Forces' and eventually lost his presidency. In the Ivory Coast, Houphouët Boigny, who had hoped to deal with the demand for pluralism with cosmetic changes, was eventually obliged to accede to a multi-party system and to fight elections, much to his distaste. President Kaunda of Zambia, who had opposed multi-partism adamantly, was obliged to accept it and to fight an election in which he was soundly beaten. In Zimbabwe, President Robert Mugabe was obliged to end the state of emergency in force since independence and to release political prisoners. He found that even his own party, ZANU-PF did not support his bid to change Zimbabwe into a one-party state, and in September 1990 he set aside his plans to that effect.

One of the most remarkable steps in the movement towards democracy was taken by Mozambique where a highly destructive civil war had raged for over 16 years between the political formation in power, the Mozambique Liberation Front (Frelimo) and its challenger, the Mozambique National Resistance (Renamo). A peace process initiated by the 1992 Rome Accords culminated in a national election conducted between October 27, and 29 1994. The election which was keenly watched by 7,000 United Nations peace-keepers and 2,400 election observers, was taken very seriously by Mozambicans who seemed anxious to utilize the rare opportunity to vote. According to the National Election Commission, over 90 per cent of the estimated 6.4 million voters voted, despite 75 per cent illiteracy and the complications of 14 parties on the ballot. The election was by all accounts one of the most orderly and peaceful elections in Africa. It returned Chissano's Frelimo to power with over 50 per cent of the vote, while Renamo, led by Afonso Dhlakama, got 30 per cent. Dhlakama threatened to reject the election results in the way that Savimbi had done in Angola, but he came under heavy pressure from Western governments as well as South Africa and Zimbabwe and relented, deciding to cooperate for democratic stability in Mozambique (*Africa Report 1994*, 39 (6), Nov.).

In March 1990, Madagascar legalized a multi-party system. Niger Republic did the same in July 1990. Following popular protests, one of Africa's longest-serving autocrats, President Traore of Mali, was forced out of office in March 1990 after 24 years. There are holdouts, of course: General Abacha in Nigeria relying on force, Mobutu of Zaire hoping to survive by the use of force and the manipulation of social pluralism, Biya of Cameroon and Eyadéma of Togo trying to maintain power through a spurious legitimacy of rigged elections. But they are swimming against a tide which is very strong and getting stronger.

In what must be the critical threshold of democratization, between January 1990 and December 1991, 26 additional African countries adopted the multi-party system. Between 1990 and 1993, 22 countries held multi-party elections.

The situation at the end of 1989, when 35 of the 45 countries in Africa were under military and single-party rule and the rest under personal rule or limited pluralism, has been completely reversed. Discounting the countries in civil war, there are no legal single-party systems and there are only two military regimes.

However, one should be careful not to read too much into this. It is well to remember that there are really two intertwined democracy movements in Africa. One is the popular movement which is concerned with a 'second independence' from the African elite. It is about empowerment to avoid political oppression and to promote economic well-being, and it is more concerned with concrete rights and the social upliftment of the poor and the culturally deprived. For the peasants and urban masses of Africa, human rights and multi-party elections do not offer very much. While their human rights may be legally guaranteed, oppressive poverty allows them no sense of efficacy or the means to realize their rights; they may chose among parties and candidates but there is no choice in ignorance; they are free to take part in politics, but their daily struggle for survival is so totally absorbing that this is no more than a theoretical possibility.

The popular democracy movement has been subsumed by an elite movement which is more visible and more articulate. It is supported by the political class, especially those out of power. It seeks a liberal democracy reduced to electoral competition. As we have already seen, the political class in Africa tends to use democracy as a strategy of power. One of the notable developments of democratization in Africa recently is that leaders who oppose democracy have found that it is not so threatening after all and that it could be exploited to legitimate and to prolong their stay in power by staging elections which they could control. Arap Moi of Kenya, Paul Biya of Cameroon, Jerry Rawlings of Ghana, Blaise Compaoré of Burkina Faso and Eyadéma of Togo among others have taken this option. More will take it now that it is clear that it is low-risk if taken in time and perfectly acceptable by the standards of democratic conditionality.

Multi-party elections may be an inevitable start for the democratization of Africa. But it does not get the process of democratization very far in African conditions. What will a more substantive democratization of Africa entail? Is it feasible?

Part Four

Necessary Transformations to Feasibility

State Transformation: Towards a Democratic State

The democratization of Africa requires social transformations to ensure that it does not lose its emancipatory character. For now, democratization coexists with political repression and even reinforces it. What it will take to democratize Africa is not so much democratization as a democratic revolution. What it will take is not calling into being democratic processes but pulling away certain well-embedded social and political structures and replacing them with entirely new ones.

In Africa democratization has to be about the transformation of the state before it can be about the introduction of new political processes. But what specifically is the problem of the state in Africa? Why is its present constitution inimical to democracy? Systematic treatment of this question will take us too far afield; we will deal very briefly with some aspects of it merely by way of illustration. Put simply, the problem is that the typical post-colonial state in Africa is perhaps even more than its colonial predecessor literally an instrument of oppression.

If Africa settles for democratization as multi-party electoral competition, as it is in danger of doing, then there will be no democracy despite elections, because elections will be a choice between oppressors. A state constituted as an autocracy will be undemocratic no matter who is running it. An interesting commentary on the status of democratization in Africa is that the political class, both those in power and those out of power and demanding democratization, seem to have no interest even now in transforming the autocratic postcolonial state. Those in power are quite happy to leave the state as it is, because they exercise its powers; those in opposition worry about being victims of this power, but this is mediated by their hope of capturing it, and they are all the more focused on control now that democratization is in the air, holding out prospects of a chance to compete for what they see as a worthy prize.

That this is so is clear from recent democratic transitions, for example, Burkina Faso, Cameroon, Central African Republic, Ghana, Ivory Coast, Kenya, Nigeria, and Zambia.

In all these instances, even the democratic opposition did not make an issue of the nature of the state including highly authoritarian constitutions. Countries such as Kenya, Cameroon, Zambia and Ivory Coast, which moved from single-party systems to multi-party electoral systems, did so with constitutions which maintained or reproduced the state structure and the authoritarianism of the single-party system. Countries such as Nigeria, Burkina Faso and Ghana, which made the transition from military rule, did so with constitutions which reproduced the concentration of power and the command structure of military regimes.

This phenomenon can be seen in clear relief in the Nigerian experience of democratic transitions. On October 1, 1975, Murtala Mohammed, Nigeria's military head of state, announced a five-point programme for the return of Nigeria to civil rule after 9 years of military rule. He set up a constitution drafting committee (CDC) of 51 persons drawn from academic, military and business backgrounds some of them, like Rotimi Williams, Yusuf Bala Usman and Segun Osoba, Aminu Kano, Pius Okigbo, Ben Nwabueze and Obi Wali, people who were highly respected and reputedly independent-minded.

The principles which Mohammed laid down for the CDC were interesting in that they gave the members strong encouragement to think democratically. He enjoined commitment to 'a free democratic and lawful system of Government which guarantees fundamental human rights', 'a stable system of Government through Constitutional law', 'public accountability, elimination of 'over-centralization of power in a few hands, and as a matter of principle, decentralize power wherever possible, as a means of defusing tension'. But in one notable note of discord, he urged the committee to 'discourage institutionalized opposition to the Government in power and instead, develop consensus politics and Government based on a community of all interests rather than the interest of sections of the country'. When the report of the CDC was presented on September 14, 1976, it did not generate debate on the structure of the state. Rather public debate was focused on the creation of more states and the desirability of a Federal Sharia Court of Appeal.

On October 6, 1977, a constituent assembly was inaugurated to consider that draft constitution. The constituent assembly was composed of 203 elected members, 20 members appointed to represent professional and special interest, the chairperson of the CDC and the six chairperson of the special committees of the CDC. What emerged from this constitution was an executive President with immense powers. According to Article 122, Section 2, he is the Head of State and the Chief Executive of the Federation as well as the Commander-in-Chief of the Armed Forces of Nigeria. His power as Commander-in-Chief is not merely formal. According to Article 198, Section 1, these powers 'shall include power to determine the operational use of the armed forces of the Federation'. He may attend any meeting of the House of Representatives and or Senate to give an address and make policy statements he considers to be of national importance (Article 63, Section

1). The National Assembly makes laws which the President may veto. But his veto can be overridden by a two-thirds majority.

However, the President's powers as the chief executive and control of the judiciary are so firm that the threat of veto will be invariably decisive. In addition to powers as chief executive over all ministries and parastatals, the President also controls all the federal executive bodies, namely: the Council of State, the Federal Civil Service Commission, the Federal Judicial Service Commission, the National Defence Council, the National Economic Council, the National Population Commission, the National Security Council and the Police Service Commission (Article 140, Section 1). S/he appoints their members and their chairpersons, subject to Senate confirmation or consultation with the Council of State. By his/her powers to appoint the Council of State, the National Defence Council and the National Security Council, he needs no confirmation or consultation. The powers of the President effectively obliterate the separation of powers. The President can control the judiciary through the Judicial Service Commission, and the legislature is too weak to resist the President. Even when it is able to override the presidential veto, the President can easily render the legislation unenforceable.

The Second Republic for which this constitution was written did not last very long. In 1983, it was overthrown by a military coup. On January 13, 1986, the Federal Military Government of Ibrahim Babangida started another elaborate transition to civilian rule by setting up a political bureau to recommend a form of civilian government for Nigeria along with its guiding principles. A constitution review committee was set up in 1987 to review the 1979 Constitution in accordance with the recommendations of the political bureau. In 1988, a constituent assembly was established to deliberate on the draft constitution. The assembly was composed of 450 elected and 111 nominated members. Again what came out of all this elaborate process, with a great deal of civilian input and public debate, was an illiberal constitution which gave the President an inordinate amount of power. This is all the more striking because one of the reasons why the Second Republic broke down was the failure of those who drafted the 1979 Constitution to heed the injunction of Murtala Mohammed to the effect that the constitution should 'eliminate over-centralization of power in a few hands' and avoid cut-throat political competition. The constitution concentrated so much power in the presidency that the struggle for this office could not be anything but intense and prone to lawlessness. And that was precisely what happened.

Despite this experience, the Constitution of 1989 managed to concentrate more powers in the President than the Constitution of 1979 although, it hardly seems possible to do so. Article 128, Section 2, made the President Head of State and Commander-in-Chief of the Armed Forces. He appoints the service chiefs and has operational powers (Article 216); he is chief executive with control over the federal bureaucracy and all federal parastatals. He has enormous powers of appointment and patronage (for instance, Article 169). The powers of the 1979 Constitution are not only reproduced but enhanced. To begin with, the powers of the President are expanded by virtue of the additional executive bodies which he appoints. These are: the National Boundaries Commission, the National Economic Council, the National Primary Education Commission, the Revenue Mobilization Allocation and the Fiscal Commission and the Public Complaints Commission (Third Schedule, Part 1).

The President is also more powerful under the 1989 Constitution, in that it is more difficult to impeach him. In the 1979 Constitution, impeachment was the sole responsibility of the National Assembly. Under the 1989 Constitution, the assembly must now share this responsibility with the judiciary. When the National Assembly passes a motion for impeachment procedure, it is now the Chief Judge rather than the Senate President who appoints the seven-person investigative panel. Also, the new civil service structure gives the President immense powers of patronage and appointment in the bureaucracy. It is remarkable that both the Constitutional Review Committee and the Constituent Assembly freed the President from submitting his/her ministers to Senate confirmation, preferring only consultation. It was actually the Armed Forces Ruling Council which insisted on Senate confirmation.

The concentration of power is compounded by its fusion. This is evident in the crop of constitutions with which Africa is making the transition of democracy of which the Nigerian Constitution is typical. The separation of the executive, judiciary and legislature is nominal. The executive controls the judiciary directly by the control of the Judicial Service Commission, and its powers of appointment role of the legislature, which is supposed to be the repository of the popular will in the polity, is generally devalued. It has no independence. It can make laws, but the law-making function is marginal in a constitution which is oriented less to politics and popular power than to administration; a constitution which is essentially the articulation of the executive function.

The ultimate sanction of an overriding veto which the legislature has is not effective because the President is so powerful that any law which /he or she does not want to enforce is for all practical purposes inoperative; and by controlling the judiciary, the President is an arbiter of what the law is and its proper interpretation. The marginality of African legislatures is reflected in the fact that hardly any importance is attached to legislative elections, as recent cases of Ghana, Kenya, Cameroon, Senegal and Nigeria show. As a rule, in post-colonial Africa, there is only one election for the only office that matters, which is the Presidency.

African politics is decisively shaped by the structure of the power at stake in political competition, especially the concentration and fusion of power in the Presidency. It is this power structure which makes political competition in Africa notoriously intense and prone to lawlessness. Because virtually all power is fused in one office, it becomes inconceivable to lose that office, but even more to the point is the problem that politics becomes a zero-sum game, a condition which put so much premium on power that political competitors are induced to prefer efficiency norms to legitimacy norms. In this sense, the intensity of electoral competition in Africa is a structural problem. It arises from the form and function of the state as the apparatus of virtually arbitrary power. The politics which this structure produces reinforces it. For it is a Hobbesian politics which cannot sustain democratic norms.

The echo of the colonial legacy in all this is striking. In the colonial system, power was concentrated and fused at all levels: the village chief who was the agent of the colonial government at the grassroots, the district officer, the resident and the governor. For instance, at the village level, the chief was everything: he arranged labour supply for colonial officials and settlers, assessed taxes, levied them, collected them, adjudicated cases, imposed sentences and carried them out, among other functions. With minor exceptions, this is the case in post-colonial Africa. In Nigeria, for instance, the power of the President is reproduced at the level of the state with the governor; at the level of the local government with the local government chairperson; and, at the level of most communities, in the chief or traditional ruler.

The form and content of the colonial state has remained reproduced in personal rule, the single-party state and the military regime. It is a form of state which cannot be bent to the service of democracy.

State Transformation: Towards a Liberal State

Since the democracy movement in Africa is currently being stirred in the direction of liberal democracy, what is the feasibility of liberal democracy and by extension the liberal state in African conditions?

To answer this question one must appreciate that the modern liberal state is a historical product of industrial capitalism. Its distinctive characteristic is that the mechanism of political domination is autonomized, which is to say it is relatively independent of all social classes and groups.

Political domination is constituted in this way by virtue of its contextualization in the generalization of commodity production and exchange, that is in a society which is already a market.

Market society is based on a principle of solidarity which is entirely different from those of pre-capitalist societies. Its basis of integration is the nexus of exchange relations. The complementarities and the reciprocities of exchange relations produce and sustain an organic solidarity. Hegel calls this solidarity 'the system of wants'; Marx calls it 'the interdependence of exchange relations'. In a similar vein, Adam Smith argues that bourgeois society epitomizes the development of the unique qualities of human beings, egotism, entrepreneurship and dependence. The paradox of egotism and dependence is resolved in the necessities of commodity production and exchange which the self-seeking of each binds them to all.

This society has its own logic which determines its form of government, administration and political ideology. This is reflected in the fit of capitalist economy and liberal government in Adam Smith. Smith posits that the social order created by the interdependence of commodity production and exchange is the frame of government. The state is formally engendered as a support for the liberties whose dialectics constitute this social order. The basic operational principles of the state is that 'every man as long as he does not violate the laws of justice is left perfectly free to pursue his own way, and to bring both his industry and capital into competition with those of any other man, or other men'. That is the liberal state.

The relation between the liberal state and industrial capitalism can also be seen by considering the presuppositions of generalized commodity production and exchange to see how they encapsulate the values of liberal democracy. First, the commodity bearers in exchange act self-interestedly. They are in the market to realize the exchange value of their commodities and to obtain the commodities they crave. Each is concerned with maximizing utilities and regards others only as a means to that end. However, one becomes a means only because one posits oneself as an end. One becomes a means to underscore one's egotism. Second, the exchange relation is a relation of property owners. If one does not have a commodity which has use value for another one does not participate in exchange, one offers no value and gets none. Third, the commodity bearers in exchange are free. They are free and have to be free in their action; that is, in exchange, they posit themselves as ends in exchange and out of their own free will dispose of their commodities through contractual agreements to which they freely enter. Fourth, commodity bearers are equal. They are equal in their abstraction in the market as exchangers, in the masking of qualitative distinctions behind the formal sameness of buyers and sellers. As they exchange equivalents, each person sees the other as equally worthy. The values of commodity exchange are the organizing values of liberal democracy: individualism, property, freedom and equality.

For the most part, African countries are not yet market societies, mainly because of the limited development of capitalism. Over 60 per cent of the population of Africa is rural, mostly peasants engaged in subsistence farming. Even urban Africa is not necessarily the sphere of capitalism. The real private sector in Africa, in terms of the number of people involved, is the informal sector. It accounts for more than 50 per cent of urban jobs and between 20 and 80 per cent of the labour force in Africa (MacGaffey 1988). The informal sector is not outside the capitalist exchange network (ibid.). It buys the bulk of its raw materials, usually as much as 80 per cent, from the formal sector, it sells services to the formal sector, including cheap goods. Nonetheless it also reinforces the limited penetration of capitalism. It is part of the capitalist system in the sphere of circulation, but only marginally and intermittently so in the sphere of production. It relies on family labour and apprentices, thus combining features of the household economy and the guild system which posits some means of consumption prior to production and so limits the commoditization of labour. There is a long way to go before we can say, taking Africa as a whole, that property has become capital and labour, wage labour, so that for the bulk of the population, the means of subsistence is produced as a commodity.

Because of the limited development of commodity relations in Africa, social atomization is limited as is individualism; consciousness is still considerably communal and interests are not generally perceived as being private and in potential conflict with other interests, which is the raison d'être of liberal law and the juridicalization of persons. Political society in Africa is not sufficiently homogenized to be a 'public' whose existence depends importantly but by no means exclusively on the development of commodity relations to the point of constituting society as a solidarity of exchange relations and giving its members vital common interests such as proprietorship, liberty, freedom and formal equality.

This is important because the constitution of political society as a 'public' is the basis of political participation. Political participation arises because the state is literally a 'res publica' or a 'commonwealth, because its members have common business and mutual interests in the way it is conducted. They are like stock holders in a joint stock company. Those who are not shareholders and have no interest in this collective enterprise cannot have a right to participate.

While the development of the 'public' in Africa is rudimentary, something akin to a public exists at the sub-national level. This public is a homogeneous political community with the peculiarity that its homogeneity derives from kinship and culture. We may call them primordial publics (Ekeh 1975) as opposed to the modern public of market society in which the liberal state is embedded. The uniqueness of the African state is that it has a very rudimentary modern public displaced and retarded by a multiplicity of primordial publics: ethnic, national, communal and sub-national.

These circumstances have produced a structural dualism in contemporary Africa which is problematic for the development of the liberal state. On the one hand, the local community with its primordial public inscribes a corporate political identity. It is here that most people direct their loyalty and energy into collective self-realization by joint enterprises. It is to these local communities that most people turn for security, emotional support and social welfare. In effect, they displace the state and preempt its role.

On the other hand is the rudimentary modern public at the level of the state where the transition from power to authority is proving impossible, right remains largely coextensive with power, and accountability and political participation are lacking. It is peopled by individuals and social groups who are essentially strangers to each other. Their relation rests mainly on an amoral calculus of strength and is characterized by unrelenting struggle for power. They invest nothing in the state and so have no interest in it and no responsibility to it. In most of Africa, the state is a contested terrain where different nationalities, sub-nationalities, 'ethnic groups' and communities go to fight for the appropriation of resources including power. A state which is a contested terrain in this sense can only be an anarchy of self-seeking and a theatre of war. These conditions are difficult for liberal democracy.

To end the entrapment of Africa between these two worlds is a very difficult problem. Ideally it can be solved by a radical transformation in one of two directions. One direction is for the state to become a community that is to be embedded in a modern public. This will require among other things a highly accelerated capitalist development, which does not appear to be on the cards for much of Africa. The other direction is for the community to become the state. This will entail the breakdown of African countries into something like ethnic polities, a process which could be extremely violent and traumatic. One possible compromise could be a confederal, federal or consocietal arrangement. But there are no easy solutions to this formidable problem, which is hardly recognized much less addressed.

Social Transformation of Society

To democratize Africa successfully, it is necessary not only to effect a political transformation of the state but also a social transformation of society, for social conditions in Africa are not conducive to democracy. To begin with, apart from a few countries, such as Tanzania, Botswana, Ethiopia, Mali and Burkina Faso, there is so much inequality that one may speak of a dichotomy of two societies.

One is the country of the elite, usually less than 10 per cent of the population. It is for all practical purposes 'another country' organically linked and oriented to the highly industrialized societies which it resembles. Like them, it enjoys a comparatively high real income, very high living standards and scores very high on social indicators such as life expectancy, infant mortality rates, nutritional level, literacy and educational standards. On such indicators, the score of the African elite would be far higher than the average for the highly industrialized countries, which means adult literacy rates verging on 100, life expectancy of about 76, and incomes in excess of $16,000 per annum and access to health, water and electricity.

In contrast, the rest of society, reflecting average African standards, would have, as of 1990, a life expectancy of 51 years, only 40 per cent access to safe water, 89 per cent of daily calorie requirement, and adult literacy rate of 51 per cent and real GDP per capita of $1,187 (UNDP 1992:135). The distance is much greater still when we allow for urban-rural disparities and for the fact that 69 per cent of Africa's population is rural. Only 36 per cent of this rural population have access to health services of any kind, 28 per cent to safe water and 17 per cent to sanitation (UNDP 1992:147) and, on a rough estimate, rural incomes average only between 20 to 25 per cent of urban incomes.

These socio-economic differences are also a power hierarchy. Even without democracy, the small minority at the top enjoy rights, power and commodious living. But the vast majority at the bottom suffer numerous vulnerabilities which reinforce each other: poor health, lack of education, crushing poverty, limited cultural opportunities, the rigours of the daily struggle for survival at the margins. Even if there were opportunities for democratic participation, these vulnerabilities effectively exclude them.

Mastery of the language of power is a relatively minor aspect of these vulnerabilities, but it is problem enough and is a good illustration of the problems of accessibility of democracy to the poor. The language of the coloniser is required for political competition and to manoeuvre through the minefields of opportunities and constraints for the sharing of meaning and the appropriation of values. It is part of a power hierarchy, at the top of which stands the social group which commands the language of power, leaving the rest of society who have not mastered it not only subordinate but virtually disfranchised. They are disfranchised because they do not belong to the 'interpretative community' (Fish 1980), the community which shares a common understanding of speech markers and the memory of language.

By virtue of being an interpretative community, they are also operating within the same political framework of shared values and meanings about goals, modalities, perception of reality, sense of efficacy and the like. The elite who command the colonial language form the dominant interpretative community to which all others are subordinated.

The problem of subordination is compounded by heterogeneity. In the typically plural societies of Africa, the subordinated stratum is divided by linguistic segmentation into a variety of localized 'interpretative communities' (Heller 1981). This localization of the interpretative communities, that is, their placement in location-specific linguistic paradigms of the grammar of politics, isolates these communities and renders them uncompetitive and manipulable, especially when they coincide with a territorial locale. The national language which is ostensibly a major instrument of political integration does not integrate, but rather facilitates dispersion, isolation and domination (Clark and Dear 1984).

The grammar of politics, which is central to the solidarity and identity of the political community, is an instrument of inclusion and unity as well as that of exclusion and disunity. Those in the community who speak the same grammar share a cognitive map. The political linguistic paradigm is also a Weltanschauung. It defines political experience, for the experience of the political is often much less of events than the language about events. The grammar of politics speaks not to objectivity but to commitment. The terms and meanings of this grammar commit us to a view of how the world is, how it ought to be and how it might be. It discounts the possibility of certain kinds of experience and allows others. It values, devalorizes, denies, prioritizes. It prescribes norms style, morality, rewards and punishment.

By its insistent commitment, the grammar of politics homogenizes its adherents. People get socialized or talked into accepting the world as the grammar represents it. Even when they want to dissent, it is very difficult to sustain dissent against the tide of the linguistic paradigm. To attain status, and to appropriate values, including power, one needs to speak the language of politics. Those who cannot or will not are not only likely to fail to appropriate values, they are likely to face severe penalties. The millions of people in Africa who do not speak the language of power suffer these disadvantages. The mere introduction of multi-party electoral competition will not help them very much.

The African who is slated for democracy is typically a rural dweller who lives in a society that is still predominantly communal. She is a subsistence farmer, absorbed in toiling to eke out a precarious existence. She has virtually no access to safe drinking water, health services and sanitary facilities and she is illiterate or only marginally literate. What does democratization mean in this setting and for this person? As we have already seen, what is on offer by way of democratization is multi-party elections. But where does this peasant come into this? The answer to the question seems quite obvious. Democratic elections finally give the peasant the opportunity to choose who will govern her or even to seek a mandate to govern; they give her the opportunity of making power accountable to those over whom it is exercised and to bring public policy into greater harmony with social needs.

However, this is more apparent than real. There is no chance that this peasant will be running for office. There is no chance at all that her vote is going to make power accountable to her. Her act of voting means very little as exercise of choice. More important still, what she is confronted with as options at the point of voting is framed by forces which are beyond her control in ways that are beyond her understanding and hardly relevant to her needs.

For the political elite who are the effective competitors for power, she is only part of a gesture. They are set on gaining power with her cooperation if possible and without it if necessary. What democratic elections really mean for her is that she is set up to be hunted down, captured and harnessed in the interest of someone else, a veritable ordeal. To be sure, this ordeal may be sweetened by allurements, material inducements which underline the contempt and devalorization of the voter. If the allurement is token, the ordeal of harassment is real. She has to be mobilized, herded through voter's registration, placed in protective custody, so she is unavailable to the other hunters looking for her, and produced to demonstrate the candidate's popular standing and finally guided through voting before being discarded. Her being sought after is not a mark of democratic incorporation but rather alienation; it is not a mark of power, but one of powerlessness, and her relevance is a gesture.

The processes by which she is mobilized express and reinforce her disempowerment. She is not mobilized in the market place of formally equal legal subjects who are negotiating their interests and finding common ground. The mobilisation is done through patron-client chains, leveraging parochial identities, corruption and intimidation. In the case of patron-client chain, the patrons treat the community as their turf and they keep it so by manipulation, inspiring awe or admiration, by reward and punishment. Mobilization of the community for elections is really a matter of these local notables delivering their people. Indeed, the political parties being formed in the surge for democratization are invariably networks of these notables.

A famous example of this phenomenon is the role of the religious brotherhoods in rural Senegal. The ruling party of Senegal, the Parti Socialiste, remains in power mainly because it is able to count on the 'support' of the rural population. This support is gained through the religious brotherhoods who control much of the rural population spiritually and materially, and are thus able to instruct them on how to vote through a system of voting instructions called 'Ndigel'.

In return for delivering the rural people, the Parti Socialiste government gives the marabout very lavish patronage, including huge credit on very easy terms. The marabouts in turn use some of the financial resources to tighten their control of the rural population, especially by giving credit to peanut farmers. There has been a great deal of criticism against this political use of religion, especially by the radical parties, such as the Ligue Democratique (LD), the Rassemblement Nationale Démocratique (RNP) and the And Jeff/ Parti Africain pour la Démocracie et le Socialisme (AJ/PADS).

For the election of February 21, 1993, the principal leaders of the Tijaan, Mouride and Layeen brotherhoods refrained from issuing voting instructions. But this did not really change the situation because it came in the wake of the growth of brotherhoods and intense competition among them for followers, patronage and influence. In the heat of the competition, some of the marabouts retreated into religion but others, 'the worldly marabouts', delved even more aggressively into using religion to exploit rural people for political power and economic resources (Diouf 1993:5).

All these techniques of popular mobilization underscore a serious limitation of democratization in Africa. In this context the act of voting becomes misleading. For what is happening on that occasion is no longer the practice of democracy but the exploitation of ordinary people for profit. The use of religious authority by the marabout expresses the manipulability of the people and also reinforces it, turning the democratic process into a reaffirmation of a social relation which is the very negation of democracy.

The case of bribing rural people to take voting instructions is much the same thing. The offering of the bribe for the vote is an act of contempt for the voting. It reflects the liberties which the elite take by virtue of being dominant. That some of the voters condone such contemptuous treatment is a reflection of their sense of self-worth and their domination. In the offer and acceptance of bribes which commoditize their democratic rights, they reproduce their low self-esteem and their subordination, thus turning election into bondage.

The case of ethnic appeal is equally regressive, reflecting their manipulability as well as reinforcing it. This mode of mobilisation has its own special problem. In responding to the ethnic appeal, the voters are frozen in a moment of particularity that effectively cancels the prospect of sharing in the universality, at any rate, the synthesis of universality and particularity which is the whole meaning of democratic participation and consensus-building. They are left one-sided, stunted, undeveloped, as they remain confined to their small parochial space, and in their entrapment pay for the realization of the ambitions of the elite for whom their ethnicization is just one strategy of power.

Clearly, in African conditions, democratization cannot be limited to multi-party elections. It has to address these vulnerabilities of the ordinary people who are unable to participate effectively in a democratic dispensation. By all indications, these vulnerabilities can only be addressed by social transformation, by massive social, cultural and economic upliftment of the poor in Africa. Without this there is no democracy.

If that is the case, should Africa be democratizing given its level of poverty? Or should it be seeking development? There is a school of thought which argues that the quest for democracy is futile given Africa's level of poverty, that the continent is better served by concentrating on development, at any rate, the eradication of poverty. This is a rather influential point of view. To all appearances there is considerable support for this point of view in the industrialized countries and the international development agencies, especially the Bretton Woods institutions. For this is the implication of the tendency to give economic reform a higher priority than democratization. The concerns of some Western countries, development agencies and the Bretton Woods institutions are not so much about democracy as they are about better governance performance. And better governance performance is operationalized as transparency, predictability, minimizing corruption and accountability (in the book-keeping sense, not in the sense of popular sovereignty).

Democracy entails good governance performance, but good governance performance does not entail democracy. On the contrary, as the experience of many countries, especially the East Asian countries, has shown, good governance is perfectly compatible with political authoritarianism. In the end, the point of interest in better governance performance is not democratic politics but economic development. Good governance supplies the political and administrative correlates for the operationalization of the law of value. The clear implication is that economic development has priority over democratization.

While it is the case that economic development is necessary for making democracy feasible, it is mistaken to conclude that attention has to shift from democratization and focus on this enabling condition. This mistake arises from easy assumptions about the causes of the crisis of underdevelopment in Africa and the relation of the economic to the political. What has become increasingly clear is that it is political conditions in Africa that have intensified underdevelopment. This was precisely why the West, the international development agencies and the Bretton Woods institutions started to question their traditional developmental apoliticism and to recognize the importance of addressing the political conditions of development.

Since this change was signalled by the World Bank's Long Term Perspective Study, *Sub-Saharan Africa: From Crisis to Sustainable Growth*, published in 1989, it has become conventional wisdom. The need for accelerated economic development in Africa calls for emphasis on creating enabling political conditions.

The view that Africa needs to seek economic development rather than democratization is now abstract and irrelevant in the light of the salient realities currently on the ground in Africa. One of these is that, as we have seen, the people of Africa are demanding development now and also demanding more determinedly still, democracy now. They see that both things are linked and they think that it is essential to have both now. And they are right. But even if it is granted that they need both now, can they have both and how can that be?

The conventional wisdom is to give more economic aid to democratizing countries to ensure that democratization is not defeated by the rigours of poverty and the systemic stress of economic austerity. However, this idea of buying democracy with economic aid is a non-solution. Nobody is going to give Africa enough aid to buy democracy, and democracy cannot be bought. It has to be won in struggle in a world in which people do not voluntarily give up power or treat the economic and political aspects of their lives as discrete entities.

The way to have both economic development and democratization simultaneously is to collapse both processes into one by making economic development itself a process of democratization. Economic development becomes a process of democratization by being incremental empowerment and upliftment of ordinary people. There is nothing fanciful about this because this is what development is and how it should have been conceived in the first place. Because it was not so conceived in Africa, it has faltered.

Also the dichotomy between democratization and economic development arises only because economic development had been misconceived and perverted to an exercise in alienation rather than an emancipatory experience and hence a democratic project. Development is a process of self-realization, and it is so only in so far as the people are the means and the end of development. The self-development of ordinary people is democratization at its most concrete and most profound.

The Social Transformation of Democracy

The feasibility of democracy in Africa requires yet another kind of transformation. This is the social transformation of democracy itself. One of the constraints on democratization in Africa is that the process is not taking much cognizance of the historicity of democracy and the uniqueness of Africa. This problem has arisen because there has been relatively little appreciation of the need to distinguish between the values and the principles of democracy from particular historical practices of democracy. Instead of making this necessary distinction, we have taken to conflating the historical democratic practices in the 'established democracies' with democracy. There are grave risks in approaching democratization in Africa with this frame of mind, as we are apparently inclined to do. In all probability, it will lead to distortions which will bear importantly in a negative sense on the feasibility of democracy in Africa. There is no alternative to recreating democracy anew in every historical instance. This is what all the 'established democracies' had to do, and it is what Africa has to do if it is to have a chance at democratization.

In Africa as in Europe, there can be no question of stopping at continental specificity. The marrying of democratic values and principles to social realities has to go down to country and even regional and community specificities too, for Africa is a continent of immense diversity. In what follows we discuss some of the peculiarities of contemporary Africa and try to explore in a and preliminary way how they may affect the customization of democracy to African conditions. The peculiarities we speak of are some commonalities or broad tendencies of traditional African social and political formations. 'Traditional' is used advisedly here. Africa is a blend, sometimes a confusion, of the traditional and the modern. There is nothing in Africa which can be described with any accuracy simply as traditional, any more than there is anything that can be called modern; the things to which we attach such nomenclature are ideal characteristics at different stages of transition.

Africa is not a *tabula rasa* waiting to soak up modernity. There are realities on the ground, even though it is not always clear what they are. It may be elements of a fractured traditionality, institutions and values at different stages of decay, transformation or even reconstitution, hybrid forms or new totalities. Whatever they are, the incursion of modernity whether in the way of development or democratization generally meets resistance, sometimes weak, more often fierce. As they clash, the intruding modernity may be expelled, distorted or transformed; the traditional with which it articulates may disintegrate, adapt or reconstitute itself in any number of ways. It is useful to explore briefly some points of divergence and conflict between democracy, especially the liberal democracy which is on offer, and traditional

African institutions, values and practices and also to consider how the values and principles of democracy might be creatively operationalized in the African context rather than crudely reproducing, to the detriment of democracy in Africa, an irrelevant historical practice of democracy.

Law

Law in a useful point of entry into this exercise. The concept of law including the rule of law is one of the defining characteristics of liberal democracy and, indeed, any democracy. But the prevailing conception of law, which is that of liberal democracy, is extremely difficult to relate to some African conditions.

Once more, the problem is that law in the liberal state is a phenomenon of market society. Its reason for being is that society is atomized and egotistical, interests are private and in real or.potential conflict, social relations are first and foremost exchange relations and therefore contractual; by extension, law is mainly about property.

In the liberal state, law expresses the dialectical unity of particulars and presupposes the atomized society, a social arena of private interests and their real or potential collision. That is the objective basis of the rule of law on one level. On another level, the rule of law is the political correlate of generalized commodity production and exchange. It is the political condition for the maintenance of the market and the operation of the law of value. As we have seen, the market throws up contradictions which threaten it and which have to be mediated. The rule of law mediates these contradictions; its specificity as a social fact is that it is the artifact which can deal with the contradictions in a manner compatible with the sanctification of the values of the market. The need for this artifact is that it is of the very nature of the market to prioritize formal freedom, equality and egotism.

In market society, regulation takes the form of laws which are formally promulgated, abstract rules of utility which meticulously disregard persons, emotions and feelings. Reflecting the retreat of biological persons into commodity masks, and the obliteration of all qualitative differences, as everyone collapses into the universal category buyer/seller, exchanger, bourgeois law is abstract universalistic and formalistic. Concerned about applying equally and universally, it maintains a rigorous distinction between universal categories, such as property owner, and particulars, such as the actual persons who are the beneficiaries or victims of the law. The property owner in the dock is also an actual person, but in keeping with its universalism and egalitarianism, the law deals with him or her formally and abstractly. Thus in its procedures the law relies on rational proof and avoids experiential considerations and appears more interested in logic than in truth and in formal justice rather than in substantive justice.

In the context of pre-capitalist societies which still prevail in much of rural Africa, it is more useful and more accurate to speak not of laws as such, but of rules of conduct. They are orientationally diffuse and not usually formally promulgated and coded, although there is no doubt what they are. Rules may exist as norms, customs or values. These rules essentially regulate society and the conduct of persons only incidentally, because the person exists first and foremost as a member of the group, and the strong accent on communality means that there is really nothing which is simply the private affair of a person.

This is so in a double sense: the organic ties of communal life and the strong belief that what persons do affect the well-being of the community. This is why the law in communal societies is tendentially penal rather than restitutive and why reparation and punishment involves not just the person in arbitration but kinship groups and other solidarity groups such as age-sets. (Bohanan 1957; Gluckman 1965).

While the process of regulation is always referring beyond the individual, to a social whole, there is at the same time the constant assertion of personality and its uniqueness. Far from eradicating personality and self-consciousness, African communalism heightens it, turns it into a preoccupation. The community is a strong ubiquitous presence so taken for granted that specificity (the person) is problematized. It is not just problematized, but, somewhat paradoxically, affirmed constantly in the division of labour by which society is produced and reproduced. The person cannot be abstracticized and hidden in a society of kinship which is so orientationally diffuse that the person is effectively the role.

These features engender an entirely different notion of law and the rule of law. As already noted, it is more accurate in the context of these communal societies with mechanical solidarity, to speak of rules rather than laws, rules which encompass value, norms, customs, precedence and taboos. They are capsules of the total experience as legitimized by society, including ontology, religion, morality, epistemology and ideology. Unlike bourgeois law, they are not rules of convenience. They do not deal with partial experience but with the total experience; they apply not to abstract persons but to real people, and they are not formalistic but substantive. Thus criminal proceedings and judicial arbitration admit considerations of personal factors, moral and value judgements, which are often decisive; indeed, there is a total rejection of the notion of basing the determination of judicial issues on purely rationalistic and technical criteria (Bohannan 1957; Gluckman 1965(a); Elias 1956).

That is not to say that the rule of law does not apply. Since the culture and ideology of these societies accept laws as ideographs of total experience and so admit the relevance of personal, moral and value judgements to judicial arbitration, the admission of these considerations is by definition part of due process.

The rule of law prevails in another sense. Whether rules and regulations are recognized as norms, taboos or custom, there is clarity as to what they are, and their significance is understood by everyone. The socialization process inculcates this knowledge with efficiency despite the fact that the rules and regulations are not formally promulgated or coded and despite the lack of specialized judicial institutions such as a magistracy.

There is much more objectivity in the enforcement of the regulations because everybody knows what they are; there are no specialists in the knowledge of the rules, everyone is an acknowledged expert. There is less room to hierarchize interpretation and for authoritarian control of the arbitration process, or to mystify and exploit it. In the African tradition, judicial arbitration constantly reaches beyond the individuals in arbitration to corporate entities, especially kinship groups. This tends to equalize the competitiveness of the parties and to increase the prospects of objective outcomes.

Also, laws are not just rules of convenience but the institutional structuration of the values and behavioural modes which determine, for good or ill, the material, moral and spiritual well-being of the community. A seemingly minor transgression, the violation of a taboo, a careless disregard of a custom may be life-threatening to the entire community, creating the need for elaborate rituals of restitution. The moral and spiritual significance of abiding by the rules for the entire society induces everyone to respect the law and to resist its corrupt exploitation for private benefits. These circumstances operationalize the rule of law in a manner that is at once more rigorous and more concrete.

However, this is not achieved by placing law above society, investing it with de facto sovereignty but by making law a means of the 'good life'.

The question as to whether the law stands above society and rules it or whether it is a subordinate instrumentality does not arise in the African traditional context. What prevails here must seem from the discursive practices of the West as an incomprehensible collapse of identity and difference and a harmony of contradictions. There is a clarity about what the laws are, about their sanctity, and yet they are used with the casualness of currency in the routine transactions of social existence, interpreted with infinite variety by a consciousness which locates fairness in the unique treatment of each person and each situation, a uniqueness which can be respected only by renegotiating the rules on the spot so that they are created and recreated daily.

The law is at once sacred and commonplace, consummatory and instrumental as value, unchanging and constantly improvised from day to day. It rules and serves as sovereign and subject, it strives for universality and equality by its insistent particularism. At work, here is a completely different mind-set, a unique political logic.

One of the most urgent tasks of democratization in Africa is to democratize in such a manner that law and the rule of law are relevant to social experience. By enabling and protecting, law defines the realm of freedom, prevents arbitrary power and secures order in justice, thereby contributing immensely to the sense of well-being. It is extremely alienating for people to live under a system of law which does not connect to their social experience; it gives a pervasive sense of helplessness amid a chaos of arbitrariness.

This state of affairs is one of the major contributors to the violent implosions associated with the search for meaning and identity in Africa and other parts of the Third World. One of the appeals of Islam in 'modernizing' countries is that for Moslems, it provides a legal system in harmony with social experience; by the same token one of the causes of Islamic fundamentalism is the search for meaning in the face of an aggressive technocratic culture which is contesting every space, and filling them with norms and institutions which seem to people on the receiving end arbitrary and unintelligible.

Although advocates and scholars of democratization do not seem to be concerned by the formidable problems posed by the received practice of democracy and legal systems that alienate instead of inculcating the reassuring feeling of being secure in freedom and in the consciousness that the social order is predictable and just, ordinary people are acutely aware of this problem because it oppresses them. They are trying to cope by resorting to primordial identities, by reinventing the legal systems of traditional social systems and submitting to them, by religiuns fundamentalism, by demanding institutions such as customary courts. But the problem is so important and so serious it needs to bc addressed much more systematically than this. For now this is not happening. Until it happens democratization will be alienating and shallow.

Egalitarianism, Participation and the Domestication of power

Democracy in African social conditions has to be markedly more egalitarian and participative than it is in the 'established democracies'. Contrary to popular assumptions, African traditional systems were generally egalitarian and participative. The political repression of the colonial era by the colonizing powers, including the Arabs, and in the post-colonial era by the nationalist leaders was an unusual and traumatizing experience for Africa, an experience which remains a formidable obstacle to Africa's quest for peace and development.

In the African past, there were large-scale political entities and even a few empires. But these were the exception rather than the rule, and they were alien political forms associated with conquest. The traditional African society was typically small in population and geographical spread, usually no more than a few thousand people in a territory of no more than a few square miles. Its size was regulated by the need for self-sufficiency and the maintenance of ecological balance. It was not only a society and an economy, but also a community, a community of kinsfolk. It followed the rhythm of this relationship along with that of its ecological setting. In effect, this society was not only man-made but also 'natural' and God-made.

> So it came about that all property and productive relations had to be conceived in terms of kinship relations, since it was the sum of the family groups, combined in a rural community, that was seen as having devised the saving balance with nature. This meant that political action was necessarily kinship action. But this in turn required that every individual must play an expected social role. To the ecological balance, there corresponded another in the field of human relations: an ideal balance of kinship rights and obligations.... The ideal balance of kinship relations, seen as essential to the ideal balance with nature that was itself the material guarantee of survival, called for specific patterns of conduct. Individuals might have rights, but they had them only by virtue of the obligations they fulfilled to the community (Davidson 1969:56-57).

The egalitarianism of these societies was expressed in various ways, including their attitude to work. Work was perceived to be limited by its end, namely, the servicing of needs. Work was not seen as a virtue except in so far as this was indirectly associated with it, for instance, by the legitimacy of the need it served. However, work is always a necessity to be limited. So it is not usually geared to the maximization of productivity but, rather, to a predetermined quantum of necessary product. The production of excess is often seen as a waste of time, or as carrying high opportunity costs. Excess production is undesirable because it tends to upset the equilibrium between people in society and the balance of nature. In particular, it leads to inequality between people, corrupts and destroys the harmony of their relations, bringing with it arrogance and domination, envy and submissiveness, antagonism and conflict.

The production system is a cause and effect of the egalitarianism of these societies. Since it is so strictly geared to need and does not produce wealth, it does not allow the economic stratification of society. At the same time, a consciousness which regards surplus production as a waste of time and energy, and accumulation as a threat to moral well-being and the solidarity of society, keeps production focused on the fulfilment of need. As much as possible the cultural attitudes discourage wealth. The Bembe saying that to 'find one beehive is good luck, to find two is very good luck, to find three is witchcraft' (Davidson 1967) is a typical attitude. In so far as the production of some wealth cannot be avoided entirely, these societies try to deal with this by sanctioning its rapid disappearance by public ceremonial consumption of private wealth.

Students of African traditional societies have captured this egalitarianism by characterizing them as acephalous, tribes without rulers and societies without states. One recurrent feature of these societies is a profound distrust of the coercive hierarchization of power as fixed positions of command and obedience, as is clear in the ethnographies of the Ibo, the Mossi, the Tallensi, the Lozi, the Bembe, the Tiv, the Diola, the Izo, the Ewe, the Masai, the Luo, the Makonde and the Kikuyu. In some cases, such as the Lozi and the Tallensi, so strong was the ideological commitment to egalitarianism that they feared and avoided war and sought peace by every means in order not to risk giving anyone power even for the purposes of their own protection.

It was not easy to maintain these egalitarian political systems. Some of them were transformed by contradictions into monarchies. But even in these cases the egalitarianism and distrust for political power was easily evident in their constitutional provisions. For instance, the Barotse of Central Africa balanced the power of the monarch carefully with a council of ministers, and then the council of ministers was segmented into units carefully balanced one against the other. The king was bound by strict rules of conduct and could be deposed if he failed to conform to the constraints on his power.

An illustration of this traditional republicanism of African traditional systems can be seen in the Mossi empire. The office of emperor was hereditary, and the emperor or the Moro Naba had to come from the family of previous emperors. But he was not chosen by the members of that family. He was chosen by a body of four, presided over by the prime minister, the Togo naba, who was only a commoner. The emperor shared power with four ministers, each of whom was also a governor of one of the four regions of the empire. The prime minister, a commoner, was ranked first among these four ministers. The second-ranking minister, the rassam naba or the bingo naba, always came from a slave family. His extensive powers included being the ministers of finance as well as being the high executioner and ruler of the canton of Kindighi. The third-ranking minister, the balum naba, was mayor of the palace, chief of protocol and administrator of Zitinga, the Bussu and the Gursi. The fourth minister, the kidiranga naba, the head of the cavalry, was once again a commoner. Most importantly, once the ministers were installed, they could not be removed by the king (Diop 1987:44).

What we have called the egalitarianism or better perhaps, the republicanism of African traditional systems was associated with the domestication of power. In traditional Africa, political domination was tendentially constituted as an essentially noncoercive hierarchization of political society, based primarily on a differential distribution of status which became only incidentally an asymmetrical relationship of political power. Hierarchy, not in the sense of domination and coercion but in the sense of ranking and precedence, was a pervasive feature of indigenous African political societies (LeVine 1976). It occurs through the entire range of traditional systems, from the monarchies such as the Baganda and the Yoruba kingdoms to the more typical acephalous societies such as the Tallensi and the Tiv. The hierarchy is based on criteria such as age, gender, chronology of origin, proximity in genealogy to the royal house, order of initiation into cults, secret societies or age-grade, order of marriage in polygamous marriages, athletic prowess, fitness, artistic talent, knowledge of history, oratorical ability, the possession of magical powers and reputation.

These criteria are not in themselves a hierarchy of power but a hierarchy of status, although they may become the basis for the differential allocation or appropriation of power, status and authority. The possession of these qualities may eventually be perceived as power. This is all the more so because they become the basis for the ascription of political roles, for instance, the most senior in age becoming a gerontocracy as among some Ibo peoples. For at this point, the qualities underlying these criteria become virtually indistinguishable from power.

Still, it never comes to identity because claims to seniority and competition for seniority are always directed at these criteria of hierarchy. Thus political competition does not necessarily focus directly on power but access to roles of social recognition, and political power is not appropriated directly but rather in highly oblique and ritualized manner, through complex mediations in an ascent of status.

Even when the people who gain social recognition by the prevailing criteria of hierarchy occupy political roles, make decisions and exercise power, the hierarchization and, exercise of power are refracted and blurred. For instance, when an individual gains a political office it tends to be claimed by the kinship group and invariably invested in this corporate entity through the original incumbent. The norms legitimate this corporate appropriation. Among other things, it reflects a bias against egotism, and affirmation of communalism.

Most importantly, it is legitimized as a mode of participation. The individual holds office on behalf of a group who by the collective exercise of this office or by sharing, however vicariously, in its privileges and immunities, are incorporated into the political process as active participants. This form of political participation, usually more concrete and more equitable, is not often perceived or fully understood because political participation is perceived from the perspective of social atomism and individualism.

The appropriation of office by the kinship group of the incumbent mediates hierarchization. We have to think of hierarchy within the corporate kinship group and without (that is, between groups). The person holding high office may belong to a kinship group at lower levels of the political and social hierarchy. The person of lowly origins holding no office may be associated with corporate ownership of a powerful office or may belong to a group which is high on the political hierarchy. This cross-cutting of personal status and corporate standing enables some equalization of power. In a situation where people are dominant or subordinate in changing personal situations and multiple corporate identities it is not always easy to see who is dominating whom.

In fact, the very concept of political domination is problematic in the African context, given its connotation of control, coercion and exploitative subordination, because, as we have seen, while there is order, ordination and subordination, they are contextualized in ways which are largely devoid of these connotations. In any case, the African view of hierarchy is such that we can hardly problematize the compatibility of hierarchy with freedom, equality and self-realization. For one thing, culturally, hierarchy is sanctioned in ways which make it positive and liberating and 'valuable'. It is accepted as a principle of civic virtue in the Aristotelian sense of being equally comfortable, adept and morally uplifted by ruling and being ruled. African communalism places particular emphasis on social bonding which includes attachments of clientage (Fortes 1949). For not to be so attached is license, not being ruled is not a virtue but a vice.

At the very top of the political hierarchy, the role occupant, whether monarch, chief or elder, was regarded as the incarnation of both polity and society. This was not incarnation in a metaphysical sense; the leader's person is literally society become flesh. Thus all of the leader's personal qualities become inseparable from the welfare of the community (Young 1966). If he is ill, weak, strong, virile and dynamic, so is the society.

He was controlled meticulously in regard to what he could see, where he could be, and when, how he could mate, if, when, and how he could show emotion. There was a daunting array of taboos to observe. It was taken for granted that the leader would act in the collective interest of the community. This assumption is not questioned when the community is at peace, prosperous, healthy and dynamic. However, once the society encounters serious problems of whatever nature, it was promptly questioned and the leader was blamed. This is a unique and rigorous kind of accountability which effectively transforms the leader into a scapegoat for everything, even things he could not control (Muller 1980), such as epidemic, drought and external aggression. Thus the Jukun King was expected to be killed in the event of famine or drought or if he fell seriously ill (Young 1966).

Implicit in all this is an unusual domestication of power. The leader, answerable for everything even fortuitous events and acts of nature, becomes essentially a scapegoat, the role of the weakest: a role which not only lacks power but entails subjection to oppression. As if to underline this, some of the taboos and ritual control of the behaviour of the leader amount to a public demonstration of the fact that ordinary people can humiliate the leader, deny him values. In all cases, they make the point that the leader is not subject but object, controlled in the public interest in an infinite variety of ways, not free to live or even to die. Even at the top, power and dominance become very paradoxical and elusive.

Against this background, it is odd that studies of Africa over the decades of independence never problematized the fit of the brutal authoritarianism of the post-colonial era. Rather it was readily assumed that authoritarianism sits well on Africa. Africa is yet to live through the trauma of this singular prejudice and the extraordinary violence which African leaders did to Africa with the new-found powers and coercive technology of the modern state. This violent assault on Africa, which fully matched and arguably surpassed that of the imperial powers, underlies the deepening crisis of underdevelopment in contemporary Africa. By all indications even the surge of democratization has not sensitized scholars and development agents in Africa to address this problem.

How might it be addressed? It is best to nurture a democracy that takes equality and participation seriously, much more seriously than the established democracies currently do. Current democratic practice puts all the emphasis on political rights and none on economic rights except the right to property. Even then the political rights are abstract; there is hardly any interest in the enabling conditions for the enjoyment of rights such as education and economic resources, and competitive capability. There is not enough concern with the simple fact that gross economic inequality such as exists in most Third World countries and even in some of the established democracies is making democracy impossible. Remarkably, even as the world proclaims the triumph of democracy, this condition is getting worse. In virtually all the established democracies, economic inequality is increasing and the subordinate social classes are more powerless than ever.

It is especially important to address this problem in Africa for two reasons. The first is that the problem of authoritarianism continues to traumatize Africa, and only democratization of unprecedented depth, one that reaches back to the republican traditions of African traditional systems, can change this. The second is that the popular base of the democracy movement is insistent on a democracy that actually realizes equity and participation. This is clearly the language of the demand for a second independence. As the Arusha Proclamation and the debates in the national conferences show, ordinary people want, not abstract political rights but economic rights; they want social upliftment and empowerment to fend for themselves, defend their interests and be fully part of the enterprise of forging the collective destiny.

The feasibility of democracy in Africa will depend importantly on how far democracy is recreated to reflect as much as possible the traditional notion of participation which was associated with the communal political culture of African society, which still remains strong, especially in the rural areas. This political culture demands the involvement of everyone in promoting the common good. People are required to participate, not because they are individuals whose interests need to be asserted, but because they are part of an interconnected whole. Participation rests not on the assumption of individuality but on the social nature of human beings. By this traditional conception, participation is as much as much a matter of taking part as of sharing, sharing the burdens and the rewards of community membership. It does not simply enjoin abstract rights but also secures concrete benefits. In this instance, participation is not the occasional opportunity to choose, affirm or dissent. It is rather the active involvement in the process, not the acceptability of the end decision that satisfies the need to participate.

Conclusion

In the light of these reflections it seems useful to consider briefly what may reasonably be conjectured regarding the practicalities of making democracy feasible in Africa. However, one should not be seduced by talk of practicalities into misconceptions of what this exercise is and what it might accomplish. It is not a turning from theory to action, from the abstract to the empirical. Regretfully we are still obliged to operate on the level of generality. For there is so much diversity among African countries and within African countries that it will be misleading to recommend specific practices and institutions for democracy which will be valid all over Africa. All that can be reasonably expected is highly probable responses to the generic nature of the problem, not necessarily the answer to the problem in any specific historical settings.

A Relevant Democracy

As we have seen, the democracy movement in Africa is being moved in the direction of a simple liberal democracy of multi-party electoral competition. The pressure to move in this direction will remain strong. But this is not the democracy that is most relevant to the social realities of contemporary Africa. Social democracy would be more feasible. Its advantages are an activist role for the state and strong commitment to social welfare. It places less emphasis on abstract political rights and more on concrete economic rights and also on the removal of conditions which block the democratic participation of ordinary people such as gross economic inequality. This is the democracy which the ordinary people, who have the greatest interest in democratization, want. And it is the kind of democracy they need.

If and when the democracy movement in Africa starts to move in this direction, serious contradictions will be engaged, for the ideological climate in the world today, as well as the interests of those who currently have power in Africa, is hostile to social democracy. Eventually, the democracy movement will in all probability split on class lines and the contest between the two classes will be long and bitter.

Developmental Basis of Democratization

The intensifying crisis of underdevelopment is not conducive to the advancement of democracy in Africa. Too many people are too engrossed in mere survival. The vulnerabilities of ordinary people, especially peasants, are not conducive to a democratic citizenry. For instance, lack of education is a problem because it is bad for self-esteem which is necessary for effective participation; it devalues democratic choice because there is no choice in ignorance. Economic stagnation and rigorous austerity tend. to nurture extremist politics which are not conducive to democracy.

It is agreed that the cause of democratization will be helped if there is also accelerated economic development. Some think that democratization and economic development occur sequentially, not simultaneously, and that we must chose development first. But the conventional wisdom is that democratization can be pursued simultaneously, provided democratizing countries receive massive economic aid to insulate the society and democracy against austerity. However, we have seen that this approach helps neither democratization nor development. What is required is to make development itself a process of democratization. This means making the people the end and the means of development. By this approach development ceases to be what the government and international development agencies do for ordinary people, but what the ordinary people do for themselves. It becomes their possession, their lived experience, not a received experience. In so far as they possess development and become its end, the content of development can be nothing other than the development of their potentialities, their progressive empowerment and self-realization. Once development moves in this direction, it becomes the concrete content of democratization.

Democratization of the State

Democratization in Africa has been tendentially processional, with particular emphasis on the process of selecting the managers of state power through multi-party electoral competition. This is not enough. Processional democratization needs to be supplemented with structural democratization, especially the restructuring of the state in order to ensure that democratic processes actually produce democratic outcomes. Because the state in most of democratizing Africa remains decidedly undemocratic in structure, it has been relatively easy for dictators such as Jerry Rawlings of Ghana, Arap Moi of Kenya, Blaise Compaoré of Burkina Faso, Paul Biya of Cameroon and Eyadéma of Togo to assume the mantle of democratic legitimacy through multi-party elections. Indeed, in much of Africa people are voting without choosing.

By all indications, the first crop of elections which democratic pressures have compelled will for all their limitations be an improvement on subsequent elections as the new leaders become more adept at using an undemocratic state to augment their power and incapacitate their opponents. In this connection the experience of Zimbabwe, another holdout on multi-partism is instructive. The first election which was held at independence remains the most competitive and democratic election in Zimbabwe. Every succeeding election has been less competitive and less democratic than the preceding one, because of astute use of the state and its apparatuses to weaken political opponents and to discourage the people of Zimbabwe from turning elsewhere. If the current pattern of democratization continues, more African countries will settle into a pattern in which multi-party elections become established and held routinely with a diminishing chance of dislodging the elite in power. It is essential to democratize the state in Africa, especially in the following respects:

Less Power in the Presidency

Even in the era of democratization, African constitutions give far too much power to the presidency, sometimes to the point of constituting it virtually as a dictatorship. In all too many cases, democratization has been a matter of replacing a self-appointed dictator with an elected one. It is all the more necessary to correct this, because apart from being an impediment to democracy, the concentration of power in the presidency gives politics an unhealthy intensity. Because this office is so powerful, those who compete for it readily resort to means that are unlawful, as if to indicate that for this particular office, the end justifies all means. An example of the reduction of the powers of this office is to set up the important 'independent' commissions such as the Judicial Commission, the Public Service Commission and the Electoral Commission in such a manner that the President's role in their appointment is nominal and to abolish all presidential determination of the conditions of their tenure.

Greater Balance of power

The traditional separation of powers between the executive, the legislature and the judiciary is generally lacking in democratizing Africa as power is concentrated in just one office in the executive. In African conditions the democratization of the state will require, among other things, giving substantive powers to the legislature in regard to appointments to high offices of state, the making and approval of national budgets, foreign policy and national planning and national security. As well as such substantial powers, African legislatures need an information base for the exercise of their role; they also need administrative support and financial resources independent of the presidency to carry out their duties.

An independent judiciary is essential. To facilitate this, the judiciary should be adequately funded, and funding should be by statutory allocation directly from the national budget. It should be self-accounting. The Judicial Commission that overseas the judiciary should be effectively independent of the presidency, which should have nothing to do with the appointment of its members except in a nominal way. Judges should be appointed by this independent Judicial Commission or elected, and their tenure of office should be secured by statutory instruments which the president cannot change.

Local Autonomy

The democratization of the state in Africa will benefit a great deal from a multi-tier government structure, especially local governments which are not simply administrative units but a tier of government. That means that they will have a statutory allocation of a proportion of the national revenue specified by the constitution just like the national government. The constitution should also give them specific spheres of autonomy with substantial powers to operationalize this autonomy including the power to raise revenue by taxation and other means. In some cases , the diffusion of power and the prospects of local autonomy will require proportional representation.

Law

An important aspect of the democratization of the state is the democratization of the legal system. This requires much more than an independent judiciary, for the independence of the judiciary says nothing conclusive about its quality as an instrument of justice, a guarantor of democratic rights and liberties and the rule of law. To achieve these ends, African legal systems have to be reformed radically to make them relevant to the needs of ordinary people. They are usually too intimidating and alienating to ordinary people, and their norms, values and practices are often incomprehensible to them. For the most part African workers and peasants lack the educational resources, cultural opportunities and financial resources to access justice.

Relevance of the legal system to the needs of this class of people will entail extensive use of African customary law duly reformed to remove the elements of arbitrariness arising from the corruption of arbitrary power. The use of customary law could be supplemented with the adaptation of the small claims court judicial procedures of the United States which would be simpler, less expensive and less intimidating to ordinary people.

Another necessary change is to focus judicial procedure less on formalistic justice and more on substantial justice. The received judicial systems in vogue in Africa are too ponderous, time-consuming and expensive. It is necessary to dispense with their archaic language, bizarre sartorial taste and feudal pomposity and even the geographical structuring of the court room which seems calculated to underscore the vulnerability of litigants and to inspire awe. Above all, there is need to develop institutions of legal counselling, legal aid and human rights protection.

The Rudimentary Development of Civil Society

The development of civil society in Africa is so rudimentary that political society is not constituted as a 'public', a unity of abstract legal subjects and a solidarity of complementarities and reciprocities arising from their self-seeking. Instead of political society being one public, it is segmented into a plurality of competing and alienated primary publics, because people are alienated from the state and tend to give their primary loyalty to ethnic, sub-national or communal groups rather than the state. The polity becomes a society of strangers, of social groups which have little in common, and which are so deeply suspicious of each other that they would go to any length to avoid being in each other's power. The existence of the common concerns, which is the very rationale of democratic participation, becomes problematic. As long as the state remains a contested terrain and the point of this contest is the private appropriation of state power, the state must be undemocratic and arbitrary. To tame and democratize it, the state has to be seen as something that belongs to all and not to some, something which deserves support for the service it renders, not as a fearsome exploiter or an exploitable resource.

It is best to approach this problem from two perspectives, which seem contradictory but are actually complementary. The first is to recognize the differences and antipathies and make some concession to the autonomy of these entities in order to reduce the anxieties that drive them to contest so fiercely for power in a way that makes democratic politics impossible. This can be done by recognizing not only individual rights but also collective rights. It is also necessary to allow the social groups some autonomy in their local space, although this should be done in a manner that does not assume that their differences are permanent.

The second approach is to promote trust, mutual respect and consensus-building by means of a consocietal arrangement in which government is essentially a coalition of the authentic leaders of the social groups. It is necessary for the managers of state power to demonstrate at all times that the rewards and the burdens of citizenship are being shared with equity. More important still, they have to show by humane and even-handed governance, by developing a substantial social welfare system accessible to all and by meticulous upholding of the rule of law not only that the state belongs to all, but also that it cares deeply about the welfare of all; the state has to compete successfully to capture the loyalty of the citizens from the primary groups who mainly command it.

The Challenge of Change

How are these changes to be brought about? In considering this question, it is well to remember that they have to be effected in class-divided societies in which power and wealth are concentrated in a small elite while the rest of the society is very poor and subject to vulnerabilities associated with lack of access to health, education, cultural opportunities and basic amenities. Related to this is the consideration that all these changes involve moving against the logic and tendencies of these societies. They entail bringing ordinary people to the centre, privileging them and removing their vulnerabilities. In addition, they entail a radical redistribution of power and resources away from the small elite which currently monopolizes them to the masses. Unfortunately, those who have the power to effect the changes which democratization requires have a strong interest in resisting these changes, and those who have an objective interest in the changes do not have the power resources to effect them. Power and desirable change are pulling in diametrically opposite directions.

The challenge is to bring them into alignment. How can this be done? One option is to persuade the elite to accept these changes. This is apparently not a realistic option. In view of the vigour with which the factions of the political elite in power all over Africa resisted the first wave of democratization, the modest democratization achieved in Africa came with a very high price in conflict, social disruption and violence. And the resistance continues, even though it is clear by now that democratization has so far not significantly changed the distribution of power in much of Africa, and only in isolated instances has it come close to changing the ruling elite in power as opposed to the government in office. The changes in the second wave of democratization will be more threatening to the ruling elite. Therefore, they are going to be resisted more vigorously, still albeit with more sophistication this time, since they are now obliged to operate within democratic forms.

This time, the resistance will be reinforced from two sources. The first is elites which had fought for democratization because of their exclusion from power. They support democracy mainly as a strategy of power, as the opening that will enable them to compete for power. It is highly suggestive that they have shown little or no interest in going beyond electoral competition to those transformations which will give depth to democracy. By all indications, they want to inherit the system through democracy, not to change it, especially in ways that will reduce the amenities and prerogatives of power. That is why, as the experience of Nigeria, Ghana, Cameroon, Kenya, Togo, Zaire, Zimbabwe and Ivory Coast has shown, many of them are easily co-opted.

The second source of reinforcement will be the international community, including the 'established democracies' which have settled into a democracy of abstract rights and multi-party electoral competition. In the conservative environment of the post-Cold War era, the popular empowerment and welfare-oriented democracy which Africa must eventually strive for is likely to be seen as resurrecting the spectre of socialism.

That leaves the option of effecting the changes through the agency of ordinary people who have an objective interest in them. Given their weaknesses and their lack of access to economic resources and state power, they can only marshal the force to advance democracy through the development of their own political consciousness, organization and struggle. This will not easily happen. For one thing, the limited democratization which has taken place will to some extent disguise and even conceal the political oppression of the people and deradicalize consciousness. Besides, the international environment will be less supportive of this phase of democratization. The elite still has considerable leeway for manipulating primordial loyalties and traditional solidarity groups. And the daily struggle for survival will continue to make such heavy demand on the masses that there will be little room for politics.

However, the chances are that, in the end, the battle will be joined because electoral democracy will not satisfy the needs which impelled the ordinary people of Africa to insist on a second independence. While the masses want concrete economic and social rights, it offers them only abstract political rights; while they want empowerment and more control over their lives and destiny, it offers them ritual participation; while they want self-realization in recreating the principles of democracy anew in their cultural and historical setting, it offers them alienation by reducing democracy to a historical practice of democracy.

It is conventionally assumed that the liberal democracy which is on offer to Africa will facilitate economic growth in Africa by operationalizing market values and unleashing competitive efficiency. But this underrates the political disarticulation of Africa caused by the legacy of political repression, the high premium on power and the unbridled political competition which goes with it, and the exploitation of primordial loyalties.

In most parts of Africa, there is not even the political coherence for the capitalist project. Even if a modest growth rate is achieved, it will, in prevailing circumstances, be associated with the persistence and even some increase in uneven distribution which is going to play very badly with the masses who are already troubled and putting their bodies on the line for change. Improved growth performance will be modest at best, and not nearly enough to avert the coming confrontation.

Even though liberal democracy is currently dominant, it is unlikely to prevail because it reflects the values of the leadership and not those of the base. The element that may well be decisive is that the democracy movement in Africa is riding on popular consciousness which is yet inarticulate, as yet unclear how its values will find concreteness. Eventually the movement will mature to reflect the interests and the values of the popular consciousness driving it. When this happens, its character will change; it will be more concerned with the social and material upliftment of ordinary people, more with concrete economic and social rights, than abstract political rights, and it will try to realize democratic values in institutions which are more harmonious with indigenous culture and historical experience.

Still, it will be rash to assume the outcome of the impending struggle. What is clear enough is that this struggle will determine the fate of democracy in Africa. But more important, it will determine the fate of Africa. Democracy has never been as important to the fate of any people as it is to Africa. If the democracy of the elite prevails, Africa would have democratized in form but not in content, and in a way that is largely irrelevant to its social realities.

Wearing its new mantle of democratic legitimacy, Africa will plod on in the old ways, unable to create the political conditions that will finally enable the development project to take off, unable to enlist its greatest but long-neglected resource, namely, the energy of its people, in the battle against intensifying underdevelopment; unable to achieve the capacity to stem the rising tide of violent conflict and descent into chaos; and unable to become a going concern in the modern world.

But if the democracy of the 'popular' democracy movement prevails, Africa would have achieved the conditions for generating the negotiated consensus which will enable it to be more coherent and less prone to violent conflict, more able to pursve collective projects, especially development.

Just as important is the likely effects of the triumph of the democracy of the base on democracy itself. It will reinvigorate democracy, recreate it as a powerful instrument of social engineering and enduring political morality central to the possibility of civilisation. It would appear that it is in the lowly and struggling regions of the world, such as Africa, that the historic mission of democracy will be finally vindicated or betrayed.

Bibliography

Adejuyibe, O., 1974a, 'The size of state and political stability in Nigeria', *African Studies Review*, XVI (2).

Adejuyibe, Omdale, 1974b, *The Ethnic Nations of Nigeria*, Seminar Paper, Department of Linguistics, University of Ibadan.

African Development Bank, 1993, *Governance and Development in Africa: Issues and the Role of the African Development Bank and other Multilateral Organizations*. Abidjan, Côte d'Ivoire: ADB.

Ake, C, 1969, 1981, *Social Science as Imperialism: The Theory of Political Development*. Ibadan: Ibadan University Press.

Ake, C, 1978, *Revolutionary Pressures in Africa*, London: Zed Press.

Ake, C., 1967, *A Theory of Political Integration*, Homewood: The Dorsey Press.

Ake, C., 1981, *A Political Economy of Africa*. Harlow: Longman.

Ake, C., 1985, 'The Nigerian state: Antimonies of a periphery formation', in C. Ake, (ed.), *Political Economy of Nigeria*, London: Longman.

Ake, C., 1991, 'Rethinking African democracy', *Journal of Democracy*, 2 (1).

Ake, C., 1993, 'What is the problem of ethnicity in Africa?' in *Transformation*, 22:1-14.

Ake, C., 1994, 'A world of political ethnicity', in R. van den Berg and U. Bosma (eds.), *Historical Dimensions of Development Change and Conflict in the South*, The Hague: Ministry of Foreign Affairs.

Alesina, A. and Rodrik, D., 1993, 'Distributive politics and economic growth', mimeo, Harvard University, October.

Alesina, A., *et al.*, 1992, 'Political instability and economic growth', NBER Working Paper 4173, Boston.

Almond, A. and Verba, S., (eds.), 1980, *The Civic Culture Revisited*, Boston: Little, Brown.

Almond, A. and Verba, S., 1963, *The Civil Culture: Political Attitudes and Democracy in Five Nations*, Princeton, Princeton University Press.

Amsden, A., 1985, 'The state and Taiwan's economic development', in Peter B. Evans *et al. Bringing the State Back In*. Cambridge: CUP.

Anderson, B., 1983, *Imagined Communities: Reflections on the Origin and Spread of Nationalism*, London, Verso Editions and New Left Books.

Anyang' Nyong'o, Peter, 1992, 'Africa: The failure of one-party rule', *Journal of Democracy*, 3 (1), January.

Arendt, H., 1958, *The Human Condition*, Garden City: Doubleday.

Aristotle, 1981, *The Politics*, Harmondsworth: Penguin.

Awolowo, O., 1974, *Path to Nigerian Freedom*, London: Faber and Faber.

Ayittey, G.B.N., 1991, *Indigenous African Institutions*, Ardsley-on-Hudson, NY: Transnational.

Babangida, Gen. Ibrahim Badamasi, 1993, 'Laying the foundation of a viable democracy and the path of honour', address to the nation, June 26, in *Newswatch*, July 2, 17-19.

Bachrach, Peter and Botwinick Aryeh, 1992, *Power and Empowerment,* Philadelphia: Temple University Press.

Bamishaiye, A., 1971, 'Ethnic politics as an instrument of unequal socio-economic development in Nigeria's First Republic', *African Notes, Bulletin of the Institute of African Studies,* University of Ibadan.

Bangura, Y., Gibbon, P., and Ofstad, A. (eds), 1992, *Authoritarianism, Democracy and Adjustment. The Politics of Economic Reform in Africa.* Uppsala: The Scandinavian Institute of African Studies, no. 26.

Banton, M., 1960, *West Africa City, A Study of Tribal Life in Freetown,* London: OUP.

Banton, M., 1983 and 1993, *Racial and Ethnic Competition,* Modern Revivals in Sociology Series London: Ashgate pub.

Barber, J. (1991) 'Zimbabwe's regional role', *Conflict Studies,* 24 (3), July/August.

Bardhan, P., 1993, 'Symposium on democracy and development', *Journal of Economic Perspectives,* Summer.

Barkan, J., 1984, 'Development through self-help', *The Forgotten Alternatives, Rural Africana,* 19-20 (Spring-Fall).

Barkan, J., 1994, 'Can established democracies nurture democracy ahead?', Paper presented at Nobel Symposium on Democracy's Victory and Crisis, Uppsala University, August 27-30.

Barth, F., 1959, *Political Leadership Among the Swat Pathans,* Monographs of Social Anthropology, London: School of Economics.

Barth, F., 1969, *Ethnic Groups and Boundaries: The Social Organisation of Culture Difference,* London: George Allen and Unwin.

Bates, R., and Krueger, A. (eds), 1993, *Political and Economic Interactions in Economic Policy Reform.* Oxford and Cambridge: Blackwell.

Bayart, J.-F., 1989, *L'etat en Afrique: la politique du ventre,* Paris: Fayard.

Beetham, D., 1981, 'Beyond liberal democracy', *Socialist Register,* 190-206.

Berelson, B., 1952, 'Democratic theory and public opinion', *Public Opinion Quarterly,* 16 Autumn:313-30.

Berelson, B., Lazarfeld, P.F. and McPhee, W., 1954, *Voting,* Chicago: University of Chicago Press.

Berg-Schlosser, D., 1984, 'African political systems: Typology performance', *Comparative Political Studies,* 17 (1) (April).

Berlin, I., 1969, *Four Essays on Liberty,* Oxford: OUP.

Berman, B., 1984, 'Structure and processes in the bureaucratic states of colonial Africa', *Development and Change,* 15:161-202.

Bernal, V., 1988, 'Coercion and incentives in African agricultural development: Insights from the Sudanese experience', *African Studies Review,* 31 (2):89-108.

Bhalla, S.S., 1994, 'Freedom and economic growth: A virtuous cycle?', paper presented in *Democracy's Victory and Crisis: A Nobel Symposium,* Uppsala University, August 27-30.

Bhatnagar, B. and Williams, A.C., (eds.), 1992, *Participatory Development and the World Bank—Potential Directions for Change,* World Bank Discussion Paper 183, Washington, DC.

Bienen, H. and Herbst, J., 1991, 'Authoritarianism and democracy in Africa', in D.A. Rostow and K.P Ericson (eds) *Comparative Political Dynamics: Global Research Perspectives.* London: Harper Collins.

Bohannan, P.J., 1957, *Justice and Judgement Among the Tiv,* Oxford: OUP.

Bollen, K., 1979, 'Political democracy and the timing of development', *American Sociological Review,* 44:572-87.

Bollen, K., 1980, 'Issues in the comparative measurement of political democracy', *American Sociological Review*, 45:370-90.

Bollen, K., 1990, 'Political democracy: Conceptual and measurement traps', *Studies in Comparative International Development*, 25:7-24.

Bollen, K., and Jackman, R., 1985, 'Political democracy and the size distribution of income', *American Sociological Review*, 50:438-57.

Brass, P., 1976, 'Ethnicity and national formation', *Ethnicity*, 3 (3).

Bratton, M. and Van de Walle, N., 1992, 'Popular protest and political transition in Africa', *Comparative Politics*, 24 (4):419-42.

Bratton, M. and Van de Walle, N., 1992b, 'Toward governance in Africa: Popular demands and state responses', in Goran Hyden and Michael Bratton (eds) *Governance and Politics in Africa*. Boulder: Lynne Rienner, 27-56.

Bratton, M., 1989, 'Beyond the state: Civil society and associational life in Africa', *World Politics*, xii, (3), April.

Bratton, M., 1992, 'Zambia starts over', *Journal of Democracy*, 81-94.

Bratton, M., and Van de Walle, N., 1992a, 'Popular protest and reform in Africa', *Comparative Politics*, 24 (4), July.

Bratton, M., and Van de Walle, N., 1994, 'Neopatrimonial regimes and political transitions in Africa', *World Politics*, August.

Brett, E., 1973, *Colonialism and Underdevelopment in East Africa, 1919-1939*, London: Heinemann.

Brittan, S., 1975, 'The economic contradictions of democracy', *British Journal of Political Science*, 5(1):129-59.

Buell, R.L., 1928, *The Native Problem in Africa*, New York: The Macmillan Company.

Burnheim, J., 1985, *Is Democracy Possible?*, Cambridge Mass: Polity Press.

Callaghy, T., 1984, *The State Society Struggle: Zaire in Comparative Perspective*, New York: Columbia University Press.

Car, S., 1989, *Technology for Small-Scale Farmers in Sub-Saharan Africa*, Washington, DC: The World Bank.

Cernea, M., 1987, 'Farmer organisations and institution building for sustainable development', *Regional Development Dialogue*, 8 (2).

Cernea, M., 1981, 'Modernization and development potential of traditional grass roots peasant organisations', in Attir et *al.*, *Directions of Change: Modernization Theory, Research and Realities*, Boulder: Westview.

Chabal, P. (ed.), 1986, *Political Domination in Africa: Reflections on the Limits of Power*, Cambridge: CUP.

Chalker, L., 1991a, 'Good government and the aid programme', speech to Overseas Development Institute/Chatham House, June.

Chalker, L., 1991b, 'Giving aid to the Third World with strings attached', *The Sunday Times*, August 18.

Chambers, R. and Ghildyal, B., 1986, 'Agricultural resource-poor farmers: The farmer-first and last model', *Agricultural Administration*, 20.

Charlick, R., 1992, 'The concept of governance and its implications for AID's development assistance program in Africa', *Associates in Rural Development*, Washington, D.C., June.

Charlton, R., 1993, 'The politics of elections in Botswana', *Africa: Journal of the International African Institute*, 63 (3): 330-70.

Chazan, N., 1989, 'Planning democracy in Africa: A comparative perspective on Nigeria and Ghana', *Policy Sciences*, 22: 325-57.

Chazan, N., Mortimer, R., Ravenhill, J. and Rothchild, D., 1992, *Politics and Society in Contemporary Africa*. Boulder: Lynne Rienner.

Chrétien, J.P., 1985, 'Hutu et Tutsi au Rwanda et au Burundi', in Jean Loup Amselle and Elikai Mbokolo, (eds.), *Au Coeur de l'Ethnie*, Paris: Editions la Decouverte.

Christopher, W., 1993, 'The United States and Africa: A new relationship', 23rd African-American Institute Conference, Reston, Va, USA, May 21.

Cleaver, K., 1993, *A Strategy to Develop Agriculture in Sub-Saharan Africa and a Focus for the World Bank*, Washington, DC: The World Bank.

Clough, M., 1992, *Free at Last? US. Policy Toward Africa and the End of the Cold War*, New York: Council on Foreign Relations.

Cohen, A., 1981,'Variables in ethnicity', in C. Keyes (ed.), *Ethnic Change*, Seattle: University of Washington Press, 307-31.

Cohen, A., 1985, *The Symbolic Construction of Community*, Chichester: Homewood.

Cohen, J. and Rogers, J., 1983, *On Democracy*, New York: Penguin.

Cohen, Joshua, 1989, 'Deliberation and democratic legitimacy', in A. Hamlin and Philip Petit, *The Good Polity*, Oxford: Blackwell.

Cohen, Y., 1985, 'The impact of bureaucratic-authoritarian rule on economic growth', *Comparative Political Studies*, 18 (1), April: 123-36.

Coleman, J., 1958, *Nigeria: Background to Nationalism*, Berkeley: University of California Press.

Coleman, J. S., 1960, 'The politics of sub-Saharan Africa' in G.A. Almond and J.S. Coleman, eds. *Politics of the Developing Areas*, Princeton: Princeton university press.

Collinson, M., 1980, 'A low cost approach to understanding small farmers, *Agricultural Administration*, 8.

Conner, W., 1973a, 'The politics of ethnonationalism', *Journal of International Affairs*, 27:1-21.

Conner, W., 1973b, 'Ethnonationalism in the First World: The present in historical perspective', in M. Esman, *Ethnic Conflict in the Western World*, Ithaca, Cornell University Press, 19-45.

Connolly, William, E., 1991, 'Democracy and Territoriality', *Millennium*, 20:463-84.

Corcoran, P.E., 1983, 'The limits of democratic theory', in G. Duncan (ed.), *Democratic Theory and Practice*, Cambridge: CUP, 13-24.

Coulter, P., 1975, *Social Mobilization and Liberal Democracy*, Lexington, Mass: Lexington Books.

Crozier, M., Huntington S.P., and Watanuki, J., 1975, *The Crisis of Democracy: Report on the Governability of Democracies to the Trilateral Commission*, New York: New York University Press.

Cutright, P., 1963, 'National political development: Measurement and analyses', *American Sociological Review*, 28:253-64.

Cutright, P., and Wiley, J.A., 1969, 'Modernization and political representations: 1927–1966', *Studies in Comparative International Development*, 5:23-44.

Dahl, G., and Hjort, A., 1984, 'Development as message and meaning', *Ethnos*, 3-4.

Dahl, R.A., 1956, A *Preface to Democratic Theory*, Chicago: University of Chicago Press.

Dahl, R.A., 1957, The concept of power, *Behavioural Science*, 2(3):201-15.

Dahl, R.A., 1971, *Polyarchy: Participation and Opposition*, New Haven: Yale University Press.

Dahl, R.A., 1979, 'Procedural democracy', in P. Laslett and J. Fishkin (eds.), *Philosophy, Politics and Society*, Fifth Series, New Haven: Yale University Press, 97-133.

Das Gupta, J., 1989, 'India Democratic becoming and combined development', in L. Diamond, J.J. Linz and S.M. Lipset, (eds.), *Democracy in developing countries: Asia*, Boulder: Lynne Rienner, 53-104.

De Nevers, R., 1993, 'Democratization and ethnic conflict', *Survival*, 35 (2): 31-32.

De Tocqueville, A., 1945, *Democracy in America*, vol. 2, New York: Vintage (Original work published in 1840).

De Vos, G. and Romannuci-Ross, L., (eds.), 1975, *Ethnic Identity*, Palo Alto: Mayfield.

Decalo, S., 1990, *Coups and Army Rule in Africa: Motivations and Constraints*, Second Edition. New Haven: Yale University Press.

Decalo, S., 1992, 'The process, prospects and constraints of democratization in Africa', *African Affairs*, 91:7-35.

Deng, F., 1994, 'Anatomy of conflicts in Africa', Paper delivered at Clingendael Institute Seminar on Conflict and Development, March, 22-24.

Devereux, G., 1975, Ethnic identity: Its logical foundations and its dysfunctions', in G. de Vos and L. Romanucci-Ross, (eds.), *Ethnic Identity*, Palo Alto:Mayfield.

Di Palma, G., 1990, *To Craft Democracies: An Essay on Democratic Transitions*, Berkeley: University of California Press.

Dia, M., 1993, *A Governance Approach to Civil Service Reform in Sub-Saharan Africa*, World Bank Technical Paper 225, Washington, DC.

Diamond, L., 1980, 'The social foundations of democracy: The case of Nigeria', unpublished PhD. dissertation, Stanford University.

Diamond, L., 1987, 'Class formation in the swollen African state', *Journal of Modern African Studies*, 25 (4), December: 567-96.

Diamond, L., Linz, J.L. and Lipset, S.M., 1987, 'Building and sustaining democratic government in developing countries: Some tentative findings', *World Affairs* 150 (1): 5-19.

Diamond, L., 1988a, *Class, Ethnicity, and Democracy in Nigeria: The Failure of the First Republic*, London: Macmillan; Syracuse: Syracuse University Press.

Diamond, L., 1988b, 'Introduction: Roots of failure, seeds of hope', in L. Diamond, J.J. Linz, and S.M. Lipset, (eds.), *Democracy in Developing Countries: Africa*, Boulder, Lynne Rienner, 1-32.

Diamond, L., Linz, J.L. and Lipset, S.M., 1990, *Politics in Developing Countries. Comparing Experiences with Democracy*. Boulder: Lynne Rienner.

Diamond, L., 1992, 'Promoting democracy', *Foreign Policy 87*, Summer: 30-31.

Diamond, L., 1992a, *Economic Development and Democracy Reconsidered*.

Diamond, L., 1993, 'The globalization of democracy: Trends, types, causes and prospects', in R. Slater, B. Schutz and S. Dorr (eds.), *Global Transformation and the Third World*, Boulder: Lynne Rienner.

Diamond, L., 1994, 'Promoting democracy in the 1990s', Paper presented at Nobel Symposium on Democracy's Victory and Crisis, Uppsala University, August 27-30.

Dick, G.W., 1974, 'Authoritarian versus non-authoritarian approaches to economic development', *Journal of Political Economy*, 82 (4) (July-August).

Diop, C.A., 1987, *Black Africa: The Economic and Cultural Basis for a Federal State*, Chicago: Lawrenceville Books.

Diouf, M., 1993, 'Senegal's February 1993 Elections: New factors in the political arena', *CODESRIA Bulletin*, no 2, pp. 4-7.

Donelly, J., 1984, 'Human rights and development: Complementary or competing concerns?', *World Politics*, 36 (2), (January).

Doornbo, M., 1972, 'Some conceptual problems concerning ethnicity in integration analysis, *Civilisations*, 22 (1).

Downs, Anthony, 1957, *An Economic Theory of democracy*, New York: Harper and Row.

Drysek, John, 1990, *Discursive Democracy*, Cambridge: CUP.

Dunn, J., 1969, *The Political Thought of John Locke*, Cambridge: CUP.

Durkheim, E., 1993, *Division of Labor in Society: Some Notes on Occupational Groups*, Reprint Series in Social Sciences Series, Irvington Publishers.

Duverger, M., 1974, *Modern Democracies: Economic Power versus Political Power*, Illinois: The Dryden Press.

Economist, 1991, 'Freedom and prosperity', June 29.

Edelman, M., 1977, *Political Language*, New York: Academic Press.

Ekeh, P., 1975, 'Colonialism and two publics in Africa: A theoretical statement', *Comparative Studies in Society and History*, 17:91-112.

Elias, T.O., 1956, *The Nature of African Customary Law*, Manchester: Manchester Univ. Press.

Enloe, C., 1983, *Ethnic Development and Political Conflict*, Boston: Little Brown.

Ergas, Z., (ed.), 1987, *The African State in Transition*, Basingstoke: Macmillan.

Eriksen, T.H., 1991, 'Ethnicity versus nationalism', *Journal of Peace Research*, 28:263-78.

Evans-Pritchard, E.E., *et al*, 1961, *The Institutions of Primitive Society*, Oxford: OUP.

Fabian, J., 1986, 'Language and colonial power', chapter 4 of *Labour and Language in Katanga*, 92-111.

Fairley, N., 1987, 'Ideology and state formation: The Ekie of southern Zaire', in I. Kopytoff, (ed.), *The African Frontier: The Reproduction of Traditional African Societies*, Bloomington: Indiana University Press.

Fallers, L.A., 1966, *Bantu Bureaucracy: A Century of Evolution among the Basoga of Uganda*, Chicago: University of Chicago Press.

Fanon, F., 1988, *The Wretched of the Earth,* Grove Atlantic.

Fatton Jr., R., 1990, 'Liberal democracy in Africa', *Political Science Quarterly*, 105, Fall: 455-78.

Figleye J., and Burton, M., 1989, 'The elite variable in democratic transitions and breakdowns', *American Sociological Review*, 54:17-32.

Financial Times, 1990, 'Survey of Nigeria', March 19.

Fish, S., 1980, *Is There a Text in this Class? The Theory of Interpretative Communities*, Cambridge Mass: Harvard University Press.

Forde, D. with Kaberry, P.M. (ed.), 1967, *West African Kingdoms in the Nineteenth Century*, Oxford: OUP.

Forde, D., (ed.) 1954, *African Worlds: Studies in the Cosmological Ideas and Social Values of African Peoples*, Oxford: OUP.

Fortes, M. with E.E. Evans-Pritchard, (eds.), 1940, *African Political Systems*, Oxford: OUP.

Fortes, M., 1945, *The Dynamics of Clanship among the Tallensi*, Oxford: OUP.

Fortes, M., 1949, *The Web of kinship Among the Tallensi*, Oxford: OUP.

Foucault, M., 1977, *Discipline and Punish*, London: Allen Lane.

Friedman, M., 1962, *Capitalism and Freedom*, Chicago: University of Chicago Press.

Frischtak, L.L., 1993, 'Antinomies of development: Governance capacity and adjustment responses', Private Sector Development Department Working Paper, World Bank, Washington, DC.

Furnivall, J.S., 1949, *Progress and Welfare in South East Asia: A Comparison of Colonial Policy and Practice*, Reprint of the 1941 edition, Cambridge: CUP.

Gerson, P., 1993, *Popular Participation in Economic Theory and Practice*, Human Resources Development and Operations Policy Working Paper Series HROWP18, *World Bank*, Washington, DC.

Gluckman, M. (ed.), 1962, *Essays on the Ritual of Social Relations, Custom and Conflict in Tribal Africa*, Manchester: Manchester University Press.

Gluckman, M. 1963, *Order and Rebellion in Tribal Africa*, London: Cohen.

Gluckman, M. 1965, *Politics, Law and Ritual in Tribal Society*, Oxford: Blackwell

Gluckman, M. 1965a, *The Ideas in Barotse Jurisprudence*, New Haven: Yale University Press.

Goodin, R.E., 1992, *Motivating Political Morality*, Oxford: Blackwell.

Goody, J., 1971, *Technology, Tradition and the State in Africa*, Oxford: OUP.

Goody, J.A., 1962, Death, Property and the Ancestors, Cambridge: CUP.

Goody, J.A., 1966, *Succession to High Office*, Cambridge: CUP.

Griffiths, S.I., 1993, *Nationalism and Ethnic Conflict: Threats to European Security*, Oxford: OUP.

Grossman, H.I. and Noh, S.I., 1988, *Proprietary Public Finance, Political Competition and Regulation*, IMF Seminar Series, No 8:1.

Gulhati, R., 1989, 'Impasse in Zambia: The economics and politics of reforms', *Analytical Case Studies*, no. 2, Washington, DC: IBRD.

Gurr, T., 1994, Peoples against states: Ethnopolitical conflict and the changing world system', *International Studies Quarterly*, 38 (3), September: 347-337.

Gurr, T.R. and Monty, M., 1990, *Ethnopolitical Conflicts Since 1945: Report of a Global Survey*, US Department of Defence: Academic Research Support Program.

Habermas, J., 1976, *Legitimation Crisis*, trans. from German by Thomas McCarthy London: Heinemann.

Haberson, J. and Rothchild, D., 1991, 'Africa in post-Cold War international politics: Changing agendas', in Harbeson and Rothchild, (eds.), *Africa in World Politics*, Boulder: Westview.

Hadenius, A., 1992, *Democracy and Development*, Cambridge: CUP.

Hadenius, A., 1994, 'Assessing democratic progress in Africa', paper presented to IPSA Berlin, August 21-25.

Haggard, S., 1990, *Pathways from the Periphery: The Politics of Growth in the Newly Industrializing Countries*, Cornell University Press.

Haggard, S., and Kaufmann, R., 1992, 'Economic development in new democracies', in Joan M. Nelson *et al.* (eds) *The Politics of Adjustment: International Constraints, Distributive Politics, and the State*. Princeton: Princeton University Press.

Haggblade, S.P., Brown Hazel, J., 1989, 'Farm-non-farm linkages in rural Sub-Saharan Africa', *World Development*, 17 (8).

Harbeson, J. and Rothchild, D. (eds.), 1995, *Africa in World Politics*, Second Edition. Boulder: Westview Press.

Harsh, E., 1991, 'Democracy in Africa', *Development Forum*, July-August.

Hayek, F.A., 1976, *The Road to Serfdom*, London: Routledge and Kegan Paul.

Hechter, M., 1976, 'Ethnicity and industrialization: On the cultural division of labour', *Ethnicity*, 3: 214-24.

Hegel, F., 1942, 1975, *Philosophy of Right*, trans. by T.M. Knox, Oxford: OUP.

Heilbrunn, J.R., 1993, 'Social origins of national consciousness in Benin and Togo', *Journal of Modern African Studies*, 31 (2): 277-99.

Helliwell, J., 1992, 'Empirical linkages between democracy and economic growth', NBER Working Paper #4066, Boston.

Herbst, J., 1991, *The Politics of Reform in Ghana, 1982-1991*. Berkeley: University of California Press.

Herskovits, M.J., 1938, *Dahomey, An Ancient West African Kingdom*, 2 vols., London: Books on Demand.

Hirst, P., *Associative Democracy* (Amherst: University of Massachusetts, 1994).

Hodgkin, T., 1957, *Nationalism in Colonial Africa*, New York: New York University Press.

Hogg, A., 1990, 'Frightened Moi vows he will cull democratic "rats"', *The Sunday Times*, July 8.

Holden, B., 1974, *The Nature of Democracy*. London: Nelson.

Holloway, J., and Picciotto, S., 1979, *State and Capital: A Marxist Debate*, Texas: University of Texas Press.

Horowitz, D.R., 1985, *Ethnic Groups in Conflict*, Berkeley: University of California Press.

Horton, R., 1962, 'The Kalabari world view: An outline and interpretation', *Africa*, xxxii, (2).

Horton, R., 1969b, 'Stateless societies in the history of West Africa', in J.A. Ajayi and M. Crowder, (eds), *History of West Africa*, Harlow: Longman.

Huntington, S.P. and Nelson, J.M., 1976, No Easy Choice: Political Participation in Developing countries, Cambridge Mass.: Harvard University Press.

Huntington, S.P., 1968, *Political Order in Changing Societies*, New Haven, Yale University Press.

Huntington, S.P., 1991, *The Third Wave: Democratization in the Late Twentieth Century*. Oklahoma: University of Oklahoma Press.

Huth, P., 1995, *Standing Your Ground: Territorial Disputes and International Conflict*, Ann Arbor: University of Michigan Press.

Hyden, G., 1983, *No Shortcuts to Progress: African Development Management in Perspective*, Berkeley: University of California Press.

Jackman, R.W., 1973, 'On the relation of economic development to democratic performance', *American Journal of political Science*, 17:11-21.

Jackman, R.W., 1975, *Political and Social Equality: A Comparative Analysis*, New York: Wiley.

Jackson, R.H, and Rosberg, C.G., 1982, *Personal Rule in Black Africa: Prince, Autocrat, Prophet, Tyrant*, Berkeley: University of California Press.

Jaycox, E., 1985, 'Africa: Development challenges and the World Bank's response', Lecture at the Smithsonian Institution, Washington, DC.

Jaycox, E., 1992, 'The challenges of African development', Washington DC: World Bank.

Joseph, R., 1987, *Democracy and Prebendal Politics in Nigeria: The Rise and Fall of the Second Republic*. Cambridge: CUP.

Joseph, R., 1989, *Beyond Autocracy in Africa*. Emory University: African Governance Programme, Carter Center Working Paper Series.

Joseph, R., 1990, *African Governance in the 1990s*. Emory University: African Governance Programme, Carter Center Working Paper Series.

Joseph, R., 1991, 'Africa: The rebirth of political freedom', *Journal of Democracy* 2 (4), Fall.

Kasfir, N., 1979, *The Shrinking Political Arena: Participation and Ethnicity in African Politics, with a case study of Uganda*, Berkeley: University of California Press.

Kenyatta, J., 1962, *Facing Mount Kenya*, New York: Random House.

Keyes, C., 1981, 'The dialectic of ethnic change', in C. Keyes, (ed.), *Ethnic Change*, Seattle: University of Washington Press.

Kopytoff, N., 1987, *The African Frontier: The Reproduction of Traditional African Societies*, Bloomington: Indiana University Press.

Krause, K., 1990, 'Controlling the trade in conventional arms', *International Journal*, Spring.

Kuper, H., 1961, *An African Aristocracy: Rank Among the Swazi*, Oxford: OUP.

Kuper, L., 1982, *Genocide: Its political Use in the Twentieth Century*, University of Michigan: Books on Demand.

Kuper, L., n.d., *An African Bourgeoisie: Race, Class and Politics in South Africa*, University of Michigan: Books on Demand.

Lal, D., 1987, 'The political economy of economic liberalization', in *The World Bank Economic Review*, 1 (2), January: 273-300.

Lamb, G. and Kallab, V., (eds.), 1992, *Military Expenditure and Economic Development: A Symposium on Research Issues*, World Bank Discussion Paper 185, Washington, DC.

Lancaster, C., 1991, 'The new politics of US aid to Africa', *CSIS Africa Notes*, January 28.

Lancaster, C., 1991/92, 'Democracy in Africa', *Foreign Policy*, 85:148-65.

Landau, D., 1993, *The Economic Impact of Military Expenditure'*, Policy Research Paper WPS 1138, World Bank, Washington DC.

Landell-Mills, P., ,1992, 'Governance, cultural change, and empowerment', *The Journal of Modern African Studies*, 30 (4):543-67.

Lange, A. and Charles W., 1981, *Etnisk Diskriminering och Social Identitet*, Helsingborg: Publica.

La Palombara, J., ed., 1963, *Bureaucracy & Political Development* (Studies in Political Development) Vol. 2 Princeton University Press.

Le Vine, R., 1976, 'Patterns of personality in Africa', in G. Vos (ed.), *Response to Change: Society, Culture and Personality*, New York: Van Nostrand.

Lemarchand, R., 1992, 'African transition to democracy: An interim (and mostly pessimist) assessment', *Africa Insight*, 22 (3):178-185.

Lemarchand, R., 1992a, 'Mobutu and the national conference: The arts of political survival', paper presented at US State Department conference on Zaire, Washington, DC, March 12-13.

Lemarchand, R., 1992b, 'Africa's troubled transitions', *Journal of Democracy*, 3 (4): 98-109.

Lewis, P., 1992, 'Political transformation and the dilemma of civil society in Africa', *Journal of International Affairs*, 46 (1):31-54.

Lijphart, A., 1980, *Democracy in Plural Societies: A Comparative Exploration*, Yale Univ. Press.

Lijphart, A., 1984, Democracies: Patterns of Majoritarian & Consensus Government

Lindblom, C. E., *Politics & Markets: The World's Political-Economic Systems*, NY: Basic Books.

Lindblom, Charles E., 1980, *Politics and Markets: The World's Political-Economic Systems*, New York: Basic Books.

Linz, J.J., 1987, *The Breakdown of Democratic Regimes: Crisis, Breakdown and Reequilibration*. Baltimore: Johns Hopkins Press.

Lipset, S.M., 1959, 'Some social requisites of democracy: economic development and political legitimacy', *American Political Science Review*, 53:69-105.

Lipset, S.M., 1960, *Political Man: The Social Bases of Politics*, Garden City, New York: Doubleday.

Lipset, S.M., 1981, *Political Man: The Social Bases of Politics*, Second Edition Baltimore: Johns Hopkins University Press.

Lipset, S.M., Seong, K-R and Torres, J.C., 1991, 'A comparative analysis of the social requisites of democracy, unpublished paper, Hoover Institution, Stanford University.

Lively, J., 1975, *Democracy*. Oxford: OUP.

Locke, J., 1963, *Two Treatises of Government*, Cambridge and New York: CUP.

Lonsdale, J., and Berman, B., 1980, 'Crisis of accumulation, coercion and the colonial state: The development of the labour control system in Kenya', *Canadian Journal of African Studies*, 14, 1:55-77.

Mabogunje, A., 1985, *Last Things First: A Reappraisal of the Fundamentals of Nigeria's Development*, Lagos: Niran Modern Printers.

MacGaffey, J., 1988, 'The Endogenous Economy', unpublished paper, Washington DC: The World Bank.

Machiavelli, N., 1975, *The Prince*, Harmondsworth: Penguin.

Mackintosh, J., 1991, *Dissertation on the Progress of Ethical Philosophy, Chiefly During the Seventeenth & Eighteenth Centuries*, 19th Century British Philosophy Series., Thoemmes Press

Macpherson, C.B., 1962, *The Political Theory of Possessive Individualism*, Oxford: Clarendon Press.

Madison, J., 1966, *Reflecting on Representation*, in Marvin Meyers (ed.), *The Mind of the Founder: Sources of the Political Thought of James Madison*, Indianapolis: Bobb-Merrill, 501-9.

Madison, J., 1966, *The Federalist Papers*, New York: Doubleday.

Malinowski, B., 1945, *The Dynamics of Culture Change*, ed. P.M. Kaberry, New Haven: Yale University Press.

Mamdani, M., 1992, 'Africa: democratic theory and democratic struggles', Paper presented at the seminar on Social Movements, State and Democracy, New Delhi, October 5-8.

Markovitz, J.J., 1986, *Studies in Power and Class in Africa*, New York: OUP.

Marsh, R.M., 1979, 'Does democracy hinder economic development in the latecomer developing nations?' *Comparative Social Research*, 2.

Martin, D.M., and Omar Hashi, F., 1992a, *Gender: The Evolution of Legal Institutions, and Economic Development in Sub-Saharan Africa*, World Bank Staff Working Paper 3, Africa Technical Department, Washington, DC.: World Bank.

Martin, D.M., and Omar Hashi, F., 1992b, *Women in Development: The Legal Issues in Sub-Saharan Africa Today*, World Bank Staff Working Paper 4, Africa Technical Department, Washington, DC. World Bank.

Martin, G., 1993, 'Preface: Democratic transition in Africa', *Issue*, 21 (1-2): 3.

McCracken, J., 1966, 'Coercion and control in Nyasaland: Aspects of the history of a colonial police force', *Journal of African History*, 27, 1. pp. 127-47.

McCrone, D.J. and Cnudde, C.F., 1967, 'Toward a communications theory of democratic political development: A causal *model*, *American Political Science Review*, 61:72-79.

McGowan, P. and Johnson, T.H., 1984, 'African military coups d'état and underdevelopment: A quantitative historical analysis', *Journal of Modern African Studies*, 22 (4): 633-66.

McGowan, P. and Johnson, T.H., 1986, 'Sixty coups in thirty years: Further evidence regarding African military coups d'état', *Journal of Modern African Studies*, 24 (3): 539-46.

McNeil, W., 1985, *Polyethnicity and National Unity in World History*, Toronto: University of Toronto Press.

Middleton, J., with Tait, D. (eds.), 1959, *Tribes Without Rulers: Studies in African Segmentary Systems*, London: Routledge.

Middleton, J., with Winter, E.H. (eds.), 1963, *Witchcraft and Sorcery in East Africa*, London: Routledge.

Mill, J.S., 1976, *M. de Tocqueville on Democracy in America*, in Geraint L. Williams (ed.), *John Stuart Mill on Politics and Society*, London: Fontana. 186-247.

Miller, David, 1992, 'Deliberative Democracy and Social Choice', *Political Studies*, 40 (special issue): 54-67.

Miller, David, 1993, 'Deliberative Democracy and Social Choice', in David Held (ed.), *Prospects for Democracy*, Cambridge Mass: Polity Press, 74-92.

Molomo, M.G., 1990, 'The political process: Does multi-partism persist due to the lack of a strong opposition?' *Southern Africa: Political and Economic Monthly*, 3 (7): 6-7.

Montville, J., (ed.), 1990, *Conflict and Peacemaking in Multi-Ethnic Societies*, Toronto.

Mudimbe, V., 1988, *The Invention of Africa: Gnosis, Philosophy and the Order of Knowledge*, Bloomington: Indiana University Press.

Mullins, A., 1987, *Born Arming: Development and Military Power in New States*, Stanford, Stanford University Press.

Murphy, W., and Bledsoe, C., 1987, 'Debating in common idiom: Variant traditions of genesis among the Basu of Eastern Zaire', In I. Kopytoff, ed., *The African Frontier: The Reproduction of Traditional African Societies*, Bloomington: Indiana University Press.

Nadel, S.F., 1942, *A Black Byzantium*, Oxford: OUP.

Nadel, S.F., 1952, 'Witchcraft in four African societies: An essay in comparison', *American Anthropologist*, 54.

Nkrumah, K., 1973, I Speak of Freedom, Panaf Books.

Nnoli, O., 1978, *Ethnic Politics in Nigeria*, Enugu: Fourth Dimension.

Norton, D.L., 1991, *Democracy and Moral Development*, Berkeley: University of California Press.

Nyerere, J.K., 1974, *Freedom and Development*, Nairobi: OUP Eastern Africa.

Nzouankeu, J.M., 1993, 'The role of the national conference in the transition to democracy in Africa: The cases of Benin and Mali', *Issue*, 21 (1-2): 44-50.

O'Donnell, G., 1973, *Modernization and Bureaucratic-Authoritarianism: Studies in South American Politics*, Politics of Modernization Series, no. 9, Berkeley: University of California, Institute of International Studies.

O'Donnell, G., and Schmitter, P.C., 1986, *Transitions from Authoritarian Rule: Tentative Conclusions about Uncertain Democracies*, Baltimore: Johns Hopkins University Press.

Odinga, O., n.d., *Not Yet Uhuru*, Nairobi: Eastern Educational Pub.

Offe, C., 1984, *Contradictions of the Welfare State*, London: Hutchinson.

Ojo, G.J.A., 1966, *Yoruba Culture*, London: University of London Press.

Okamura, J.Y., 1981, 'Situational Ethnicity', *Ethnic and Racial Studies*, 4 (4).452-65.

Olsen, N.E., 1968, 'Multivariate analysis of national political development', *American Sociological Review*, 35:699-712.

Olson, M. Jr., 1991, 'Autocracy, democracy and prosperity', in Richard J. Zeckhauser, (ed.), *Strategy and Choice*, Cambridge, Mass: MIT Press, 131-57.

Olzak, S. and Nagel, J., 1986, 'Introduction, competitive ethnic relations: An overview', in S. Olzak and J. Nagel, (eds.), *Competitive Ethnic Relations*, New York, 1-14.

Orizu, N., 1980, Without Bitterness, Nwamife Publishers.

Pateman, C., 1985, *The Problem of Political Obligation: A Critique of Liberal Theory*, Cambridge Mass: Polity Press.

Pereira, D.P., 1937, *Esmeraldo de Situ Orbis*, trans. and ed., T. Kimble and H.George, London: Hakluyt Society, 2nd series, vol. LXXIX, no. 132.

Peterson-Royce, A., 1992, *Ethnic Identity, Strategy of Diversity*, Bloomington, Indiana Univ.ersity Press.

Plamenatz, J., 1963, *Man and Society*, vol. 1, London: Longman.

Plato, 1974, *The Republic*, Harmondsworth: Penguin.

Polsy, N., 1963, *Community Power and Political Theory*, New Haven: Yale University Press.

Powell Jr, G. B., 1982, *Contemporary Democracies: Participation, Stability and Violence*. Cambridge, Mass.: Harvard University Press.

Przeworski, A. and Limongi, F., 1993, 'Political regimes and economic growth', *Journal of Economic Perspectives*, 7 (3), Summer:51-69.

Przeworski, A. and Limongi, F., 1994, 'Democracy and Development' paper presented in *Democracy's Victory and Crisis Nobel Symposium*, August 27-30.

Putnam, R.D., 1992, *Making Democracy Work: Civic Traditions in Modern Italy*, Princeton: Princeton University Press.

Radcliffe-Brown, A.R., and Forde, D. (eds.), 1950, *African Systems of Kinship and Marriage*, Oxford: OUP.

Rakner, L., 1992, *Trade Unions in Process of Democratisation: A Study of Party Labour Relations in Zambia*. Bergen: CMI Report Series R, 6.

Rey, P., 1966, 'The lineage mode of production', *Critique of Anthropology*, 3.

Riker, William H., 1982, *Liberalism against Populism*, San Francisco: Freeman.

Riley, S.P. and Parfitt, T.W., 1987, 'Party or masquerade? The All People's Congress (APC) of Sierra Leone', *Journal of Commonwealth and Comparative Politics*, 25 (2), July.

Robinson, P.T., 1992, 'Grassroot legitimation of military governance in Burkina Faso and Niger: The core contradictions', in Goran Hyden and Michael Bratton (eds.) *Governance and Politics in Africa*. Boulder: Lyne Rienner, 143-65.

Rothchild, D. and Olorunisola V.A. (eds.), 1983, *State Versus Ethnic Claims: African Policy Dilemmas*, Boulder: Westview Press.

Rueschemeyer, D., 1991, 'Different methods—Contradictory results? Research on development and democracy', in C.C. Ragin, (ed.), *Issues and Alternatives in Comparative Social Research*, Leiden, Brill: 9-38.

Rummel, R., 1994, *Death by Government*, New Brunswick: Transition Publishers.

Rustow, D.A., 1970, 'Transitions of democracy', *Comparative Politics*, 2:337-363.

Samoff, J., 1994, 'Structural adjustment, poverty and democracy', Paper presented to IPSA, Berlin, August 21-25.

Sandbrook, R., 1985, *The Politics of Africa's Economic Stagnation*, Cambridge: Cambridge University Press.

Sandbrook, R., 1988, 'Liberal democracy in Africa: A socialist-revisionist perspective', *Journal of African Studies*, 22 (2).

Sandbrook, R., 1993, *The Politics of Africa's Economic Recovery*. Cambridge: CUP.

Schatzberg, M.G., 1991, *Mobutu or Chaos: The United States and Zaire, 1960-1990*, Lanham, MD: University Press of America, and Philadelphia: Foreign Policy Research Institute.

Schmitter, P.C., 1994, 'Dangers and Dilemmas of Democracy', *Journal of Democracy*, 2 April.

Schumpeter, J., 1978, *Capitalism, Socialism and Democracy*, London: Allen and Unwin.

Senghor, L.S., n.d., *Nation et voie Africaine du socialisme*, New York: French and European Publications Inc.

Shaw, W.H., 1986, 'Towards the one-party state in Zimbabwe: A study in African political thought', *Journal of Modern African Studies*, 24 (3), September.

Siebel, H., and Massing, A., 1976, *Traditional Organizations and Economic Development*, New York: Praeger.

Singer, J.D., 1994, 'Armed conflict in the ex-colonial regions: From classification to explanation', paper delivered at the Clingendael Institute Seminar on Conflict and Development.

Sirowy, L. and Inkeles, A., 1990, 'The effects of democracy on economic growth and Inequality: A review' in *Studies in Comparative International Development*, 25 (1), Spring:126-57.

Skalnes, T., 1993, 'The politics of economic reform in Zimbabwe', unpublished PhD. dissertation, Department of Political Science, University of California, Los Angeles.

Sklar, R. and Whitaker, C.S., 1991, *African Politics and Problems in Development*. Boulder: Lynne Rienner.

Sklar, R., 1986, 'Democracy in Africa', in P. Chabal (ed.) *Political Domination in Africa*. Cambridge: Cambridge University Press.

Sklar, R.L., 1969, 'Institutional and political conditions of pluralism', in Leo Kuper and M.G. Smith, (eds.), in *Pluralism in Africa*, Berkeley: University of California Press, 26-66.

Sklar, R.L., 1987, 'Development democracy', *Comparative Studies in Society and History*, 29:686-714.

Smith, M.G., 1960, *Government in Zazzau*, Oxford: OUP.

Smith, M.G., 1965, 'The Haousa of Northern Nigeria', in James L. Gibbs Jr, *Peoples of Africa*, New York: Holt, Reinhart and Winston.

Smock, A., 1971, *Ibo Politics, The Role of Ethnic Unions of Eastern Nigeria*, Cambridge, Mass: Harvard University Press.

Southall, A., 1985, 'The heart of ethnic anthropology', *Cahiers d'Etudes Africaines*, 25 (4):100.

Stavenhagen, R., 1994, 'Ethnicity based conflicts', paper delivered at UNRISD-UNDP Seminar on Ethnic Diversity and Public Policy, New York.

Stepan, A., 1988, *Rethinking Military Politics*, Princeton: Princeton University Press.

Tilly, C., (ed.), 1975, *The Formation of Nation States in Western Europe*, Princeton: Princeton University Press.

Tilly, C., 1990, *Coercion, Capital and European States AD 900–1990*, Cambridge: Basic Blackwell.

Toennies, F., 1971, *Ferdinand Toennies on Sociology Pure, Applied, & Empirical Sociology* Edited by Rudolf Heberle, Heritage of Sociology Ser., University of Chicago Press

Toennies, F., 1988, *Community & Society*, 'Introduction' by John Sample, Transaction Books, U. S.

Truman, D.B., 1951, *The Govenmental Process*, New York: Knopf.

Turrittin, Jane, 1991, 'Mali: People topple Traoré', *Review of African Political Economy*, 52, November: 97-103.

United Nations Development Program (UNDP), 1991, *Human Development Report 1991*, New York: OUP.

United Nations Development Programme (UNDP), 1994, *Human Development Report 1994*, New York: UNDP.

United Nations, 1981, *Popular Participation as a Strategy for Promoting Community Level Action and New Development*, New York: UN.

Uphoff, N.R. Meinzen-Dick, and St Julien N., 1985, *Improving Policies and Programmes for Farmer Organization and Participation*, WMS Professional Paper no. 1.

US Agency for International Development (USAID), 1990, *The Democracy Initiative*, Dec.

Vail, L., (ed.), 1989, *The Creation of Tribalism in Southern Africa*, London: James Currey.

Van de Walle, N., 1994, 'Political liberalization and economic reforrn in Africa', *World Development*, 22 (4), April.

Van den Berghe, P.L., 1970, *Race and Ethnicity: Essays in Comparative Sociology*, New York, Basic Books.

Van den Berghe, P.L.,1981, *The Ethnic Phenomenon*, New York: Elsevier.

Van Nelson, J., 1964, *The Politics of Kinship: A Study in Social Manipulation Among the Lakeside Tonga of Nyasaland*, Manchester: Manchester University Press.

Vansina, J., 1966, *Kingdoms of the Savannah*, Madison University of Wisconsin Press.

Vengroff, R., 1993, 'Governance and the transition to democracy: Political parties and the party system in Mali', *Journal of Modern African Studies*, 31 (4):541-562.

Vengroff, R., 1993, 'Governance and the transition to democracy: Political parties and the party system in Mali', *Journal of Modern African Studies*, 31 (4):541-562.

Wade, R., 1991, *Governing the Market: Economic Theory and the Role of Government in East Asian Industrialization*, Princeton: Princeton University Press.

Wallerstein, I., 1990, 'The construction of peoplehood: Racism, nationalism, ethnicity', in E. Balibar, and I. Wallerstein (eds.), *Race, Nation, and Class: Ambiguous Identities*, London: Verso.

Weber, M., 1978, *Economy and Society*, 2 vols., Berkeley: University of California Press.

Weber, Max M., 1980, *Protestant Ethic & the Spirit of Capitalism*, Simon & Schuster Trade.

Weiss, H., 1967, *Political Protest in the Congo*, Princeton: Princeton University Press.

Whitehead, N.L., 1992, 'Tribes make states and states make tribes: Warfare and the creation of colonial tribe and state in north-eastern South America 1498-1820', in Brian Ferguson and Neil L. Whitehead (eds.), *War in the Tribal Zone: Expanding States and Indigenous Warfare*, Santa Fe: School of American Research Press.

Wilks, I., 1967, 'Ashanti government' in D. Forde with P.M. Kaberry, eds., *West African Kingdoms in the Nineteenth Century*, Oxford: OUP.

Wilson, M., 1936, *Reaction to Conquest*, Oxford: OUP.

Wilson, M., 1951, *Good Company: Nyakyusa Age-Group Villages*, Oxford: OUP.

Wolpe, H., (ed.), 1980, *The Articulation of Modes of Production*, London: Routledge Kegan Paul.

Woods, D., 1992, 'Civil society in Europe and Africa: Limiting state power through a public sphere', *African Studies Review*, 35 (2):77-100.

World Bank, 1989, *Sub-Saharan Africa: From Crisis to Sustainable Growth*, Washington DC: World Bank.

World Bank, 1991, *Managing Development: The Governance Decision*, Washington, DC.

World Bank, 1992, *Governance and Development*, Washington DC.: The World Bank.

World Bank, 1993, *The East Asian Miracle: Economic Growth and Public Policy*, Policy Research Report, July. Washington, DC.

World Bank, 1994, *Adjustment in Africa: Reforms, Results and The Road Ahead*, New York: Oxford University Press, for the World Bank.

Young, C., 1990, 'The shattered illusion of the integral state: The case of Zaire', unpublished paper.

Young, C., 1991, 'Self-determination, territorial integrity, and the African state system', in F. Deng and I. Zartman, (eds.), *Conflict Resolution in Africa:* Washington DC: The Brookings Institution.

Young, M.W., 1966, 'The divine kingship of the Jukun: A re-evaluation of some theories', *Africa*, xxxvi, 2.

THE PUBLISHER

CODESRIA is the Council for the Development of Social Science Research in Africa head-quartered in Dakar, Senegal. It is an independent organisation whose principal objectives are facilitating research, promoting research-based publishing and creating multiple forums geared towards the exchange of views and information among African researchers. It challenges the fragmentation of research through the creation of thematic research networks that cut across linguistic and regional boundaries.

CODESRIA publishes a quarterly journal, *Africa Development*, the longest standing Africa-based social science journal; *Afrika Zamani*, a journal of history; the *African Sociological Review*, and the *African Journal of International Affairs (AJIA)*. Research results and other activities of the institution are disseminated through 'Working Papers', 'Monograph Series', 'New Path Series', 'State-of-the-Literature Series', 'CODESRIA Book Series', the *CODESRIA Bulletin, KIBARU* and *CIVIC AGENDA.*